Prospects of a Golden Age

BOOKS BY JOHN DOS PASSOS

Novels

FIRST ENCOUNTER
THREE SOLDIERS
STREETS OF NIGHT
MANHATTAN TRANSFER
CHOSEN COUNTRY
U.S.A.: THE 42ND PARALLEL
NINETEEN NINETEEN
THE BIG MONEY
DISTRICT OF COLUMBIA: ADVENTURES OF A YOUNG MAN
NUMBER ONE
THE GRAND DESIGN
MOST LIKELY TO SUCCEED
THE GREAT DAYS

Travel Narratives

ROSINANTE TO THE ROAD AGAIN
ORIENT EXPRESS
IN ALL COUNTRIES
JOURNEYS BETWEEN WARS
STATE OF THE NATION
TOUR OF DUTY
THE PROSPECT BEFORE US

Historical Narratives

THE GROUND WE STAND ON
THE HEAD AND HEART OF THOMAS JEFFERSON
THE MEN WHO MADE THE NATION

Plays

THE GARBAGE MAN
FORTUNE HEIGHTS
AIRWAYS, INC.

Verse

A PUSHCART AT THE CURB

Charles Willson Peale, then the leading patriotic painter in America, celebrated Yorktown by painting Washington with Tench Tilghman, the genial Marylander who had just retired as the commander-in-chief's aide, and Lafayette. ". . . the Marquis seeing the picture the other day, generously offered to give me a sitting that it might be made more compleat. . . . I have made in the distance a View of York & Gloster with the British army surrendering. . . . And in the middle distance I have introduced French & American officers with the colors of their nations displayed, between them the British with their colors cased. These figures serve to tell the story at first sight . . ." he wrote Governor Paca on September 7, 1784, announcing that the picture, which the Maryland assembly had ordered three years earlier, was nearly finished.

Prospects

John Dos Passos

PRENTICE-HALL, INC.

JOHN DOS PASSOS

# of a Golden Age

ENGLEWOOD CLIFFS, N.J.

119628

Occasional excerpts from *The Head and Heart of Thomas
Jefferson* and *The Men Who Made the Nation* are used by
permission of Doubleday & Company, Inc.

PRINTED IN THE UNITED STATES OF AMERICA 73130

Foreword

☼

THE FOUNDERS OF AMERICAN INSTITUTIONS CAME OF A TOUGH AND agile race. They were men of many varied intellectual and manual skills. They combined shrewdness and efficiency with public spirit.

How did they learn to manipulate the society they lived in so successfully? How did they get to know so much? How did they manage to pack so much work into a day? These are the questions you keep asking yourself when you read their letters and diaries.

Part of the answer is that their experience was direct, at the fingertips. There were great readers among them, students and theorists, but without exception they had dealt from boyhood with the practical realities of life on a virgin continent.

They were settlers and farmers and plantation managers. They were surveyors. They were horsemen. They rowed boats and sailed ships. They were lawyers and merchants and printers and craftsmen and medical practitioners. The breadth of their interests included the fine arts and the burgeoning sciences. They produced a school of painting and a style of architecture. They tinkered with inventions. When the need rose they proved themselves skilled fighters on land and sea. Their daily occupations taught them the handling of other men.

Government they considered the noblest preoccupation of man. The aim of government was the happiness of the governed. Happiness to the eighteenth century Americans meant something more than an improved standard of living. It meant dignity, independence, selfgovernment. It meant opportunity for the young, a serene old age and fearlessness in the face of death.

This book is an effort to illustrate some snatches and samples of the lives of some of the men of the great generation of 1776 and of the generations that followed immediately after. It was their skills, coupled with a profound belief in themselves and in man's capacity, that made their achievements possible. Refreshing our schoolbook knowledge of their adventures and of their aspirations may help us not to forget what great things men are capable of.

John Dos Passos

CONTENTS

✺

List of Illustrations

☼

COLOR PLATES

HALF-TONE PLATES

LINE DRAWINGS

Picture Credits

✵

Part *1*

THE GENERATION OF
1776

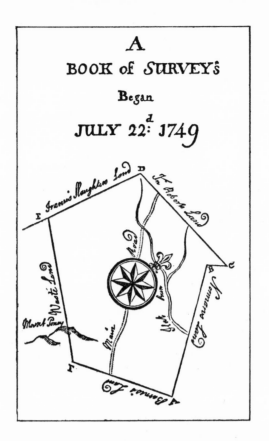

A
BOOK of SURVEYS
Began
JULY 22:ᵈ 1749

A People of Surveyors

CHAPTER 1 ✪

LAND WAS THE OBSESSION DURING THE YEARS WHEN THE MEN OF George Washington's generation were growing up. When they cleared the Virginia forests by burning the brush and girdling the great trees the early settlers uncovered a rich loam that grew magnificent tobacco. Rains washed it away. Hot summer winds blew off the dry humus. Hasty cultivation without manure exhausted what was left. All through the middle eighteenth century the landhungry gentry were moving inland out of Tidewater, with their oxcarts laden with plows and grubbing hoes and broadaxes, and their ladies riding with handkerchiefs tied over their faces against the dust, and their gangs of slaves and horses and cattle and pigs herded by poorwhite overseers, to lay out fresh plantations in the wilderness. Even in the comparatively settled regions of the Northern Neck planters were forever on the move. Boys learned to carry a surveyor's chain almost as soon as they could walk.

George Washington was raised from the cradle amid talk of fortunes in unspoiled land to the westward. When he was three his father left Pope's Creek plantation and moved further up the Potomac to the farm then called Epsewasson on Little Hunting Creek. When he was not quite seven the family moved again, this time to Ferry Farm on the Rappahannock. There Augustine Washington died.

George inherited his father's great frame and powerful hands. As soon as he was old enough to cut loose from his uncongenial mother's apronstrings he took to spending as much time as he could with his halfbrother Lawrence at the fine new mansion Lawrence was building for himself at Epsewasson which he had renamed Mt. Vernon.

Along with Thomas Lee, Lawrence Washington had become one of the moving spirits of the "Ohio Company" chartered for settlement and speculation in lands "to the westward of the Great Mountains." Educated in England, trained in the military arts under Admiral Vernon during the expedition against Cartagena, he married into that grand family of Fairfaxes who held the proprietary grant to the entire Northern Neck of Virginia. In spite of the hacking cough he never could throw off he cut a dashing figure in Fairfax County society. The Fairfax connection was busy with carving out the valley lands they were discovering in the northern marches of their grant. It was in the company of his handsome brotherinlaw George William Fairfax that young George Washington first rode into the wilderness on a surveying trip. He was just turned sixteen.

Never a man of letters, George Washington was a constant note-taker. He learned early to keep books. He had been raised in the belief that it behooved a man of parts to keep a journal.

He was already shaving. It was natural even at sixteen that on this first excursion as a man on his own he should record what he did and what he saw. "Fryday, March 11 1747-8," he wrote in a round boyish hand. "Began my Journey in company with George Fairfax, Esq.: we travelled this day 40 miles . . ."

Next day they crossed the Blue Ridge . . . "to Capt. Ashby's on Shannandoah River. Nothing remarkable happen'd."

The day after was Sunday: "We went through most beautiful Groves of Sugar Trees, & spent ye last part of ye Day in admiring ye Trees & richness of ye Land."

Monday they went to work. The pack train was sent on to a certain Captain Hite's house near Frederick (now Winchester). "Went ourselves down ye River about 16 miles to Capt. Isaac Pennington's (the Land exceeding rich and fertile all ye way—produces abundance of Grain, Hemp, Tobacco, &c) in order to lay off some land on Cates Marsh & Long Marsh."

A heavy rain interrupted their next day's survey . . . "It increasing very fast obliged us to return. It clearing about one o'clock & our time being too Precious to lose, we a second time ventured out & worked hard till night . . . We got our suppers & was lighted into a Room & I not being so good a woodsman as ye rest of my company, strip(p)ed myself very orderly and went into ye Bed, as they called it, when to my surprize, I found it to be only one thread bear blanket with double its weight of vermin, such as Lice, Fleas, &c. I was glad to get up (as soon as ye Light was carried from us.) I put on my cloths & lay as my companions. Had we not been very tired I am sure we would not have slept much that night. I made a Promise not to sleep so from that time forward, chusing rather to sleep in ye open air before a fire."

Next morning they finished their first survey and rejoined their baggage at Frederick. "We cleaned ourselves (to get Rid of ye Game we had catched ye night before). I took a Review of ye Town and then returned to our Lodgings where we had a good Dinner prepared for us. Wine & Rum Punch in plenty, & a good Feather Bed with clean sheets, which was a very agreeable regale."

So refreshed they set out into the back country up the Potomac valley. The rain kept plaguing them. At a settler's shack beside a ford they found the river "about six feet higher than usual" and rising. They waited a couple of days camped out in an open field until losing patience they swam their horses across the Potomac, ferried their baggage in a canoe, "and Travelled up Maryland side all ye Day in a continued Rain to Col. Cressap's, right against ye mouth of ye South Branch about 40 miles . . . I believe the worst road than ever was trod by Man or Beast."

Continued rain kept them under shelter at Cresap's Old Town trading post. There George saw his first Indians. His excitement broke out from the stiff wording of his diary. He threw grammar to the winds.

"We were most agreeably surprized when the sky cleared on the third day at ye sight of thirty odd Indians coming from war with only one scalp. We had some Liquor with Us of which we gave them Part, it elevating their spirits, put them in ye humor of Dauncing, of whom we had a War Daunce. There manner of Dauncing is as follows, viz: They clear a Large Circle and make a great Fire in ye middle. Men seats themselves around it. Ye speaker makes a grand speech, telling them in what manner they are to daunce. After he has finished there best Dauncer jumps up as one awaked out of a sleep, & Runs and Jumps about ye Ring in a most comicle manner. He is followed by ye Rest. Then begins there musicians to Play. Ye music is a pot half full of water, with a Deerskin stretched over it as tight as it can, & a goard with some shott in it to rattle & a Piece of a horse's tail tied to it to make it look fine. Ye one keeps rattling & ye others drumming all ye while ye others is Dauncing."

"Nothing remarkable on thursday" he wrote on Friday—he had been out two weeks and was settling down to the backwoods life—"but only being with ye Indians all day. So shall slip it." Even the Indians had lost their novelty.

They swam their horses back across the Potomac, ferried their packs in the canoe again and continued upriver to Patterson's Creek. They followed its rocky banks inland till they came to a cabin where they camped. This was the residence of Solomon Hedges Esquire, his Majesty's Justice of the Peace for Frederick County. "When we came to supper there was neither a Cloth upon ye Table nor a knife to eat with; but as good luck would have it, we had knives."

From Solomon Hedges' they rode across the hills of the Potomac's South Branch to lay out in lots some rich bottom lands belonging to the valley settlers. There George met his first Pennsylvania Dutch. Some of the men shot wild turkeys along the way. George missed his.

The weather continued horrible. They walked the lines all day and huddled in a tent at night. One blowing rainy night "our straw catched a Fire yt we were laying on. I was luckily preserved by one of our Men's awakening." Next night was even more "blustering." This time the tent blew down and they were obliged to "Lie ye Latter part of ye night without covering."

Monday April 4: "We did two Lots & was attended by a great Company of People, men & Women and Children that attended us through ye woods as we went, shewing their antic tricks. I really think they seem to be as ignorant a set of people as the Indians. They would never speak English but when spoken to they speak all Dutch."

That night the surveyors' tent blew down again.

Day after day they carried on their survey between showers of rain. They were still having trouble with the tent. Once it became "so Intolerably smoky that we were obliged all hands to leave ye Tent to ye Mercy of ye wind and fire." The sixteen year old was having the time of his life. "We camped this Night in ye woods near a wild Meadow, where was a large stack of Hay. After we had Pitched our Tent & made a very large Fire, we pulled out our knapsack in order to Recruit ourselves. Every one was his own cook. Our Spits was forked Sticks, our Plates was a large Chip; as for Dishes, we had none."

They completed their work on the parcels of land along the South Branch of the Potomac they had been ordered to survey. Their provisions ran out. Saying goodbye to the backwoodsmen, George and Mr. Fairfax set off to ride "over Hills and Mountains" homeward. Crossing the Blue Ridge they saw "a Rattled snake, ye first we had seen in our journey."

This was young Washington's life and his seasoning until he turned twenty. The fall after his first surveys he wrote a friend who lived in the settled country to thank him for a letter. "Yours gave me the more pleasure, as I received it

among a parcel of barbarians and an uncouth set of people . . . Since you received my letter in October last I have not sleep'd above three nights or four in
a Bed, but after walking a good deal all Day, I lay down before the fire upon a
little Hay, Straw, Fodder or Bearskin, which ever is to be had, with man, wife,
and children like a parcel of dogs and cats; and happy is he who gets the Berth
nearest ye Fire. There's nothing would make it pass off tolerably but a good reward. A doubloon is my constant gain every day that the Weather will permit
my going out and sometimes six pistoles . . . I have never had my clothes off,
but lay and sleep in them, except the few nights I have lay'n in Frederic Town."

Association with the Ohio Company was an education in frontier land
operations. Its founder had been that astute promoter Thomas Lee of Stratford
Hall who had succeeded "King" Carter as resident manager of the Fairfax holdings. The Company's London representative was John Hanbury who was a power
in the Board of Trade. The wealthy Nelsons of York on the York River owned
shares, as of course did George Washington's connections by marriage, the Fairfaxes. Thomas Cresap, a crusty Yorkshireman who had fought and wrangled his
way against bitter odds to a commanding position as an Indian trader on the
Maryland frontier, managed the company's trading post at Wills Creek. John
Mercer, the Carters, Gawin Corbin of Peckatone, Lomaxes and Thorntons and
Tayloes: every great landowner in the Northern Neck was involved. The Treasurer, descendant of three generations of Masons in the Potomac region, was
thoughtful George Mason of Gunston Hall, who was later, as the philosopher of
American liberties, to draft a Bill of Rights for Virginia.

The Ohio Company was far from being alone in the field. Lawrence Washington's last years after he took over on Thomas Lee's death were harassed by the
lawsuits of rival concerns in Pennsylvania. At the same time lobbyists for another
Virginia company had appeared at Williamsburg. While the shareholders in
the Ohio Company fixed their hopes on the valley of La Belle Rivière, the promoters of the Loyal Land Company were particularly interested in the level lands
rumored to stretch westward from the Virginia mountains. Most of these men
operated plantations in the new county of Albemarle. Among them was Thomas
Jefferson's father, Peter.

Peter Jefferson was one of the founders of Albemarle County and so became associated in the surveying business with Colonel Fry the County Lieutenant.
Joshua Fry was an Oxford man of some learning who had sailed overseas to teach
mathematics at William and Mary. Captivated by frontier life he had learned
the trade of surveyor. It was in partnership with Fry that Peter Jefferson surveyed the western end of the Virginia-North Carolina line and produced one of
the first reasonably accurate maps of the huge dominion of Virginia. The two

men were associated in another notable survey. That was the running of the line from the headwaters of the Rappahannock to the headwaters of the Potomac which finally established the most disputed western boundary of the Fairfax grant.

The journal of this survey still exists. It was kept by a nearsighted young man named Thomas Lewis, a son of the Ulsterman John Lewis, who had travelled down the wagon road from Pennsylvania a few years before and built himself a great log house at Bellefont in the headwaters of the Shenandoah and there founded the frontier clan of the Lewises.

The party was out two months. Peter Jefferson, Thomas Lewis, a Captain Winslow who had been in those mountains before, and a man named Brook did the actual work of surveying while Colonel Fry and the commissioners for the Crown and for the Fairfaxes rode from point to point by the easiest trails they could find. Meanwhile the surveyors struggled through the thickets and briars of the settled valley lands and over range after range of mountains. It was strenuous work. When they first started climbing the Blue Ridge "the mountains made Such a Dismal appearance that John Thomas one of our men took Sick on Same & So returned home."

They started in the middle of September. After being out with the party a couple of weeks Colonel Fairfax "not being able to undergo the foutage (fatigue) of the Journey Returned home." From the Shenandoah Valley they toiled across the range that Peter Jefferson named "The Devil's Backbone" on his map. Two more ranges and they were in sight of the South Branch of the Potomac. "Fine Lands" Peter Jefferson noted along this river on his map.

"This mountain Exceeding high it was with great Difficulty we could get our horses over," Lewis complained in his journal, "We were very much put too for want of water we Could find no other than a Standing puddle wherein the Bears used to Wallow."

There were already settlers in the "fine lands" along the South Branch. The surveyors "went to see Coburn who with his wife & Miller a Bucksom lass Repay'd the Visite in the Evening we Spent very merily." A little further on they camped for the weekend. "This Being the farthest setlement we were Obliged to Lie By in order to be supply'd with a fresh Cargo of provision that the Farrier might have time to fasten our horses Shoes & the men have time to wash their Shirts &c."

It was after they left the last settlements in the upper branches of Looney Creek that the toughest part of their journey began. Instead of finding too little water they found too much. Their line ran through an upland swamp: "This River was calld Styx from the Dismal appearance of the place being Sufficen to Strick terror in any human Creature ye Lorals"—rhododendron—"Ivey"—what we now call mountain laurel—"& Spruce pine so Extremly thick in ye Swamp through

which this River Runs that one cannot have the Least prospect Except they look
upwards the Water of the River of Dark Brownish Cooler & its motion so Slow
that it can hardly be Said to move its Depth about 4 feet the Bottom muddy &
the Banks high, which made it Extremely Difficult for us to pass the most of the
horses when they attempt'd to asend the farthest Bank tumbling with their
loads Back in the River."

The men had to carry their powder, bread and bedding over on their shoulders. By the time they reached dry ground it was dark: "Could not find a plain
Big enough for one man to Lye on no fire wood except green or Roten Spruce
pine no place for our horse to feed And to prevent their Eating of Loral tyd them
all up least they Should be poisoned."

No wonder young Lewis, scratching down his notes with a quill clutched
in weary fingers by the light of the campfire, forgot his spelling and punctuation.

Peter Jefferson was so impressed that he entered the name of the River Styx
on his map and indicated "Laurel Thickets" in large letters.

After fighting their way through the swamps and the ridges of the laurel
thickets they found to their dismay that they had crossed the divide. They were
fording streams that were "running to the left hand or West ward . . . so that
Instead of Crossing the Branches of Potowmack we Crost those of Missisipia."
They had swung too far west and had to toil their way up over the mountains
again.

After more than a month's punishing travel, ragged and bearded, sweat-
stained and weary, they reached the blazes Captain Winslow had left in a grove
of trees when he had surveyed the main branch of the Potomac three years before.
At the headspring "We Dined on a loyn Roasted Venison about three O Clock
at the Spring head Drank his Majesty's health."

Before starting out to recheck their line on the homeward trail, the leaders
of the party cut their initials on the marked trees about the spring. First on a great
beech they cut GR for King George to the west and FX for Lord Fairfax to the
east. Every man had his jackknife out. Joshua Fry cut his name on a beech. Peter
Jefferson cut PJ on a small spruce pine and again on a beech with the date. Lewis
left his own name on the smooth huge silvery trunk of the beech where the
previous expedition had left their marks. "This Done we bid adue to the head
Spring about ½ hour after nine oClock Our Course Directing to the head of
Rapahanock Being S-46-E."

The promoters of the Loyal Land Company lacked the wealth and power
of the Northern Neck planters who backed the Ohio Company. Instead of hiring
others to carry the chain and transit across the mountains they had to bear the

brunt of the work themselves. Peter Jefferson and his good friend Fry spent most of their lives on these punishing expeditions.

Dr. Walker, the versatile physician and naturalist and merchant and explorer who was another leading spirit of the enterprise, added surveying to his other accomplishments. It was as a surveyor that he had gone along with Colonel Patton of Augusta County on an exploring trip down the Clinch River into what is now Tennessee. John Findley, who was years later to guide Daniel Boone into the bluegrass country, was one of the hands on this trip. An active surveyor had to be an explorer in those days.

Another year, shooting buffalo and elk and deer and bear and wild turkeys and geese for meat as they travelled, Dr. Walker himself led a party across Cumberland Gap and helped build the first white man's cabin in Kentucky. These were men who grappled with the forest at first hand.

Thomas Jefferson spent his boyhood among tales and rumors of these explorations and of the friendly Indians his father met on his travels. Their chiefs were frequent visitors at Shadwell. He was early interested in their languages and customs. He was too young to be taken along on surveying trips, but this father, so Jefferson tells us in his autobiography, took great pains to train him in shooting and riding and woodcraft. Squirrel hunting in the hills across the river he must have often imagined himself, like his father and his father's friends, following the warriors' path beyond the barrier of the Blue Ridge that closed his horizon to the westward. Years later when he was studying the law at Williamsburg, as a normal step in the course of a Virginia landowner's career, he himself took out a license as a surveyor.

Just about all the neighbors who frequented Shadwell were involved with the Loyal Land Company. Many a time over the wine after dinner the skinny red-headed boy must have pricked up his ears at deep talk of exploration into the Western Waters. That may well have been why, though he never went west himself, he all his life retained a ready sympathy for the pioneers who did. When Peter Jefferson died leaving Thomas the head of his family at fourteen, the friends he charged in his will with the care of his son's education were all westernminded men. Their first act as guardians was to send young Thomas to school with their friend and associate, the Reverend James Maury who was Rector of the church Dr. Thomas Walker, one of Thomas's guardians and an executor of his father's estate, had built on his own land at Castle Hill.

This James Maury was a member of one of those learned Huguenot families exiled from France that spread culture and scholarship wherever they went in the old world or the new. He kept a Latin school at the rectory near Castle Hill. In spite of the poor repute in which parsons were held in Virginia in those days he seems to have been highly respected among the Albemarle planters. There's a hint of the scope of the plans these Albemarle county surveyors were laying for further exploration to the westward in a letter he wrote his uncle in England telling how Joshua Fry had been much stirred by reading, in a book by a man named Cox, which dealt with the navigation of the Mississippi, that passage by water was possible with only short portages from the great river's northernmost tributaries to a river that flowed west into the South Sea, "And I presume," wrote the Reverend Maury, "the Credit which Col. Fry gave to Mr. Cox & his recommending these Matters to the Consideration of Governor & Council, gave birth to a grand Scheme formed here about three Years ago . . . Some Persons were to be sent in Search of that River Missouri, if that be the right Name of it, in order to discover whether it had any such Communication with the Pacific Ocean: they were to follow that River if they found it, & make exact Reports of the Country they passed through, the Distance they travelled, what sort of Navigation those Rivers and Lakes afforded, &c. &c. And this Project was so near being reduced into Practice that a worthy Friend and Neighbor of mine,"—this was Dr. Walker—"who had been extremely useful to the Colony in the many discoveries he has made to the westward, was appointed to be the chief Conductor of the whole Affair: had, by order of their Honors"—the Governor's Council of Virginia—"drawn up a List of all the necessary Implements and Apparatus for such an Attempt, & an Estimate of the Expense; & was upon the Point of making all proper Preparations for setting out, when a sudden Stop was put to the further Persecuation of the Scheme for the Present, by a Commencement of Hostilities between this Colony & the French & their Indians, which rendered a Passage through the interjacent Nations with whom they are ever tampering, too hazardous to be attempted."

The good schoolmaster went on to explain to his uncle that he considered this project so deep a secret that he had instructed the person who was carrying the letter to England to throw it overboard in case there was danger of his ship being captured by the French.

The long period of peace with the Indians which made frontier settlement comparatively easy for the American settlers was over. The frontiersmen of Great Britain's American colonies were finding themselves unwillingly caught up in the worldwide war for supremacy between Great Britain and France.

But Maury was looking far into the future: "What an exhaustless fund of Wealth would here to be opened, superior in Worth to Potosi & all the other South American Mines! What an extent of Region! What a—! But no more.— These are visionary Excursions into Futurity, with which I sometimes used to feed my Imagination, ever dwelling with Pleasure on the Consideration of whatever bids fair for contributing to extend the Empire & augment the Strength of our Mother Island, so that would be diffusing Liberty both civil & Religious & her daughter Felicity the wider, & at the same time be a Means of aggrandizing and enriching this Spot of the Globe, which every civil & social Tye binds me to have the tenderest Regard for. But these pleasing Expectations, if not entirely vanished, are much weakened and suspended, till Heaven decide the Controversy between the two mighty Monarchs now contending, in some sort, for the Empire of the World."

Surveying the wilderness, the mischances of war against the Indians and the French, and difficulties with the faraway government at Westminster were the training school of the frontiersmen of the American generation of 1776. Men who dared venture out beyond the settlements had to put forth every effort of muscle and brains. The great continent lured them on through danger and privation.

Land had from the first been the consuming passion of every settler on the Atlantic fringes of the American forest. Better land for their crops kept beckoning them westward. As far back as the early days in Rhode Island Roger Williams had deplored "a depraved Appetite after the great Vanities, Dreams and Shadows of this vanishing Life—great Portions of Land—Land in this Wilderness, as if Men were in great necessity and danger for want of great Portions of Land." The appetite grew with feeding.

Honor and wealth and the part he might play in the building of a civilization in the wilds all hinged on a man's getting title to land. To get title the country had to be explored, lines run, metes and bounds set, claims registered with the colonial governments. Through the years since the first settlements the British Crown had made grant after grant based only on the dimmest hearsay knowledge of American geography. In the western extension of almost every province the grants conflicted.

The surveyor was the indispensable man. The moment that French power was broken in America, from Georgia to Maine survey parties began hacking their way through the back country again, running their lines with compass or transit.

In the Connecticut hills there grew up a family of Allens. There was Ethan and Heman and Heber and Zimri and Ira and Lydia and Lucy. His mother, Ethan Allen used to say, had, like Mary Magdalen, been delivered of seven devils. He counted himself as the eighth. When the children were tiny the father moved up country into the Housatonic Valley. There they farmed and raised hogs and were teased by tales of great lakes and broad lands to the northward and westward. When news came of the French and Indian War the settlers at Cornwall built themselves a stockade. Ethan, the eldest of the Allen boys, marched off with the militia to the relief of the fort on Lake George.

Ethan was a tall man of enormous physical strength. He read and he thought about what he read. He was a declared freethinker, a humorously profane talker and great tosspot and brawler in taverns. He could talk anybody into almost anything.

Ethan came back from serving in the militia full of tales of the marvelous lands on Lake Champlain that would be open for settlement once the French were driven off. He couldn't wait to found his fortune; he started an iron furnace in Salisbury and lead mines in Northampton.

The Allens were an enterprising lot. When the defeat of the French opened up the whole continent for the English to settle they moved inland to find themselves land. Ethan went into promoting the New Hampshire grants, Levi took to trading in furs and skins and penetrated as far as the Maumee towns seven hundred miles northwest of Detroit.

When Levi came back to the settled country he and Heman set up a factory in Salisbury to make deerskin shirts and breeches. Ira Allen worked for them for wages.

Ira was the youngest. His nickname was Stub. He seems to have been the runt of the family, but he and Ethan had more than their share of the brains and the enterprise. Ethan was the orator and brawler and leader of men. Ira was the quiet, scheming kind. Ethan promoted their land speculations. Ira did the surveying.

Ethan was already deep in speculation in the New Hampshire grants. In spite of a Royal Order in Council turning over to New York the great tract of mountainous land between Lake Champlain and the Connecticut River, the Wentworths who governed New Hampshire were still selling what they called "rights" to unoccupied lands there. For a number of years both Albany and Portsmouth furnished deeds to all comers and let the settlers fight the conflicts out among themselves. The Wentworths offered easier terms and most of the Green Mountain settlers, being Connecticut people like the Allens, preferred to deal with New Englanders.

It was as a sort of posse to keep the Yorkers, as they called them, off the lands granted by New Hampshire, that Ethan Allen first organized his Green Mountain Boys. His right hand man in that organization was a Captain Remember Baker who, like George Washington, had learned his soldiering in the war against the Indians and the French. He was a cousin of the Allens and a surveyor by profession and from him young Ira Allen learned the rudiments.

Winters Ira worked for his brothers Heman and Levi herding pigs or milling deerskins. Summers he went surveying. By the time he was twenty he'd scraped up the cash and the credit to join in taking up rights to ten thousand acres up in the wilds north of Bennington. The Allens were all of them handy with credit.

To establish his rights Ira had to find them, to lay out their metes and bounds and to make sure that no damned Yorker should get there before him. With Remember Baker in the fall of 1771 he set out to find some tract supposed to be near Castleton township. The settlers already established there weren't much help. They wanted the open meadows for themselves.

None of the Allens ever paid much attention to other people's notions. "On the North side of Castleton, on Sucker Brook, I discovered an excellent tract of intervale," Ira wrote in his autobiography, "finding no lines we surveyed this, with some other lands near to our rights, to the great mortification of some people in Castleton . . . Continuing our line to Meeds brook, we cut off fifteen hundred acres of land surveyed for Castleton, which added to the vexation of the Castleton people." Obviously the vexation of the Castleton people gave Ira no pain.

To make sure of his point of departure for this survey he had to find the exact location of the old military trail to Crown Point. He went off with five days provisions in his pack leaving Baker and his boy to make camp on Sucker Brook. Any game they might take meant that their supplies would last just that much longer. Ethan was a great hunter for the splurge and the sport of it but Ira hunted for the pot.

"I took a little gun with me more for the purpose of making fire than hunting . . . The day was calm, and the leaves so dry that a man might be heard to walk at forty rods distance. After continuing march about four miles I discovered a large buck at about 14 rods distance. His head was down (in pursuit of a doe as I suppose) which prevented his discovering me till I was preparing for a shot at him, as he stood fair broadside . . . The powder being damp the buck leaped off unhurt and stopped in a small hollow . . . I therefore prepared another shot, extremely vexed at having my gun so out of order . . . At this instant the old buck advanced towards me. By the time I could prime, he came in full sight and stopped behind trees, so that I had about eight inches of his body to shoot at. To shoot him through the guts would be of no use to me. I must therefore cut his backbone or all was lost. I leveled for it and had the good fortune to break his back at about eighteen rods distance. I loaded my gun and advanced to him . . . Having only five charges of powder I did not choose to spare another on him. I set down my gun and drew a small knife and took him by the horn, and turned his head around, and put my knife to cut his throat. As soon as it cut the rough thick skin, he gave his head a shake which threw me a rod and wrenched my left arm much, and I lost my knife, so that it took me some time to find it. I then made at the buck again, when he set his hair forward, changing the color of his eyes to a frightful hue."

Ira had to use up another charge of powder and ball to kill the great buck. He had hardly managed to get him skinned when he saw another. This one he promptly shot through the heart. "I drew this buck to the other, and took off his skin & hung up the venison with my hat over it to preserve it from ravens &c, and returned to Baker and found him near dark making his camp."

There was plenty game moving that day. "Baker had also a singular encounter," Ira wrote later. "He found it necessary to measure a line a short distance over a high ridge. He took the fore end of the chain, tally sticks & hatchet, with his compass, with which he was much incumbered. As he went down the hill he saw at the root of a tree, some signs as though there were raccoons there. As he came close to the tree he discovered a bear's paws in the hollow. The bear attempting to come, Baker dropped his compass &c and took his hatchet in both hands; but in attempting to bring it back for a blow, he was prevented by a bush, when the bear coming forward, faster than he expected, instead of striking her in the head, he struck her in the neck. She started back with difficulty & Baker got out the hatchet, for it was in her neck to the helve, and had cut some large bloodvessles. Every time Baker could get a stroke at her he did till she bled to death. He then got the body out of the tree, skinned, and hung up the meat. Thus ended the adventures of the day."

Surveying was no work for weaklings. A woodsman needed a strong stomach.

"Baker and I continued our surveys till we were out of provisions, though we had stores at Castleton, several miles distant. Our arrangements would take three days to complete. Baker, being an old soldier in the former French war, thought to drive me out of the woods to bring provisions from Castleton by saying he could live very well on fresh bear meat without bread salt or sauce . . . I answered if he could live so I could. Neither would be the first to give back; and we got supplies of bear meat roasted and ate for three days, completed our business and returned to Castleton.

"I returned to Salisbury, and spent the winter dressing leather for my brothers as aforesaid, until about the first of March, when I undertook to learn the Surveyors art. I spent Seven days with a Master, when some other business took me off."

Next summer he arrived at Bennington on his way to another survey in May. There he found Ethan and his Green Mountain Boys in a tizzy over a warning some Quakers had sent them that Governor Tryon of New York was advancing with a force of the King's troops to dispossess the New Hampshire settlers. They induced Ira to ride unobtrusively over to Albany to see whether they ought to arm themselves for defence or not. He found to everybody's great relief that the troops were bound for Detroit.

Back in the woods with Remember Baker it wasn't long before they were as usual out of provisions. This time Baker suggested they try living for three days off suckers out of the brook. "The fish operated on Baker like physic," Ira noted with satisfaction—there was a lot of malice in the Allens—; "so that he was just able to get into Castleton, when he roundly swore he would never again try such measures with me. I then commenced Surveyor for myself, and never after went to a master to learn a rule but made several rules, which are recorded in my old woods book."

Ira Allen was going through one of those spells of ill health that so often attack growing adolescents. The measles had interfered with his study of the surveyor's manual the year before. Now he was stricken with boils. He was staying with his brother in Ethan's new house in Poultney. In spite of his boils he was the one who rode over to Crown Point to find out what kind of mischief a New York surveyor named Cockburn was up to in the Onion River country. (What was then called the Onion River is now the Winooski.) Ira already thought of it as his private preserve. He was brokenhearted that he wasn't well enough to go off in pursuit of the scoundrelly interloper. His brother Ethan and Remember Baker were making it hot for the Yorkers' surveyors. When they caught one they stripped off his shirt and beat him with birch twigs till he fainted.

The days Ira had to lay up nursing his boils gave him leisure to contemplate the future of the fine lands he'd had only half a look at. "While lame I contemplated the extent of the New Hampshire Grants," he wrote in retrospect, "and probable advantages that might arise from being contiguous to Lake Champlain, and determined to interest myself in that country; as soon as able to ride. I set out to purchase some lands in the towns contiguous to Onion River that were owned in Connecticut. At Bennington I met with my brother Ethan, who exerted himself to discourage me; yet I proceeded to Salisbury, and informed Heman of my intentions. He also advised against it . . ."

In the end young Ira convinced them both. He raised enough money from his brothers to buy the rights which laid the foundations for the immense holdings of their Onion River Company. But before the Allens could take over they had to run the Yorkers out.

Though he was still weak from his boils Ira made his way up Lake Champlain by boat. At Skeensborough Remember Baker met him.

"Baker arriving we set out for Onion River. A few hours after I was taken with a dysentery that was severe for three days and nights and reduced me to be very weak. Baker advised me to steep white oak bark in water, and take it to check its operation. But I declined, considering that my constitution was throwing off the

When Charles Willson Peale painted his first portrait, in the uniform of
an officer of the Virginia regiment in 1772 George Washington still had
a little of the youthful woodsman about him.

In spite of failing health it was George's half brother Lawrence who by his fortunate marriage and high-flown connections placed the Washingtons among the leading families of the Virginia colony.

Trader, shipowner, land speculator, Thomas Lee built Stratford Hall and there founded the great clan of the Lees.

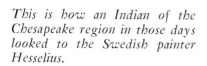

This is how an Indian of the Chesapeake region in those days looked to the Swedish painter Hesselius.

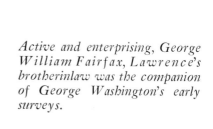

Active and enterprising, George William Fairfax, Lawrence's brotherinlaw was the companion of George Washington's early surveys.

*George Mason, who first codified
American liberties, was all his life a
western-minded man.*

*George Mason's brilliant younger
brother Thomas Mason ran across
William Buckland in England. He induced the young craftsman to come
to America to work on Gunston Hall
for his brother George who was as
fastidious an amateur of architecture
as he was of the grammar of freedom.*

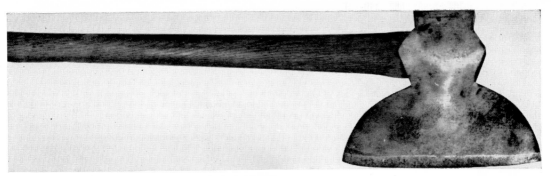

The broadaxe that cleared the forests.

Portrait of a man who may be Ethan Allen.

Ira Allen, surveyor, state builder, historian.

In Virginia and Maryland tobacco was king: transportation.

Tobacco receipts took the place of currency: curing and storage.

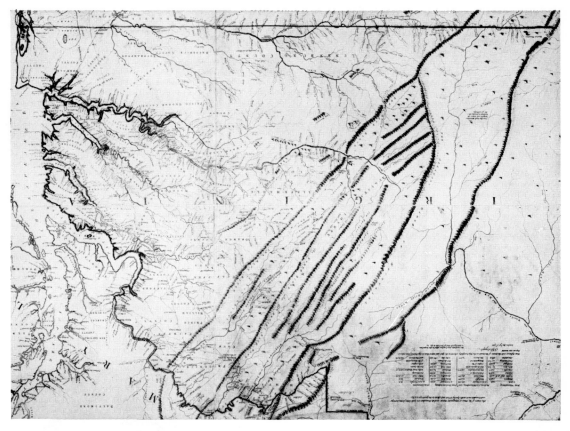

The region of the dreadful laurel thickets set down in Fry and Jefferson's epoch-making map of Virginia.

Engraving from Fry and Jefferson map.

Flag carried at the siege of Louisbourg in the 1745 expedition under Sir William Pepperell.

effects of the measles, boils, &c., as was intended by Doctr. Fay; which I really effected, and I never enjoyed better health in my life."

Before he could take any pleasure in the country he had to chase down those scoundrelly Yorkers who were trying to get it away from him.

"We proceeded to Shelburn and stopped at Acres Point, being wind-bound, when Baker and I. Vanornam set out through the woods to see the lands and find New Huntington corner, which Baker had seen when in pursuit of Cockburn; and to see if they could discover any signs of N. York surveyors in the woods. We were to meet at the falls of Onion River as soon as the wind would admit. The other men with me went on with the boat to said falls. On landing, I found a camp with some provisions &c. that induced me to suppose that a New York surveyor was in the woods." Ira was bound he would catch him alive. "I carefully left the camp, leaving no signs of our having been there, and went down the river about two miles to a large intervale, and there formed a camp. I left a sentinel to look out for Baker at the falls and to see who might come to camp. My sentinels not being old soldiers, were inattentive, and Baker passed them; and, not finding me, or any signs of my being there, was very hungry and ate some of said stores. After we met, we continued a sentinel and waited some days for the party to come in."

To Ira's great distress his prey slipped through his fingers. "When they arrived, Capt. Stevens the Surveyor discovered that somebody had been there, and before we could attack the camp, and made his escape with most of his party, leaving two men in the camp, which we made prisoners of. Not being able to learn certainly where Stevens was gone, we waited till near dark; when we took Stevens' boat, stores, and prisoners, and set out for our camp. In the twilight, two boats were discovered coming towards us, who turned and made off faster than we could pursue; nor could we discover their numbers &c. We hurried them by our stores &c, which we had taken the precaution in some measure to secrete. It was then agreed to remain there for the night and keep a lookout."

The New York surveyor was a man of some stomach himself: "In the morning before sun rise we discovered two boats coming up the river towards us, which proved to be two bark canoes, four of his men and ten Indians, all well armed with guns &c. and our whole party was seven men. Capt. Baker had a cutlass, Vanornam, a gun and I a case of pistols. These were all the arms we had; nevertheless, we determined to defend the ground. I prepared our men with axes, clubs, &c., and arranged ourselves on the bank about two rods from the water, tying our prisoners to a pole behind. Stevens was the first man out of the canoes, and while the rest were getting out, he came up the bank with a hatchet in his hand, with large pistols in his pocket, and made towards Baker, brandishing his hatchet. Baker opened his breast, inviting him to strike, if he dared. Stevens demanded why his men were tied. Baker answered it was his pleasure. Stevens drew a scalping knife from his bosom, and turned towards them, not daring to attempt to strike Baker, as Vanornam's gun was pointed on him. When about 30 feet of me, I presented a pistol at him, with a solemn word that death was his portion instantly if he stepped one step farther, or attempted to touch the pistols in his pocket. At this, he stopped with a pale countenance, & by this time, his party appeared prepared to come up the bank; when I spoke to Vanornam, who had been a prisoner with the Indians, to tell the redmen in their own language, that they and we were brothers, that they were welcome to hunt &c., on our lands when they pleased, that this was a land quarrel, that did not concern them. Vanornam spoke to them in their own language to that effect, and they instantly leaped to their canoes, leaving Stevens and his men prisoners."

The New York surveyor was nonplussed: "Stevens then asked me whether I should have fired if he had not stopped. I told him I should for I had no notion of being a prisoner & tryed by the Supreme Court of New York by the acts of outlawry &c."

The government at Albany had passed a sentence of outlawry on the Allens and their associates.

Ira couldn't help showing off a little; it was this sort of gesture that was his brother Ethan's specialty:—"Then pointing the same pistol to a small mark, less than a dollar, in a pole, about the same distance as Stevens was from me, observing that I would suppose that pole to be his body and the mark his heart, I fired. The ball (by chance) struck the pole about half an inch under the mark."

In the end everybody behaved fairly reasonably. "There being a truce between Govr. Tryon and the people of the district of the New Hampshire Grants, we thought it would not be politic to inflict corporial punishment on Stevens. He and his men were dismissed, on pain of death never to come within the district of the New Hampshire Grants again. Their boat, stores &c. were also returned to them and we parted."

At last Ira could feel that the land was his. "While waiting for the surveying party to come out of the woods, I explored the intervales below the falls of said Onion river, and pitched my tent by a large pitch pine tree nearly opposite to an island, about one and a half miles below the falls, from which I had observed large intervales on both sides of the river, when I first went up, and landed for the first time I ever set my foot on the fertile soil of Onion river, at the lower end of the meadow now known by the name of the old fields, where I discovered from my boat an opening like cleared lands. In consequence, I directed my men to refresh themselves with spirits and water, while I went to view the lands. I went up the open meadow, where the blue joint grass &c. was thick, till in sight of a large and lonely elm. Computing the open field about fifty acres, I was much pleased with this excursion, promising myself one day to be the owner of that beautiful meadow."

Back in the settled country Ira was finally able to convince his brothers that they must settle the Onion River country before the Yorkers did. "Capt. Baker came from Arlington to confer on these matters and five of us agreed to join in partnership, viz, Ethan Allen, Remember Baker, Heman Allen, Zimry Allen and Ira Allen. The plan then was to purchase lands, and furnish stores to commence settlement in the towns of Burlington, Williston, Shelburn, Colchester, Essex and Jericho. Baker and myself were to repare to Onion River in the Spring to see to business there, Ethan Allen to remain at Bennington, Poultney &c. to manage political affairs; for the country or district of the New Hampshire Grants was in a state of war with the colony of New York, not in reality with the body of the people of the colony, but with the governor, council, Court Sycophants and land jobbers."

Next spring Ira marked a road through from the lake shore to his promised land. "This road was soon after cut out so as to make a bridle road . . . Thus in a short time, I led a people through a wilderness of 70 miles; about the same distance that it took Moses 40 years to conduct the children of Israel." That same summer Ethan and a company of Green Mountain Boys built a block fort at New Haven Falls. Meanwhile Ira and Remember Baker were finishing another blockhouse at the falls of the Onion River. "The fort was built over a boiling spring for certainty of water. We made double doors, blocks for the windows, and every part proof against small arms. We never walked out without at least a case of pistols. In this situation we were a terror to the New York claimants."

That was how it happened that the Allens and their Green Mountain Boys were already on a war footing when they heard of the occupation of Boston by British troops and of the fighting at Lexington and at Concord Bridge. It was the most natural thing in the world that Ethan Allen should surprise the small British force at Ticonderoga "in the name of the Great Jehovah and the Continental Congress."

Remember Baker was the first man killed on Lake Champlain during the Revolutionary War. Ethan managed to get himself captured in a rash effort to storm Montreal and wrote the story of his captivity up in a book and came home the national hero; but it was Ira who did the spadework of building a state out of these outlaw settlements in the Green Mountains.

"Then ambition, vigor of youth, with a firm constitution united to acquire a character and fortune" Ira noted with understandable pride in his autobiography. He was a modest man: he admitted to a lack of booklearning. He let his brothers push themselves forward as leaders, but in the meetings and conventions that established first a state they called New Connecticut, and then independent Vermont, Ira Allen's name usually appeared as clerk. He developed a knack for writing. It was Ira who wrote the resolutions that other men presented. It was Ira who drafted their constitution and wrote his state's first history.

As a member of the Committee of Safety, to which the Windsor Convention turned over the government while its members got out of the way of Burgoyne's advancing redcoats, Ira Allen played a great part in preparing the resistance at Bennington that gave Burgoyne a foretaste of Saratoga. Later, while Ethan filled the air with bluster, Ira was the unseen spider who wove the web of intrigue by which the Green Mountain Boys, pitting New York against New Hampshire, and Carleton in Canada against the Continental Congress, managed to maintain their independence and to keep title to their lands, until such time as they could get themselves admitted to the union more or less on their own terms, as the fourteenth state.

The surveying adventures the Allens and George Washington and Peter Jefferson and the Lewises noted down in their journals were not too different from the adventures of hundreds of other pioneers who carried the chain through the virgin lands of Kentucky and Tennessee and Western New York and Pennsylvania and Ohio. The Americans were a people of surveyors; surveyors who made their own rules. The needs of the time turned surveyors into statebuilders.

Tobacco factors put in a good deal of care and taste on the labels that distinguished their product: an early brig.

A Seafaring People

CHAPTER 2   ✺

I̲T WAS DURING THE BOYHOOD AND YOUTH OF MOST OF THE MEN OF the generation of 1776 that the English speaking people established their preponderance in the world. The England their fathers and grandfathers had known was a minor island power that owed to the rough waters of the channel its freedom from domination by the Court of Versailles. As the eighteenth century advanced the British Isles gradually detached themselves from continental Europe. Englishmen's hopes lay in the ship lanes that led east to India and west to America. As settlements prospered along the American coast and in the islands of the Caribbean a seafaring society developed with its hub in the North Atlantic.

What was still spoken of with enthusiasm as the Glorious Revolution of 1688 had driven the last vestiges of feudalism out of England with the oldfashioned Stuart kings and brought the men of the wharves and countinghouses into positions of new importance in the kingdom. The elder Pitt's masterful strategy had cleared the seas of the French and established the British merchant as arbiter of empire. English had become the language of the sea.

Englishmen were feeling their oats. "Our Men are the stoutest and best," exulted Defoe early in the century "because strip them naked from the Waist up-wards, and give them no Weapons at all but their Hands and Heels and turn them into a Room, or Stage, and lock them in with the like Number of other Men of any Nation, Man for Man, and they shall beat the best Men you shall find in the world."

The merchants and seamen of the American seaboard played their part in the growth of this commercial empire. Outside of London, only Bristol and Glasgow could match the importance of Philadelphia and Boston as trading ports. New York and Charleston and Newport ranked high among centers of British shipping. Quite a proportion of the shipping in the Atlantic trade was American owned and a much larger proportion was American built.

Defoe again, in an unexpectedly lyrical outburst, described the place ship-building held in the economy of early eighteenth century England. It was even more important to the colonial ports: ". . . The Ship is built, fitted out for a Voyage; thousands of Tradesmen and Workmen subsist on the petty Demands of the Captain or other Persons who direct the Voyage; the Timber, the Plank; the Iron Work; the Masts; the Rigging, the Tar and Hemp, the Flax and Oyl, all pass through different and numberless Hands, till they center in the Builder's Yard; there the Frame of a Vessel is set in the Stocks. What Hands are employed to creat the beautiful useful Form of a Ship! and what Art to perfect and launch her into the Water!

"The Carpenters, Caulkers, Mastmakers, Joyners, Carvers, Painters, Smiths &c finish the Hull; the Tradesmen are employed to furnish and fit her out; the Sail Makers, Rope Makers, Anchor Smiths, Block Makers, Gun Founders, Coopers, and (for a Thousand such things too trifling to mention, tho' absolutely needful), the Ship Chandler, and at last the Brewer, Butcher, Baker &c for Provision to victual her and help on the Voyage.

"All these, supported by the glorious Head of Commerce called the Mer-chant, are employed at the Outset of the Ship but know nothing how to manage the Ship in the Ocean, how to cause her to find her Way on the wild and path-less Surface of the Water; they fit her out and deliver all to the Commander &c. But as to the sailing Part, that belongs to another Class of People called the Sailors or Navigators; and when the Tradesmen have put the Ship into their Hands, their Work is done, till the Ship returns and they begin all again; So the Circle is continued, forever the Same."

American shipbuilding originated in New England with the launching of
Governor Winthrop's "Blessing of the Bay" in the third year of the Massachusetts
colony. By the middle of the eighteenth century stocks clustered around the
tidal creeks of the Merrimac and Cape Ann and the North Shore where small
sloops were built for the coastwise traffic and lateen rigged ketches for the
fishermen and an occasional great ship for the London trade. As early as 1648
a Boston shipyard had produced a 400 ton vessel. Even in Lord Nelson's day such

Paul Revere's view of the busy codfish capital.

a ship would have been considered sizeable. In spite of the American mechanics
earning higher wages, ships could be built two or three pounds sterling a
ton cheaper in New England than in the old country. The stocks followed
the retreating fringes of the forest inland. Small boats were often built in forest
clearings eight or ten miles from the water. When snow came enormous droves
of oxen hauled them on sledges to the rivers for launching.

The eighteenth was a century of booming trade interrupted by intermittent
war between England and France. In wartime the merchantmen took cannon
aboard and turned into privateers. Privateering was hazardous but rewarding.

In the Atlantic theatre the sugarproducing islands of the Caribbean were
the bone of contention. Sugarcane, planted and cut by slave labor out of the

West African forests, brought in enormous profits. For a century the West Indies were virtually the only source of sugar for the growing sweet tooth of Europe. Cane was so profitable that the plantation owners had no time for anything else. Furnishing the West India planters with provisions and lumber became the daily business of American shipmasters.

An engraving that celebrates the vigorous industry of colonial America.

Especially after the Peace of Utrecht in 1713 turned over Newfoundland to the British, the New England codfisheries, centered in Marblehead and Gloucester, became the main supplier of food for the slaves that worked the sugarcane. Yankee ships brought home in return molasses which they distilled into rum. Boston and Newport were the centers of distilling. A great deal of the rum found its way to the West African coast to pay for more slaves.

One of the conveniences of the West India market was that the planters were not too choosy about the quality of the fish they bought for their slaves. The better grades of dried cod went to Madeira and the Canaries and the Southern European seaports to be exchanged for wine and lemons and salt for American consumption. Often the master was instructed to sell the ship itself if a buyer offered the right price, and to bring his goods home in some cheaper bottom. Profits were invested in bills of exchange collectible on the London market. American exporters were always in need of credit in England. The mother country was the source of all the tea, and of the manufactured goods which the seaport merchants retailed in America and the hemp and iron castings essential to the rigging and building of ships.

It was on the whole a three way trade. Boston to the West Indies, to England and back to Boston again. A great deal depended on the skipper's judgment. Here are the instructions John Hancock's uncle Thomas, from whom that worthy was to inherit his fortune and his standing among Boston merchants, wrote for one of his captains:

Boston, Dec^{er} 20th 1743

Capt. Simon Gross

You having the Command of the Charming Lydia Brigantine and She in all Respects fitt for the Sea, My Order to you is that you take the first wind & weather for Sailing and proceed to the West Indies. You have Liberty to go to any of the English Islands, & if you think it Safe to any of the french Islands. But I advize you to proceed direct to St. Eustatia—(a tiny islet off St. Kitts which the Dutch ran as a free port. It was the center of free trade operations which the Trade Lords considered to be smuggling)—where you will hear how the Markets Govern, and advise with Mr. Godet on your affairs, after which you will be able to form a better Judgement where will be the best place to make a voyage & so proceed accordingly. You have Invoice & Bill of Lading Inclosed Consigned (to) yourself, you are to procure a Load of Molasses & proceed back to Boston & if you have more Cargo than Loads you, then Ship it on the best Terms you Can in Molasses or bring it in Indigo. I'd have you unload at Nantaskett—(to keep the cargo away from the prying eyes of the customs)—if no man of War there. You are Interested Oneeighth in the Cargo & are to have one eighth of the neat proceeds of Returns, I doubt not of your making the best Sale of everything . . . Make all possible Dispatch that you may be here early for the Land—(that is for a trip to Newfoundland to buy salt cod)—See that your Casks be good and well Stow'd, bring me some fruit for the officers—(I imagine this refers to the customs officers who had to be kept in good temper)—if any to be had, be prudent & saving of Expenses—Should it happen that you Can get bills of Exchange on Holland or England for your Cargo at a good price & a good freight for Holland or England take it, advising me thereof that I may Insure, or if you have Opportunity to Sell Vessell & Cargo for Bills on Holland or England at a price you think may answer you have my Liberty. You have Liberty also in every Respect to act as you think Shall be most for my Interests. But if you come back to this Place a Load of Molasses will be the best

Cargo you can bring here, write me by all Opportunitys. The Good Lord
protect you & our Interests, from all Dangers & Enemies & Give you Conduct
& prudence in all things to act for the Best, I wish you a Good Voyage and
am your Owner.

Along with these instructions went a keg of salmon, six kegs of oysters, a
barrel of apples, a barrel of pears and other delicacies for the Mr. Godet whose
advice was to be sought. He was Thomas Hancock's trusted agent in those parts.
Along with the delicacies went a letter asking his opinion: Should Captain Gross
risk going to Cap François, the great sugar port of what is now Haiti, for his
molasses in view of the imminent danger of the outbreak of war with the French?

Many shipowners weren't as fortunate in their captains as Thomas Hancock presumably was in Captain Gross. About the same year a Quaker merchant
in North Carolina was writing a fellow Friend, Richard Waln in Philadelphia:

"If thou be concerned with Spanton in the sloop Ranger I fear thee will
be a sufferer from the bad account I hear of him, he left Eden town about
the 20 June with a Strumpet on board not bound for Jamaica as he gave out but
bound for Madeira."

Codfish, lumber, provisions and rum were the chief exports of New England
until an ingenious Nantucketer discovered that he could melt the oil out of whale
blubber as well at sea as ashore. Building brick tryworks on board ship gave the
whalers range. American whalers started to scout the Arctic and to push their
voyages further and further into the South Atlantic.

Whale oil was the source of illumination. It furnished the raw material of
most candles and of the oil people used in their lamps. Its price fluctuated on the
London market. Boston merchants built themselves faster and faster ships to
try to win the race with oil across the Atlantic every fall. The first ship that tied
up at Bristol or London sold its cargo for the highest price. Whaleoil became a
major factor in the trade with the home islands.

Meanwhile the middle colonies furnished furs, that came into New York
down the Hudson, and wheat, flour and salt meat and lumber and barrelstaves.
Virginia and Maryland, loading their great hogsheads in a thousand creeks and
inlets in the Chesapeake, had a monopoly of tobacco.

Tobacco was by far the most important export from the Chesapeake
region, but its economy, though equally based on slave labor, was not quite as
limited to one crop as that of the islands: "Our Trade" Governor Gooch of Virginia wrote home in 1740, "besides Tobacco & Lumber, Pitch & Tarr, Skinns &
Furrs to Great Britain; is, a little Tobacco, Beef, Pork, Wheat, Indian Corn,
Candles made of Myrtle-Wax" (a kind of bay) "to the British Islands in the
West Indies; for which we have in Exchange, Sugar, Rumm and Molasses, and

sometimes Money. To the Madeira Islands we send Wheat and Indian Corn with some Candles and bring back their Wine, but in this Commerce the Ballance much against us, is paid in Bills of Exchange."

Money was even rarer in Maryland and Virginia than in New England. The common currency consisted in receipts and inspection certificates for tobacco. The bulk of the Indian Weed went to England to cover the charges the English merchants chalked up against the planters when they shipped them out manufactured goods.

Charleston and Savannah shipped indigo and rice. All the colonies furnished naval stores. Through the vast coastal forests from Maine to Georgia inspectors went about marking the king's arrow on the straightest pines to set them aside for masts for the Royal Navy.

Cash was always scarce. The whole Atlantic commerce was built up on barter. The merchants were their own bankers. Bills of lading were the medium of exchange. The process was complicated by the rules and regulations issued by the Trade Lords in London to enforce the Navigation Acts which aimed, according to the mercantilist creed, to protect the mother country's monopoly of trade with the colonies. Skill in smuggling and evading red tape and duties became an important part of the merchant's equipment. Smuggling and privateering gave American merchants and seacaptains a very special kind of training. It was a tough school but it made for seamanship and sharp wits.

This was a world where brains and nerve and coolheaded calculation counted. Young men with these qualities found careers opening for them in the counting house and on the quarter deck.

Robert Morris of Philadelphia was the sort of man who rose to fortune in the Atlantic trade. He was born in Liverpool. His grandfather was a common seaman. He seems to have been brought up by his grandmother. The story was that as a boy he was apprenticed to a nailmaker.

His father had left home early and sailed west to make his fortune and set himself up as a tobacco factor in the then flourishing port of Oxford on the Eastern Shore of Maryland. There he'd made himself a reputation as a high liver and congenial spirit. He was considered a man of brains and enterprise. He was credited with inaugurating the system of tobacco inspection before shipment through which the Maryland and Virginia planters preserved the reputation of their product in the London market. The chief blemish on his character, according to his contemporaries, was the cruelty with which he treated his servants.

When young Robert Morris was about thirteen his father felt himself prosperous enough to send for his son. He arranged for his schooling in Philadelphia.

He was to have the best education the city afforded and to be brought up in the mercantile business.

The elder Morris seems to have felt that his menage at Oxford was not quite the place for a growing boy. He had set up housekeeping there with a lady named Sarah Wise whom he had not taken the trouble to marry. Or perhaps the first Mrs. Morris was still alive in the old country.

In spite of everything the Board of Trade in London could do, the colonists would manufacture goods. Here they are producing shoes which soon became a great export from New England.

When young Robert Morris was about sixteen his father came to an untimely end through an ironic accident. He had been dining, possibly too well, with the master of the ship *Liverpool*, which, presumably, was loading tobacco in the river. It was the custom to salute distinguished guests with a round of cannon when they were rowed ashore after the festivities. As his guest was leaving the ship the captain was to signal the gunner when to fire. Some said that this time a fly lit on the captain's nose and that when he raised his hand to brush it off the gunner thought he was giving the signal to fire. Anyway the gunner let fly too soon, before the ship's boat was out of harm's way, and poor Mr. Morris the tobacco factor was hit with a pad of burning wadding that splintered his arm. The wound became infected and he died. A certain Mr. Callister wrote friends in Philadelphia that he had eased Mr. Morris's last hours by reading him Plato's *Phaedo* and that his faithful dog Tray had never left his bedside. He added that Tray refused to be comforted and pined away after his master's death.

In his will Robert Morris senior left his son about twentyfive hundred pounds in Maryland currency. His daughter by Sarah Wise was provided with a hundred pounds and another hundred was left "to the infant with which she was then with child." When this infant turned out to be a boy whom the mother named Thomas, young Robert Morris took charge of him and brought him up.

His father's Philadelphia friends even before his father's death had arranged to apprentice young Robert with the Willings family, notable Bristol merchants established in Philadelphia. He served as a supercargo on trading journeys to Europe and the West Indies then became the firm's indispensable man.

Flaking the cod.

When the Willing firm was reorganized after young Thomas Willing came back from London, where like the sons of so many colonial merchants he had read law in the Temple, Morris, although he was only twenty-one, was taken in as a junior partner. He had made good use of his father's little legacy in private adventures on the Willing ships, and he had already a substantial sum to invest. He and young Willing became firm friends.

Thomas Willing was a cautious thoughtful individual who in later life was known in Philadelphia as "old squaretoes." His conservatism combined with Morris's reckless enterprise made the classical combination for a business partnership. The firm of Willing and Morris was successful indeed.

Morris became one of the great men of fast growing Philadelphia. His hearty sanguine manner made him friends in all directions. He married Mary White, a lady from a respected Maryland family who was reputed a great beauty. He acquired a town house on Front Street and a country house across the Schuylkill. This place "The Hills" was known for its fruit and for the products of the vegetable garden and greenhouse. His table became famous for good food and good drink and cheerful entertaining. "You see I continue my old practice of mixing business and pleasure" he wrote one of his friends "and ever found them useful to each other."

MARYLAND No

A tobacco stamp illustrated the sort of wharf that Robert Morris Sr. managed at Oxford.

It was natural that he should push to the fore in the Philadelphia Committee of Merchants during the Stamp Act agitation. He sat in the Pennsylvania Assembly. He was appointed to the Continental Congress. Though, possibly under the influence of his cautious friend Willing, who was suspected of being a bit of a Tory, he opposed the Declaration of Independence as untimely, when the day came to sign the document he put his name to it in a bold scrawl at the head of the Pennsylvania delegation.

With his practical knowledge of shipping he immediately became the most active member of the Secret Committee on Commerce and of the Marine Committee that handled naval affairs. He saw to it that his firm's network of correspondents in the West Indies and in European ports became indispensable in the procurement of war materials.

The salt Atlantic breezes blow through his correspondence. He knew ships and he knew seamen. When his family feelings weren't involved he was a shrewd judge of men. There's a strong sense of common knowhow in such a letter as John Bradford wrote him from Boston a month before the Declaration of Independence. Bradford, an agent of Morris's maritime committee, had been instructed to find a ship and a skipper to run to Europe for a cargo of munitions.

"The day I received your letter," wrote John Bradford, "I set out for Beverly where I fix'd on Just such a Brig as you described sent in by Manly some time since. She's not a year off the Stocks and said to be the fleetist sailing vessel in America." He would provide her with "every small sail that is needful." He had picked out "a Master so recommended by the Salem gentlemen that he appears to have every qualification you required a master of that vessel to have, and if his Face is an Index to his mind, he must be a fine fellow." He knew the Bay of Biscay like the palm of his hand. This was important because he must evade the British cruisers and run his cargo into Bilbao. The Spaniards paid in gold.

Bradford added that he was loading the brig with salt cod and whalebone and beeswax for the Spanish market, and adding ten or twelve tons of logwood (a tropical wood from Honduras, used by dyers) which he understood was selling well in Holland. As he wound up he asked Mr. Morris to present his compliments to several gentlemen he was acquainted with who were members of the Continental Congress and announced himself as "penetrated by the honor conferred on me by that august body" in intrusting him with this mission.

It was this training in illegal trade that enabled American merchants and seamen to outsmart and outsail the British during the Revolutionary War. For a whole century they had been evading the Navigation Acts. War conditions added only a slight extra hazard to their smuggling ventures. At the same time it immensely increased the profit of successful journeys.

Robert Morris's efforts in behalf of the United States did not escape criticism among convinced patriots.

Joseph Reed of Pennsylvania wrote of him "Those who know him will also acknowledge that he is too much of a man of the world to overlook certain private interests . . . It seems to have ever been a ruling principle with him to connect the public service with private interest and certainly he has not departed from it at this time of day."

Part of the confusion over Morris's honesty as a public servant arose from the complexity of the commercial dealings of the time. Bookkeeping was rudimentary. American merchants had to deal with the fluctuating paper currencies of thirteen separate provinces. Morris would trade so many hogsheads of tobacco estimated in Maryland paper currency, say, for a shipload of molasses in St. Kitts estimated in pounds sterling. Bills of lading would have to pass as a medium of exchange, so that half the time he would be using the bill of lading for the shipload of molasses to meet an obligation for a shipment of straw hats held by a merchant in Leghorn, which would be exchanged for powder and muskets in Rotterdam. Bills of exchange circulated that could be met part in cash, part in commodities, part in credit. Due to the slowness in communications years might

go by before any particular transaction was completed and liquidated. Add to
that the hazards of wartime captures and confiscations and the custom, so as not
to have all their eggs in one basket, of a number of shippers sharing in a shipload
of goods. "The commonest things," Morris wrote to a friend, "become intricate
when money has anything to do with them."

Everything depended on the individual merchant's personal standing in the
worldwide commercial community, what Robert Morris, in the parlance of the
time, spoke of as his "integrity." It was considered ethical for a merchant, who
had in his hands a shipload of lumber consigned to him, say, in Boston, to exchange
it, if he saw the chance for a good deal, with the bill of lading for a shipload of
hides in Cadiz, without consulting the original owners, who might be merchants
in St. Eustatius or in Baltimore or in Savannah, or the State of Pennsylvania
or the Continental Congress. Sometimes he was not too curious to find out
whether he was using the negotiable paper of the United States for a speculation to
his own advantage, or whether he was using his credit for the benefit of the
United States.

He would hardly have been human if he hadn't encouraged the legend to
grow that he was risking his private fortune to finance the revolution. To a
certain extent this may have been true; to a large extent the opposite was true.
Of one thing we may be sure: the commercial career of Robert Morris became
interlocked with the successes and failures of the American cause.

Robert Morris treated the Continental Congress and the State of Pennsylvania as he would commercial partners. While he procured them the munitions
they needed he indulged in profitable speculations on his own.

As early as the fall of 1777 Willing and Morris dissolved their main partnership, though they remained associated in a number of enterprises. It is likely
that the cautious Willing was already finding Morris's speculations a little giddy.
The failure of young Thomas Morris may have had something to do with Willing's
decision to dissolve the partnership. Robert Morris had given his bastard halfbrother "the best education that could be obtained in Philadelphia," and brought
him up in his own counting house and, in hopes of launching him on a career
as successful as his own, sent him off to Europe to represent Willing and Morris
and the United States in a number of delicate negotiations. Thomas took to drink
and gambling, fell into the hands of sharpers, and finally died in France in a
desperate fit of dissipation. Morris stood up for him manfully, but he had to admit
in the end that his halfbrother had made a mess of every matter put into his
hands and had cost both the firm and the United States a great deal of money.
This was not the way "old squaretoes" believed in doing business. It is possible
too that Willing was suffering some doubts that winter about the success of the

Gray's Inn Creek shipyard on the Eastern Shore of Maryland in the mid-eighteenth century.

The Bethel, *a New England privateer.*

A merchant's counting house.

Crossing a raging bar.

At the height of his fame as the richest man in America Robert Morris was painted by C. W. Peale. Through the window you can see l'Enfant's marble palace, which helped bring about his ruin.

West's early patron, William Henry, the Lancaster gunsmith, in West's still provincial early style.

Clérisseau's Ruins of Rome. C. L. Clérisseau, archeologist, architect, draftsman, was a French pupil of Winckelmann. Years later he helped Jefferson with his plans for the Virginia capitol.

The painting that caught the eye of George III and helped set the London style.

George III and Benjamin West Fishing, by Joseph Farrington. This picture is said to represent the fortunate painter and the unhappy monarch fishing together in a quiet English stream.

Smibert's portrait of Bishop Berkeley.

Part of the preliminary cartoon for Copley's Floating Batteries at Gibraltar.

Copley's horror picture Brooke Watson and the Shark *besides being an extraordinary piece of composition in its own right represented the avant garde of the romantic movement that was to fill the canvases of the early nineteenth century with contorted agonies.*

The result of Captain Watson's lucky bet. The stars and stripes are hard to see in the reproduction, but they float from the stern of his ship.

William Pitt the elder, the builder of empire, the idol of the colonials, glorified in a toga.

Peale's "Princeton" Washington. Since nobody remembered what General Mercer looked like, Peale substituted Mercer's deaf-mute son Billy for his father. Billy was one of the painter's apprentices.

47

Gilbert Stuart:
Portrait of the Artist as a Young Man.

Stuart in his old age.

American cause. When Howe occupied Philadelphia he chose to remain in the city as a noncombatant.

Morris on the other hand was thoroughly committed to independence. As a merchant by this time he was quite able to stand alone. His investments were scattered over the middle and southern states and all of the Atlantic ports. He had profitable dealings in rum and salt fish and flour with William Bingham in

A Robert Morris bill of exchange.

Martinique. He was speculating in tobacco with Carter Braxton in Virginia. He was involved in nine major partnerships in various American seaports, as well as in numberless smaller enterprises. His name was enough to attract capital to almost any venture. With Willing he set up a bank to finance procurement for the Pennsylvania troops. Even before the fighting began he was reputed to be one of the richest men in America. During the years of the war his knowledge of the sea lanes, his reckless enterprise as a speculator and merchant, his practical feel for money, were all put to the service of the Continental cause.

The tea party that so embittered Copley's life.

A People of Limners

CHAPTER 3 ☆

IF, IN THE YEARS JUST BEFORE THE AMERICAN REVOLUTION, YOU had asked some lounger in a London coffeehouse who the two greatest Americans were, he would have told you without hesitation: Benjamin Franklin and Benjamin West. Unless your informant turned out to be a fervent Whig he would have hesitated a little over Franklin's name, but Whig and Tory alike would have agreed that George III's court painter was one of the great artists of the age.

In America, during the years when the men of the generation of 1776 were growing up, Benjamin West's career became as much as Franklin's part of the myth of the success of rustic American virtues among courts and countinghouses of the bad old world.

The pleasures of the eye had not been as neglected as you might expect among the pioneer communities of the American seaboard. From the earliest days the settlers cultivated the popular arts they had inherited from Tudor England.

They enjoyed bright colors arranged in naive patterns that still had a mediaeval flavor. Thrown on their own resources by the difficulty and expense of importing house furnishings from England provincial artisans developed the skills their fathers had brought from overseas. Styles ran a generation behind metropolitan fashions but they tended to be simplified and made functional by the demands of a rude environment. Something of the freshness of the New World air crept into the designs that decorated the chests people kept their clothes in. Walls were painted with scenes and conventional ornaments for lack of hangings.

Religious painting was discouraged as popery but even in Puritan New England the new-rich merchants hankered after family portraits. There were a good many competent amateur painters, but a certain number of professional limners, as they were called, went about sketching in the heads of their sitters on canvases where halflengths garbed in rich costume had already been painted. The sitter could choose his clothing and accessories according to his taste and his pocketbook. Until the mid-eighteenth century these limners were mostly European immigrants who hadn't been able to make a go of it at home, but among the surveyors and seamen and statesmen of the generation of 1776 there were a number of painters who could vie with the best Europe had to offer.

Whittling and carving had long been popular with American woodsmen. Tombstones and the figureheads and poops of ships were carved in relief. Men made good livings casting weathervanes and painting signs for inns and shops. As the seaboard merchants became richer they put a great deal of money into decorating their coaches and carriages. The New Englanders, who allowed no ornament in their meeting houses, developed an ornate funeral pageantry. Pulpits were hung with sable for funeral orations. Paintings of skulls and hourglasses and of the deceased lying in state were carried in procession to the graveyard.

A young man who showed talent for drawing and painting could find ready acclaim even among the Pennsylvania Quakers. Indeed it was the Quakers who produced the first important American painter.

Benjamin West was the son of an English born Quaker who kept a rural inn a few miles west of Philadelphia, on the wagon road to the Conestoga Valley. He was the youngest of a large family of children. John West, the father, seems to have been a man of some education. He was prominent in Quaker meeting and early expressed qualms of conscience about the lawfulness of slaveholding. In later life, when Benjamin West was rich and famous and president of the Royal Academy in England, he filled the ears of his biographer with tales of a childhood which had become legendary before he was well out of his smock.

He was born in the fall of 1738. His mother, so the story went, was so moved by a Quaker preacher's description of God's imminent vengeance on the sinful peoples of Europe unless they fled the City of Destruction to found a new Zion amid the mountains and forests of America, that she was taken with labor pains right in the meeting house. The neighboring Friends interpreted this as a sign from on high that a child of extraordinary talent and virtue was coming into the world. From infancy little Benjamin was the spoiled darling of the family.

When he was seven he drew a likeness of his sister's baby Sally which was much admired. He took to drawing flowers and birds. He used to tell the story that it was the Indians who camped beside the inn on their way to and from the Philadelphia market who furnished him with his first colors. He was said to have made himself a brush by snipping hairs out of the tail of the family cat. A cousin of his father's, a Philadelphia merchant, was so impressed by the boy's productions that he sent him out a painting set and some engravings to copy.

The travelers clustered at the bar in his father's tavern marveled at the boy's precocious talent. Even the schoolmaster didn't grumble too much when little blond Benjamin played hooky from school to finish a painting. His Philadelphia cousin used to take the boy into the city to improve his mind and to show him off to his friends.

The leading portrait painter of Philadelphia at that time was a Bristol man named William Williams. When young West was shown a painting of his he almost went off his head with delight. Williams, very much flattered, showed him his pictures and drawings, lent him books about the old masters, and told his friends that such talent should be encouraged. Young West went passionately to work to paint in the style of William Williams.

This Williams was a man of great and varied talents. He seems to have dabbled in painting as a child in England. He was a rolling stone. When his father tried to make him study law he took the bit in his teeth and ran away to sea. He shipped before the mast on a privateer and was cast away on some Caribbean coast where he spent several years among the Indians. From there he made his way to the northern colonies where he wrote poetry and edited a volume of the lives of the painters and wrote the narrative, half fact and half fiction, in a style that's between Defoe and Herman Melville, which gives us one of the few pictures in English of life in the regions round the Gulf of Mexico before the coming of the white man. When this narrative was published years after Williams's death under the title of *The Journal of Llewellyn Penrose* it became one of Byron's great joys. It makes very good reading today.

In Philadelphia Williams helped construct the first American theatre and conducted art classes and taught music. According to the advertisement he ran in the papers he undertook "Painting in general, viz. History, Portraiture, Landskip, Sign painting, Lettering, Gilding and strewing Smalt." Besides he cleaned, varnished and repaired old pictures. Paintings which have come down to us show him to have been a painter of some originality and of great charm of color. A craftsman in the colonies had to be a jack of all trades to make a living.

By the time Benjamin West was fifteen he was considered a professional. The Quaker meeting his father and mother attended came, after much soulsearching, to the conclusion that though their creed banned the ornamental and the sensual they had no right to discourage any Godgiven gift. "What God has given who shall dare to throw away?" one of the members was moved to exclaim. The Friends concluded that this young man's talents were so extraordinary they must be intended for the moral edification of mankind. In the end, so West told his English biographer, John Galt, the Friends gave him their blessing in a body. The women all kissed him and the men laid their hands on his head and told him to go out into the world and testify as a painter to the light within.

He had a winning way with him. When he was sent to the Lancaster grammar school, he aroused the interest of a rich craftsman named Henry. This William Henry was one of the leading gunsmiths of a locality already famous for the manufacture of accurate rifles. He had the mechanical gift so common in the colonies. At an early date he was experimenting with a steamboat on Conestoga Creek. West painted a grimfaced portrait of him in a tight wig with a rifle in his hand, standing against a classical column and balustrade with an italianate glimpse —possibly borrowed from some print he'd seen in Williams's studio—of water and hills with even a small castle in the background. It was the Lancaster gunsmith who started him reading translations of Plutarch as the source of subjects to be treated in the grand manner. At Henry's suggestion he painted a *Death of Socrates*, using the frontispiece to Rollin's *Ancient History* as a model.

He couldn't do arithmetic. School didn't interest him. At an age when most boys were still under the schoolmaster's rod, Benjamin West travelled about the country painting portraits at two guineas for a head and five guineas for a half length. He painted in New York as well as in Philadelphia. He was a goodlooking young man with light brown hair and unusually sparkling eyes. Everywhere people were impressed by the Quaker innocence of his manner and by his industry and plain living. He must go to Rome to study, everybody told him. He worked hard to save up money for the journey.

In Philadelphia he was a favorite with the budding young geniuses of the place. There was the amiable Francis Hopkinson, with his taste for music and light verse and his scientific curiosity, who in later life was to become Jefferson's crony and one of his most amusing correspondents. Hopkinson wrote of his friend:

> "Nor let the muse forget thy name Oh West,
> Lov'd youth with virtue as by nature blest!
> If such the radiance of thy early morn,
> What bright effulgence must thy noon adorn?"

There was Jacob Duché who, before his loyalist convictions got the better of him, became the first chaplain of the Continental Congress; and Joseph Reed who was to be one of Washington's first aides and a highstrung Pennsylvania politician, and left behind him some sharp and sensitive descriptions of the personalities of the time. There was Robert Morris's brotherinlaw, William White, who was to be the first Episcopal bishop of Pennsylvania.

Thomas Godfrey who wrote *The Prince of Parthia*, the first homemade American play, was then a watchmaker's apprentice. West in his old age used to tell visitors to his London studio how he yearned for a clump of great old pines beside the Schuylkill where he used to sit fishing while his poetical friends, Hopkinson and Godfrey, recited their verses.

These young men's mentor, the learned Dr. Smith who edited the *American Magazine* and was provost of Philadelphia College, was so taken with young West, that when he discovered that he lacked the preparation needed for admission to the college, he arranged a special course for him in the classics to teach him about suitable subjects to paint as "history."

The young ladies of Philadelphia took to him too. He fell hard in love with a Miss Steel whose miniature he did, but her parents were bound she wouldn't marry a painter and locked her up. Elizabeth Shewell's relations tried the same thing, but eventually, years later, she gave them the slip, and became the painter's devoted wife.

There had been crop failures in Italy in the summer of 1759. Philadelphia merchants were taking advantage of the situation by shipping wheat and flour to Leghorn. While West was in New York painting (for ten guineas) the portrait of a merchant named William Kelly, Dr. Smith found that a friend of his was sending his son off to Italy on one of the grain ships and induced him to invite the young painter to go along. Mr. Kelly was so enthusiastic about his portrait that he not only paid for it immediately in cash, but gave West a letter of credit for fifty guineas more to help defray the expenses of his trip.

Benjamin West arrived in Italy in 1760, the year George III became King of England and the year that Thomas Jefferson started his college course at William and Mary. West was just twenty one.

A man's first sight of Rome was one of the standard great moments for eighteenth century travellers. This is how West described it fifty years later to John Galt who was obsequiously writing the great man's biography:

"When the travellers reached the last stage of their journey, while their horses were baiting West walked on alone. It was a beautiful morning; the air was perfectly placid, not a speck of vapour in the sky, and a profound tranquility seemed almost sensibly diffused over the landscape . . . the general silence and nakedness of the scene touched the feelings with solemnity approaching to awe. Filled with the idea of the metropolitan city the Artist hastened forward till he reached an elevated part of the high road, which afforded him a view of a spacious champaign country, bounded by hills, and in the midst of it the sublime dome of St. Peter's . . . Near a pile of ruins fringed and trelissed with ivy, he saw a stone that appeared to be part of a column . . . It was a mile-stone . . . He was only eight miles from the Capitol. In looking before him, where every object seemed by the transparency of the Italian atmosphere to be brought nearer than it was in reality, he could not but reflect on the contrast between the circumstances of that view and the scenery of America; and his thoughts naturally adverted to the progress of civilization . . . He thought of that remote antiquity when the site of Rome itself was covered with unexplored forests; and passing with a rapid reminiscence over her eventful story, he was touched with sorrow at the solitude of decay with which she appeared to be environed, till he adverted to the condition of his native country, and was cheered by the thought of the greatness which even the fate of Rome seemed to assure to America. For he reflected that, although the progress of knowledge seemed to intimate that there was some great cycle in human affairs, and that the procession of the arts and sciences from the East to the West demonstrated their course to be neither stationary nor retrograde: he could not but rejoice, in contemplating the skeleton of the mighty capital before him, that they had improved as they advanced, and that the splendor which would precede their setting on the shores of Europe, would be the glorious omen of the glory they would attain in their passage over America."

At an early age little Benjamin had lorded it over a schoolboy friend who was apprenticed to a tailor by telling him that he intended to be a painter when he grew up and that to be a painter was to be "the companion of kings and emperors." And so it came to pass. On his first night in Rome he was taken up by an intellectual cardinal. He had hardly settled in his hotel before a noble English amateur of the fine arts, hearing that an American Quaker had arrived to study painting, called on him and barely gave him time to dress in his best clothes before he whisked him off to a party where everybody in touch with the modern aesthetic currents of the time would be collected.

This was the group who surrounded the blind and wealthy Cardinal Albani, who, using his sensitive fingertips in default of sight, had acquired a profounder knowledge of classical sculpture and relief and of the delicate intaglios and cameos eagerly sought for among the Roman ruins, than any man living.

Cardinal Albani's librarian was Johann Joachim Winckelmann, a German scholar of enormous erudition who had become a Romanist more from the love of antiquity than of Mother Church. He had become a favorite of the Pope's, was

classifying the Vatican manuscripts and presided over the Pope's cabinet of
antiquities. Winckelmann was the moving spirit of the classical revival which, as
a sort of afterglow of the High Renaissance, was to clear Europe of the last
confusions of the ebbing baroque and to install an archaeological reworking of
classical antiquity as the grand style of the century of enlightenment.

It was the students who followed Winckelmann on his walks through the
Roman forum and through the diggings at Herculaneum and Pompeii who were

*West became the leader of the new classical school. A line draw-
ing taken from one of the paintings that pointed the way for the
grand imperialist school of David.*

to set the styles for the next fifty years. From him was to stem the delicate
classicism of the Adam brothers in England, the antiquarian reconstructions of
Clérisseau from whom Jefferson learned so much while he was minister to
France, and a whole tribe of architects whose influence was to stretch from the
Capitol in Richmond to the banks of the Ohio and from the Madeleine in Paris
to the palaces of far off St. Petersburg.

Benjamin West was landing in Rome in a moment of enthusiasm and renova-
tion in the arts. Supported enthusiastically by his American patrons he studied

there for three years. When he left he was the chief Englishspeaking practitioner of the grand classical style, which was years later, as exploited by David, to become the official art of the French Revolution and of Napoleon's empire. The Romans called West affectionately their American Raphaël.

He was elected to all the academies, he was introduced to all the visiting princes, but he never gave up his plain Quaker manners. Like Franklin he acted the noble savage. He delighted the Grand Duke of Parma by wearing his hat in his presence.

When he felt he had learned all he could at the School of Rome, West decided to take a look at the home island on his way back to Philadelphia. As it turned out he spent the rest of his life there.

Several of his American patrons were in London when he arrived. They managed to bruit his Roman reputation about so that he was introduced to Edmund Burke and Joshua Reynolds and Romney and Gainsborough and invited to frequent Dr. Johnson's club. West, for all his Quaker plainness, had a knack for social climbing.

His first reputation in London came not as a painter but as a skater. It was the Lord Howe, then still a colonel, who was later to have the ungrateful task of chastising the American rebels, who called attention to the brilliance with which West executed a flourish on the ice known as the Philadelphia salute. His first winter in London was unusually cold. An aristocratic crowd gathered to see the American painter skate on the Serpentine. They were so delighted with his skating that they went to see his painting too. They found it edifying. Eventually orders came in from a brace of archbishops and from the Dean of St. Paul's.

The colonials still spoke of England as home. West decided that London offered a better market for his wares than Philadelphia. He would settle there. To settle down he had to marry. In spite of the importunities of the Italian ladies and, so some said, the tears of the lovely Angelica Kauffmann, Reynolds' Miss Angel, who had been West's pupil in Rome, the Quaker painter was still unmarried. Through as many temptations as Joseph with Potiphar's wife he had remained true to Elizabeth Shewell to whom he had plighted his troth in distant Philadelphia. But how to get hold of her? She was pining for him on the banks of the Schuylkill but her family refused to sanction the marriage.

According to the story Bishop White loved to tell in later life he and Francis Hopkinson and Benjamin Franklin concocted a plot. Her brothers had locked West's fiancée in the house. A rope ladder was smuggled in hidden under her apron by a complaisant maid. Miss Shewell let herself down from a back window one night and was carried off in a post chaise by her three eminent abductors and placed in the keeping of West's old father, now a widower and retired from innkeeping, to whom the painter had sent money to join him in England. Together they embarked on a fast sailing ship that was already dropping down the Delaware. A few months later Benjamin West and his betrothed were married amid the plaudits of the Londoners at the church of St. Martin's-in-the-Fields.

The arbiters of the elegances of London were just beginning to admit that perhaps an Englishman could paint as well as a Frenchman or an Italian. West was invited to show at the Society of Artists. His pictures of "History" combined the rhythmic space composition he had learned from the followers of Raphael with the careful attention to antiquarian detail he had learned from Winckelmann. Something of the quiet fervor of Quaker meeting inspired his revival of Plutarch's stoic mood. To a generation nurtured on Roman virtues, reenacted on the modern stage by thespians like Garrick at Covent Garden and Burke and the elder Pitt in Parliament, the effect was irresistible. Tirelessly West turned out historical paintings full of classical accuracies with such titles as *Angelica and Medora, Cymon and Iphigenia, Pylades and Orestes,* or *The Continence of Scipio.*

It was the enthusiastic account the Archbishop of York gave the young king of West's *Agrippina Bringing Home the Ashes of Germanicus,* which he had commissioned, that first interested George III in the American artist. He invited West to bring his painting to Buckingham House, personally helped set the canvas in a proper light, and immediately picked a message from Livy as the source for another. He took to going to West's studio to watch him paint. A friendship sprang up between the two men quite different from the common courtier and monarch relationship.

From the first moment they met, the Quaker innkeeper's son and the plodding Hanoverian prince found that they had more in common than a taste for the antique. They were about the same age. They both aspired to live lives of modest middleclass rectitude. They were true to their wives. Neither of them had any taste for the leering and the coquetting and the backbiting of fashionable London society. They both loved the outdoors, and plain rustic sports, especially fishing.

Ever since he was a small boy West had quite understood that it was part of a painter's business to be "the companion of kings and emperors." His Quaker training had taught him that rank and wealth were vanities of the world and not of God. He treated the King as he would have treated any other of God's children. For George III the experience was unique. He even forgave the American painter for never denying, when the Revolutionary War came on, that his sympathies were with the colonists. Their friendship lasted as long as poor George's wits held out.

As court painter and president of the Royal Academy which he helped found, Benjamin West was considered for years the leading painter of England. He remained an innovator instead of going on repeating the fillets and togas of the classical revival. In 1771 he shocked the cognoscenti by allowing historical characters to wear modern dress. His realistic *Death of Wolfe*, scornfully spoken of at first by the critics as a "boots and breeches" picture, became the most popular painting of the century. Reproduced in thousands of engravings it stirred men and women to patriotic tears throughout the Englishspeaking world.

Accustomed from childhood to think of himself as a prodigy West took his position as greatest painter of the age quite for granted. Like Franklin he was endlessly considerate of aspiring students. His studio was always open to young Americans coming to London to study.

With Copley it started as a correspondence course.

John Singleton Copley was about the same age as West. He never knew his father. He spent most of his early life in his mother's tobaccoshop at the end of Long Wharf in Boston harbor. His mother was known as the Widow Copley and must have been a competent sort of person. From the style of his letters it is obvious that young Copley had a good grounding in the three R's. He was well read in the Bible. Maybe he went to Peter Pelham's school.

Peter Pelham was a mezzotint engraver with some reputation in London who had come to America to ply his trade. He seems to have been a widower. Settling in Boston he discovered that to find pictures to engrave he had to paint them himself. Painting and engraving did not bring in enough business to support his family. He ran a school besides where children were taught dancing, painting, and needlework as well as reading and writing. He may have taught music too since a son of his, also named Peter, who eventually moved to Williamsburg became the organist of Bruton Church and was the chief music teacher there during Jefferson's student years.

When Copley was ten his mother's marriage to Peter Pelham was announced in an advertisement published in the *Boston Gazette:*

"Mrs. Mary Pelham (formerly the Widow Copley on the Long Wharf, tobacconist) is removed to Lindel's Row, against the Quakers' Meeting House, near the upper end of King Street, Boston, where she continues to sell the best Virginia tobacco cut, pigtail, and spun, of all sorts, at wholesale and retail at the cheapest prices."

In Peter Pelham young Copley found a stepfather who suited his tastes. It's likely that the move to the quiet purlieus of the Friends' meeting house was a delight to the small boy. All his life he hated the sea and war and ships and the lowlife characters who brawled about the grogshops on the wharf. Early he had taken refuge in drawing.

His stepfather had engravers' tools and palettes and brushes and colors. He sold engravings of the admired masterpieces of the period. Furthermore whatever other painters there were in Boston frequented his place of business. There was Robert Feke, the portrait-painting sailor. There was John Smibert.

Like Peter Pelham John Smibert had left a small reputation behind him in England. The son of an Edinburgh dyer, he was apprenticed to a plasterer and housepainter at fourteen. As soon as he came of age he moved to London where he scratched up a meager living painting coaches and inn signs and coats of arms. He managed somehow to get admitted to the only London art school, James Thornhill's Academy. Hogarth was his fellow student there. Somebody became sufficiently interested in his talent as a painter to see that he got the European grand tour. One result was a copy he made of Van Dyck's portrait of Cardinal Bentivoglio, which, from its eventual restingplace in his Boston art shop, was greatly to influence the style of young American portrait painters. Back in London he made friends in the literary world but found few clients. He was described by Horace Walpole as "a silent modest man who abhorred the finesse of his profession."

When George Berkeley, the philosopher of optics, offered him the professorship of painting in the "universal college" of arts and sciences he was planning to set up in America, Smibert gratefully accepted. In Newport he painted an evocative group portrait of Berkeley and his friends. When that most romantic of educational projects failed for lack of funds, Smibert moved to Boston.

There he was socially accepted as a portrait painter and artdealer, married the daughter of a welloff merchant and became the first architect of Fanueil Hall. The conversation of Smibert and Pelham and their friends gave young Copley his first taste of that international world of art lovers and philosophers in which West felt so much at home, but it was not for long. When the boy was thirteen or fourteen both his preceptors died. His mother was again left a widowed tobacconist. This time she had an extra small boy to bring up, Pelham's son Henry.

Smibert's death left a gap in Boston society. More and more of the Boston merchants were getting to feel they were rich enough to want their portraits painted. Young as he was Copley strove to take Smibert's place. He had a living to make for his mother and halfbrother. He was a retiring young man who did nothing but work. The only sign of youthful exuberance ever reported of him was to be caught strolling on the Sabbath. He worked such long hours all week, he gravely explained to the Selectmen, that he had to have the exercise for his health.

He must paint his way out of poverty and shopkeeping. He was sick of the disgrace of poverty. What his sitters wanted was a spittin' image. In spite of inadequacies due to lack of training in anatomy and in the Italians' great gift of organized space, he developed his very personal realism.

The Bostonians were proud of their precocious young painter. In 1766, when he was twentyeight, friends induced him to send a painting to London. Skippers and shipowners kept bringing home news of the extraordinary success at Court of a young Pennsylvanian named Benjamin West. Why shouldn't a Bostonian do as well?

A Captain Bruce took Copley's portrait of his halfbrother Henry to England with him. Entitled *The Boy with the Squirrel* it was hung at the Society of Artists and so admired that the painter (under the mistaken name of William Copley) was elected a member. At first, until West identified the stretchers the canvas was tacked to as American pine and the squirrel as an American flying squirrel, none of the English artists even knew what continent the picture had come from. Immediately it became the nine days wonder of the London amateurs.

Delighted to find a brother painter among his compatriots West immediately wrote Copley begging him to come to Europe for further study. Copley answered soberly that much as he'd like to study in the Italian schools he was doing quite well at home. West continued to fill the mails with letters of advice to his new-found friend. Copley stuck to his last. He was making more money than he had ever imagined possible.

A couple of years later he was explaining to a prominent Boston merchant and his wife that his painting brought him in three hundred guineas a year. He had fallen in love with their daughter while he was painting her portrait. They were suitably impressed. He married Susannah Clarke with the full consent of her parents.

His marriage brought him happiness but immediately complicated his life. The Clarkes were highflying Tories and as an artisan and mechanic Copley was a congenital Whig. All his friends were patriots. He was a retiring man, but his hatred of war and strife was more than personal timidity; it was deeply ingrained in his whole outlook on life. Furthermore as a portrait painter it would be bad business to take sides; his sitters came from both factions.

At the time of the Boston Massacre Copley seems to have sympathized wholly with the townspeople. His young halfbrother promptly executed an engraving of the event and sent a proof to Paul Revere, the versatile silversmith who made Copley's frames for him. When Revere made his own version of the engraving and sold it like hotcakes through the colonies, Henry Pelham wrote him indignantly "If you are insensible of the dishonor you have brought on yourself by this act, the world will not be so."

Perhaps it was to escape the bitterness of all this factional strife in Boston that, in spite of his dread of travel, Copley made a portrait-painting tour to New York and Philadelphia. His reputation had gone before him. Everywhere sitters sought him out.

Returning home he found the city even tenser. His fatherinlaw Richard Clarke was one of the agents of the East India Company to whom the illfated tea was consigned. During the riots and tumults that led up to the famous tea party Clarke fled with the rest of them to Castle William. Copley took upon himself the ungrateful task of trying to get the Tory merchants and the Whig politicians to agree on some harmless way of disposing of the offending cargo. In spite of his shrinking from the rough world and his neurotic fear of the water, he travelled back and forth over choppy seas in a rowboat, carrying messages between the merchants cooped up on their fortified island and the roaring crowds in Fanueil Hall. He even nerved himself up to the point of addressing Town Meeting with a plea for moderation.

It was all of no avail. Neither party would yield. Overboard went the tea. A few weeks later, perhaps in despair of ever recovering in America the tranquility he needed for his work, Copley sailed for England. His wife and four small children were to follow if he decided he could make a living there. He did not know that he was shaking the dust of Boston forever.

When he arrived in London, Copley found Benjamin West waiting to receive him with eager hospitality. West offered him the use of his studio, invited him to dine at his house whenever he was not engaged elsewhere, and introduced him to the great and powerful. He saw to it that he should be elected to the Royal Academy. He even abandoned commissions himself to let Copley execute them.

Copley hardly met West's generosity in the same magnanimous spirit. He was a nervous selfcentered apprehensive man. Though he admitted that he'd been wellreceived he found West's English friends hard to get along with. He was no sightseer. He pined for Boston as it had been in the old days before the troubles began. His happiest moments were when he dined on salt cod with a group of Boston Tories.

Much as he dreaded travel and sightseeing and strange foods and strange faces he had to see the old masters. He set out for the continent all bundled up in scarves and kerchiefs. In Rome he spent his time copying Raphael and the Caraccis, and painted an Ascension of his own in the formal manner of the school of Rome, which was a successful exercise in space composition. Hurriedly he sopped up the Roman scene. When he found some rich Americans to commission a portrait he painted Mr. and Mrs. Ralph Izard of South Carolina seated amid the cumbersome gilt furniture of the period with not only the Colosseum but a group of neoclassic statuary in the background. In Parma he copied Corregio's *St. Jerome.* By the time he got back to London, the harsh personal realism of his American painting had given way to the fashionable eclectic style of the period.

In London he was accepted as the second great American painter. He took up "history" with enthusiasm. The success of his *Death of Chatham* almost matched that of West's *Death of Wolfe*. Copley's fatherinlaw brought over his wife and children. As out and out war settled over the colonies Copley gave up any idea of returning home. In London he continued his customary retired laborious life.

A couple of astonishing innovations came out of the marriage of his old dry style with the flashy techniques of the school of Rome. *Brooke Watson and the Shark* and *The Death of Major Pierson* opened up fresh avenues that led towards nineteenth century romanticism.

After these two extraordinary works "history" seemingly lost its appeal for him. He did a few brilliant portraits in the English manner but his work was losing its savor. He had lost the need to make spittin' images of people and things for the literalminded Bostonians. With their realism the intellectual content of his portraits faded.

He was not happy in England but he dared not go home. Henry Pelham was a Tory. All his wife's family were Tories. Copley would never quite have the courage to go back to an independent America. At the same time he could never be at home in England. As the years went on, out of nostalgia perhaps, he became an eager partisan of the American cause.

During the peace negotiations a young New Englander named Elkanah Watson came to him for a portrait. Watson had done very well for himself as one of the American merchants who trafficked in war supplies at Nantes. As soon as tensions relaxed after Yorktown he set himself up to a trip to England. Naturally the painting rooms of Copley and West were part of his tour.

In London Elkanah Watson won a hundred guineas in a lucky bet at Lloyd's. He was betting that Lord Howe would relieve Gibraltar. The historic rock had been under siege for months by a combined French and Spanish force. Lord Howe did. An incident in the campaign, the defeat of the floating batteries, was to be the subject of one of Copley's most financially successful "histories." In spite of their differences with parliament and the Crown even the most patriotic Americans could kindle to the exploits of the doughty old British admiral.

Elkanah Watson was invited to dine at Copley's. Copley evidently shared his enthusiasm for the events at Gibraltar. Watson wrote in his memoirs that he decided to spend his hundred guineas on "a splendid portrait of myself." He went on to tell how he got an American flag into the picture:

"The painting was finished in most admirable style, except the back-ground which Copley and I designed to represent a ship, bearing to America the intelligence of the acknowledgement of independence, with a sun just rising upon the stripes of the union streaming from her gaff. All was complete save the flag, which Copley did not deem prudent to hoist under present circumstances, as his gallery is a constant resort of the royal family and the nobility."

Watson had been given a ticket to the House of Lords to hear King George deliver the speech which was to be his admission of defeat in everything he had fought for in the twenty years of his reign. There along with Benjamin West he met Copley.

"I dined with the artist, on the glorious 5th of December 1782, after listening with him to the speech of the King, formally recognizing the United States of America as in the rank of nations . . . Immediately after our return from the House of Lords, he invited me into his studio and there with a bold hand, a master's touch, and I believe an American heart, attached to the ship the stars and stripes. This was, I imagine, the first American flag hoisted in England."

Meanwhile, through war and peace, Benjamin West continued to put himself out in every way to give encouragement to American painters. The names of only a few of his pupils have been remembered. There was the Matthew Pratt who crossed on the same ships as West's father and his intended bride and who did a picture of West and his pupils under the title: *The American School.*

There was John Trumbull, the Connecticut governor's son, who took over West's ambitious scheme, which as court painter he didn't quite dare carry out himself, of painting the great events of the American Revolution. In later years there were Washington Allston and Sully and Leslie and Samuel F. B. Morse and Robert Fulton and Mather Brown. In fact there was hardly an American painter who learned his trade during West's lifetime who didn't study with the imperturbable Quaker.

With the rising English school it was the same. In spite of his serene conviction, which he certainly made no effort to conceal, that he was the world's greatest painter, Benjamin West remained all his life a singularly openminded man in everything which pertained to his art. He appreciated Blake who was considered a madman by the critics. He admired young Turner. He consoled Constable when the Royal Academy turned down his early canvases. He was always telling his pupils to try something new.

The year after Copley's *Boy with a Squirrel* had, under West's sponsorship, filled London with admiration for American talents, there arrived at the painting rooms on Castle Street, Leicester Fields, a slender exuberant young man with a long crooked nose. He hailed from Maryland. He was rather foppishly dressed in a light blue suit with black stockings and beaver hat and gloves all in the latest London style. He was just off the boat, still reeling a little from the seasickness of a rough winter crossing.

This was Charles Willson Peale, the eldest son of a dissipated Cantabridgian who got himself transported to America for embezzling a sum of money from the post office. Charles Peale the father eked out a living teaching school on the Eastern Shore of Maryland where he dazzled the colonials with his fashionable erudition and filled every ear with his story of being the heir to a great estate. Charles Willson, named after the rich uncle his father hoped he would inherit from, was only eight when his father died.

Left penniless with five children Mrs. Peale moved to Annapolis. Family friends helped her. She earned a little money as a seamstress. Little Charley was sent to charity school and at thirteen apprenticed to a saddler. As he grew up his daily struggle with lack of money was enlivened by the mirage of eventual gentility and affluence to come to him from overseas.

Peale was a hardworking exuberant fellow. He married when he was twenty. Get rich schemes kept rising like bubbles in his head. He was handy with tools. He repaired watches and clocks, worked silver, made harness and painted inn signs. From decorating coaches he took to trying his hand at landscape and finally at portraiture; but the harder he worked the deeper he went into debt.

His creditors might have been a little more patient, as Peale was thought of in Annapolis as very definitely a young man with a future, if he hadn't infuriated them by opposing them politically. In Maryland the rich and landowning tended to line up with the Crown in the dispute over the Stamp Tax. The lawyers, the small merchants and artisans and sailors were vociferous against the tax. In a local election Peale became a leader of the Sons of Liberty who were trying to elect to the Assembly a young radical of Peale's own age named Samuel Chase.

Marylanders took their politics seriously in those days. His creditors first warned Peale to keep his mouth shut and then descended on him in a body. To keep out of jail he had to run for it.

Luckily his sister had recently married a seafaring man who owned a schooner. Riding his horse named Gimlet desperately along the Eastern Shore, Peale managed to cross the Virginia border before the sheriff caught up with him. He took refuge in his sister's house in Accomac County. He found Bobby Polk his brotherinlaw just about to set sail for Boston with a cargo of grain.

They arrived in Boston on a Sunday morning but were cooped up on board all day because in Boston it was against the law to stroll anywhere except to church on Sunday. Next day they explored the town.

Peale, asking the way to a color shop, found himself in Smibert's old painting room. Smibert was dead but many of his paintings were still there. They were the best Peale had ever seen.

The shopkeeper told him there was a young man named Copley in town who painted even better. Peale went to see Copley and was so delighted with his work he begged the loan of one of his paintings to copy.

Peale set up as a professional limner. In a few weeks he had scraped up enough money in Boston and Newburyport from portraits to cover his passage back to Virginia. By pledging the small inheritance his wife had coming to her he satisfied his creditors to the point of letting him return to his family in Annapolis.

There he set to work to limn the local gentry with such effect that the Governor and a number of members of the Council offered to raise a purse to finance a year's study in England for him. A seacaptain gave him free passage and there Charley Peale was in London shaking his famous countryman's hand while he stared wideeyed around the painting room at the mythological subjects that crowded the walls. He was eager to learn everything there was to learn about painting. He wanted to gulp it all down in a hurry so that he could get back to earn a living for his wife and children.

The story went around that West made Peale pose for a hand he needed, and that Peale, who hadn't recovered his land legs yet, almost fainted away on the spot. West found him lodgings and gave him a place to set up his easel. In return Peale, as all the pupils did, helped on draperies and the routine parts of the canvases and posed for figures when necessary. He is said to have posed for the Regulus in West's first commission for George III.

Peale was miserable in London. He moped for his wife. His grand hopes of coming into a fortune were dashed when he found a lawyer to search the records for him. A letter from America telling him his first baby was dead did not help. He threw himself in desperation into the study of oil painting, miniatures, modelling in plaster and scraping mezzotints. A versatile fellow by nature, necessity would turn him into a jack-of-all-trades. Through a jeweler on Ludgate Hill who made the mountings he got commissions to paint miniatures at two guineas a head.

"The novelty of sights were soon satisfied," he wrote, "when not aided by the converse with a dear friend . . . I went to only seven plays in the whole time of my stay in that city; I visited Windsor once, was in Hampton Court twice, on one party to Richmond. I partook of the amusements of the several gardens in the vicinity of London. With very few exceptions these were the whole of my wanderings from close study."

There was one of the sights of London he had vowed he would not miss. That was a look at Dr. Franklin, who was still struggling, as colonial agent, to avert a war. He had no letter of introduction but being a brash and breezy fellow he barged into the doctor's lodgings one day and brushed past the servant into the laboratory where he was told the philosopher was engaged in an experiment. Peale wrote in one of his journals that, to his great embarrassment, he surprised Franklin with a young lady on his knee. They were both so engrossed in their experiment that they didn't notice him. Blushing Peale tiptoed out and sometime later made a new entrance with a great deal of noise. He found the philosopher and the lady at opposite ends of the room. Peale wasn't so embarrassed he didn't seize the opportunity to make a sketch of the scene on the flyleaf of one of his pocket account books.

Peale's major work during his stay in England was a painting of the elder Pitt, dressed in a Roman toga and surrounded by all the emblems of Whig libertarianism, which was commissioned by the gentlemen of the Westmoreland Association in Virginia and which still hangs at the county seat at Montross. An engraving made from it had a great sale among the daily more rebellious colonials.

After eighteen months Peale set sail joyously for home. It never seems to have occurred to him to settle in England with Copley and West. Already he was a furious Whig. After the annulment of the New York charter he vowed he'd never again take off his hat when King George's coach went by. He landed in Annapolis more than ever the patriot.

Peale was a family man. The first thing he did when he got home was to teach his two younger brothers to paint just to disprove the opinion of the British aesthetes that "genius for the fine arts is a particular gift and not an acquirement." As his children grew up he taught them. Like a good American Peale believed a man could put his hand to any trade he was willing to take the trouble of learning.

He had learned a lot in England. His new portraits had dash and charm. His patrons were delighted with his work. His reputation spread fast among the American gentry, who feeling more and more the importance of the historic moment they were living, wanted their features limned for posterity. He was invited to paint Colonel Washington at Mt. Vernon.

Philadelphia was the metropolis. He moved his whole family there. "The people here have a growing taste for the arts," he wrote, "and are becoming more and more fond of encouraging their progress." He became the favorite painter of the Continental Congress.

"Peale is from Maryland," John Adams wrote Abigail, "a tender soft affectionate creature . . . He is ingenious. He has vanity, loves finery, wears a sword, gold lace, speaks French, is capable of friendship and strong family attachment."

Family men themselves the American leaders liked their artists to be family men. While Benjamin West, the Pennsylvania innkeeper's son, was becoming the court painter of old England, Charles Willson Peale the Annapolis saddler, was becoming the official painter to the rising new nation.

The illfated transparency of a triumphal arch C. W. Peale designed to celebrate the peace in Philadelphia. It burned up as soon as the lamps were lit and Peale and his helpers almost burned up with it.

The revolutionary war split the British commonwealth politically, but culturally it remained a unit. When men in the late eighteenth century spoke of the American school they continued even after the Revolutionary War to think of Benjamin West's painting rooms in London.

Political differences in those days, even discussed at the point of a musket, were not allowed to interfere too much with the basic concepts the men of the enlightenment held in common. The arts and sciences were universal. The allegiance of educated men to the "republic of letters" continued on quite a separate plane from their partisan feelings in the daily affairs of state.

Benjamin West's career was one of the great examples of the ability of an artist to remain above the battle. His Quaker background, which had taught him that wars and political commotions were "not of God" helped him maintain his

Benjamin West.

position, as did his Quaker shrewdness which allowed him to make such little adjustments to worldly pressures as did not extinguish the light within. What stands out when you read John Galt's smug eulogy is the true goodness of the man. A case in point is his treatment of Gilbert Stuart.

Stuart, a wild young man of twenty, turned up in London in the summer of 1775. He had led a rough life. His father was a Scottish millwright whom a Jacobite exile imported to Rhode Island to operate the first snuff mill set up in the colonies. Like Copley he grew up in a tobacco shop on a wharf in a seafaring town. Only for Stuart it was Bannister's Wharf in Newport. His father was an ingenious mechanic but a neerdowell. Stuart grew up in an atmosphere of shabby-genteel, somewhat bibulous poverty.

Most of his father's friends were exiled Scots of the Stuart persuasion, men who passed their glasses over the water decanter when they drank the King's health. A good many of them were men of some learning who fancied themselves fine gentlemen and encouraged the arts. Stuart was a continual truant as a boy but he learned to play the organ.

When he was found to have a talent for drawing, one of his father's friends bought him colors and brushes. He studied a little with the local instrument maker, a man named King who did portraits on the side. When a real limner, a Scot named Cosmo Alexander who claimed to have taken part in Prince Charlie's rebellion, and who talked about the grand tour and the Society of Artists, set up in Newport as a portrait painter, Stuart was taken on as his apprentice.

Alexander took the lad on a painting tour of the southern colonies and then home to Scotland with him. Evil tongues reported that the reason Alexander could wear such fine clothes and travel so freely was that he was a spy for the ministry at Westminster. Be that as it may he had hardly returned to his native Scotland when he took sick and died. Young Stuart was left destitute.

After starving for months in Edinburgh and Glasgow he shipped for America on a collier bound for Nova Scotia. A sailor's was a hard brutal life. When at last he reached Newport his memories of that time were so bitter that he would never tell about it, even to his best friends or in his most drunken moments. Benjamin Waterhouse, a scapegrace companion from the days when Stuart was chief mischiefmaker at the Episcopal charity school in Newport, who grew up to be an eminent physician, wrote: "What his treatment was I never could learn, I only knew that it required a few weeks to equip him with suitable clothing to appear on the streets."

It was to join Waterhouse, who had gone to England to study medicine, that Stuart, the day before the battle of Bunker Hill, sailed from Boston to England to study painting. In London he found that his friend had just left for Edinburgh. There followed another desperate period of poverty among dram-shops and sponging houses. He kept from starving to death till his friend returned to London by playing the organ in church. Keeping Stuart out of the clutches of the law took up most of wellconnected young Waterhouse's pocket money when he finally arrived back from Scotland. Even in his most drunken moments Stuart's friends never lost faith in his talent.

Waterhouse who, as a nephew of Dr. Fothergill was connected with all the great Quakers in England, got him commissions, but Stuart lacked the training to carry them out. He lacked the training and he lacked the habit of consistent work. Tired of living off Waterhouse he appealed to Benjamin West in an abject letter:

"The benevolence of your disposition encourageth me, while my necessity urgeth me to write you . . . My poverty and ignorance are my only excuse . . . Pity me, good sir, I have just arrived at the age of twentyone, an age when most young men have done something worthy of notice, and find myself ignorant, without business or friends . . . For some time I have been reduced to one miserable meal a day, and frequently not even that . . ."

West sent for him immediately. Stuart was everything West didn't like, he was intemperate, he was rowdy and vain; his hands trembled from nervousness and late hours; but West appreciated his talent and set to work to train him, with patience and understanding, as a painter and as a man. Though West was hardly literate himself his studio had become a school of all the accomplishments of the age. Stuart became his chief assistant. While he worked on what he mockingly called his master's ten acre canvases he learned the gentleman's vocabulary and developed his own private art of the painting of faces.

A portrait of West exhibited at the Royal Academy raised Gilbert Stuart to fame as one of the chief portait painters of the age. He started to make money. When he went back to America he arrived in Philadelphia in time to become the fashionable painter of the new Federalist society. As Peale was the painter of revolutionary and democratic America, Stuart, with his fashionable brushstroke, became the painter of President Washington's republican court.

While he trained generation after generation of American painters in his London painting rooms, West went on placidly executing, with the help of a mob of students, those ten acre canvases illustrating Bible stories that were the delight of early nineteenth century England; and that became so exquisitely boring to later generations, accustomed to see them reproduced as prize cards for all the Sunday schools, that the critics of the romantic movement dumped his whole production into the trashcan.

During George III's lucid moments, West remained the King's best friend. When his wits faded West's influence at Court faded with them. One of the first symptoms reported of one of the King's fits of insanity was when he suddenly tried to show West how to draw a lion which the court painter had inserted into a picture of Windsor Castle at the insistence of one of the young princes.

In favor and out West continued to hold his own private political opinions. Oddly for a Quaker he was seized with a great admiration for Napoleon. After the Peace of Amiens he sent a painting in a new style to the Paris Salon of 1802. Like Copley in *The Death of Major Pierson*, West now tossed off an explosive canvas which departed from all the neoclassic standards he had done so much to establish. While the friends of David were wining and dining Benjamin West as the father of the togaed school his *Death on a Pale Horse*, hung for all to see in the Salon, pointed towards the romanticism of Delacroix.

West came back from Paris full of admiration for French art. That didn't keep him from returning to the patriotic vein. The story he told was that, dining with Lord Nelson one day, Nelson said that the only picture that had ever moved him was *The Death of Wolfe*. The maimed old seadog asked him why he hadn't painted more in the same vein. West said such a subject hadn't recurred. Nelson was so fearless he added, that he feared he himself might afford him just such a subject: if he did he would paint it. Nelson filled their glasses with champagne and clinked his violently against the painter's. "Will you, Mr. West? Then I hope I die in the next battle."

His next battle was Trafalgar.

When West painted a *Death of Nelson* thirty thousand people paid to see it.

As George III's mind became more and more unstable, court intrigue robbed West of his favored position. His stipend was cut off. In spite of their Quaker sobriety the Wests kept up an expensive establishment. He had no money saved up. He faced destitution at seventyfour.

Instead of filling the skies with complaints like many an ousted courtier West went to work to paint a *Christ Healing the Sick* that brought him in twenty-two hundred guineas from prints and another three thousand when it was sold to the British Institution, and a great deal more when people paid admittance to see it.

In early nineteenth century England, West was the plain man's painter. Byron called him "the dotard West, Europe's worst daub, poor England's best." The younger critics were already beginning to jeer at his ten acre canvases. When he died at eightythree all England joined in his obsequies. His body lay in state in the great hall of the National Academy. He was buried next to Sir Joshua Reynolds among the great men of the arts and sciences in St. Paul's.

Paul Revere's tribute to his most admired leader, Samuel Adams.

A People of Lawyers
and Litigants

CHAPTER 4   ✲

L AND MEANT LITIGATION. RIGHTS AND PATENTS HAD TO BE RECORDED.
Claims conflicted.

Trade meant litigation. The complexity of the Atlantic trade where so many shares and partnerships were involved gave rise to all manner of suits. Merchants needed lawyers to guide them through the maze of changing interpretations of the Navigation Acts. The admiralty courts handled complicated problems of wartime prizes and contraband. A vessel might turn overnight from a merchant-man into a privateer. The rights and wrongs of all sorts of seizures had to be argued in the courts.

Great Britain's American colonies were a nursery of lawyers. Particularly lawyers abounded round the statehouses in Boston and New York and Philadelphia and in the rustic capitols at Williamsburg and Annapolis.

When in October 1757 John Adams presented himself to Jeremiah Gridley, who was considered the dean of the Boston legal profession in those days, to ask his help in getting admitted to the Massachusetts bar, Jeremiah Gridley read the young countryman a lecture on the complicated duties of American lawyers. Easy specialization prevailed among gentlemen of the bar in England but the American lawyer had to be a jack of all trades: "A Lawyer in this country must study Common Law, and Civil Law, and Admiralty Law: and must do the Duty of a Counsellor, a Lawyer, an Attorney, a Solicitor, and even of a Scrivener."

When Jeremiah Gridley added that these difficulties had never discouraged him, Adams suggested in his journal that perhaps the eminent jurist was suffering from "conscious Superiority." Jeremiah Gridley went on to warn young Adams against an early marriage as marriage would "involve him in expense." He shouldn't "keep much company" as that would take this attention from his books. To be a good lawyer he should pursue the study of it and not the gains.

"This Advice made such a deep Impression on my Mind," noted Adams wryly in his journal, "that I believe no Lawyer in America ever did so much Business as I did afterwards, in the seventeen years that I passed in the Practice at the Bar, for so little Profit."

John Adams was then a stocky blue-eyed young man of twentythree. Born in his father's comfortable farmhouse at Braintree within the smell and sound of the salt sea, he had studied at Harvard, and being a bookish fellow had narrowly escaped training for the ministry. He came of a family of farmers; honest yeomen they were condescendingly called by the highflying Boston merchants.

Putting a boy through Harvard was an arduous venture for the rustic Adamses of Braintree. John Adams responded to his parents' sacrifices with a fierce ambition to amount to something in the world.

His reading had stuffed his head with Cicero and Plutarch and the antique Romans. "I long to study sometimes but have no Opportunity," he wrote in his journal. "I long to be a Master of Greek and Latin. I long to persecute the mathematical and philosophical Sciences. I long to know a little of Ethics and moral Philosophy. But I have no Books, no Time, no Friends, I must therefore be contented to live and die a miserable obscure Fellow."

He knew he had intellect. He knew he had learning and the habits of thrift and hard work of his farming family. He lacked money and connections and social position. A generation before, the ministry would have been the calling open to him, but now it was the law that seemed to offer the opportunities. John Adams began to haunt the court house days when the circuit judges were sitting.

Fortunately for him a brilliant though flighty lawyer named James Putnam had recently hung out his shingle in Worcester where John Adams, the year after he graduated from Harvard, was earning a precarious living teaching school. Putnam was a man of some reading and wit. Adams found him congenial. He drank tea with him and Mrs. Putnam, and spent evenings at his house. He went shooting with him one Saturday afternoon. At last he decided to enter his office as an apprenticed clerk. That was how a young man studied for the bar in those days. John Adams signed a contract to serve Mr. Putnam for two years and to pay him one hundred pounds "when convenient." He would board with the Putnams and pay his board in cash. Coke's Lyttleton was his daily reading thenceforth.

When his two year apprenticeship was up, in spite of some flattering offers from Worcester, where he won the respect of the citizens by his dogged application to business, he moved back to his parents' house at Braintree. Worcester was too much out of the world for him. "The air of Worcester appeared to be unfriendly to me to such a Degree" he wrote in his journal "that I panted for the Want of Breezes from the Sea."

Boston he knew was crowded with lawyers. He hoped to drum up a practice among the farmers of Suffolk County, where his family was known.

The very day he settled back into family life in his father's house he started reading Justinian. Putnam had instructed him in the Common Law. Now he would use his knowledge of Greek and Latin to get a grounding in Civil Law. "I have read about ten Pages in Justinian and translated about four Pages into English," he wrote at the end of that October day; "this is the whole of my Day's Work. I have smoked, chatted, trifled, loitered away this whole Day almost;—by much the greatest Part of this Day has been spent in unloading a Cart, in cutting Oven Wood, in making and recruiting my own Fire, in eating Victuals and Apples, in drinking Tea, cutting and smoking Tobacco, and in chatting with Dr. Savil's Wife at their House and at this." Young Dr. Savil and his wife, who was a cousin of John's, were tenants in an extra house the elder Adamses owned next door. Their conversation added a great deal to the liveliness of life in Braintree. "Chores, Chat, Tobacco, Tea, steal away Time" John Adams added happily. He was enjoying every moment. "But I am resolved"—serious things must come first—"to translate Justinian and his Commentator's notes by daylight, and read Gilbert's Tenures by night, till I am a Master of both . . . on a Sunday I will read the Enquiry into the Nature of the Human Soul, and for Amusement I shall sometimes read Ovid's Art of Love to Mrs. Savil . . . This shall by my Method."

But none of this was helping him earn a living. To earn a living he had to be admitted to the bar. Through youthful diffidence he had come away from Worcester without demanding a certificate of studies or a letter of recommendation from Lawyer Putnam. His college friend Sam Quincy was going to be sworn in as a lawyer when the Superior Court next met in Boston. He suggested that John Adams come along and get himself sworn in at the same time.

John Adams rode into Boston thoroughly ill at ease: "Arrived about half after ten; went into the Court House and sat down by Mr. Paine at the Lawyers' Table."

This was Robert Treat Paine whose father was pastor of a church at Weymouth. He was a competitor of Adams', who described him as "an impudent, ill bred, conceited Fellow," but admitted that he had "Wit, Sense, and Learning and a great Deal of Humor and even some Virtue and Piety."

"I felt shy, under Awe and Concern!" John Adams went on "for Mr. Gridley, Mr. Pratt, Mr. Otis"—James Otis of Writs of Assistance fame—"Mr. Kent and Mr. Thacher were all present, and looked sour." These were the lights of the Boston bar, feeling much too important in their gowns and tie wigs to notice a new young snip from the country.

Even his friends were standoffish. "I had no Acquaintance with anybody but Paine and Quincy, and they took but little Notice."

John Adams attended court steadily all that day. In the evening Sam Quincy took pity on him and introduced him at the house of a friend: "There I saw the most spacious and elegant Room, the gayest company of Gentlemen, and the finest Row of Ladies that I ever saw." He still felt shy and out of place. He knew he had it in him to make striking and amusing remarks. "But the Weather was so dull, and I so disordered," was how he put it in his journal, "that I could not make one half the Observations that I wanted to make."

Next morning he felt bold enough to ask the assistance of the formidable Jeremiah Gridley. Mr. Gridley seemed favorably disposed. He told the aspirant lawyer to put in an appearance at the next session of court. When the day came John Adams sat in the back of the court house beside Sam Quincy. He was thoroughly disconsolate. He knew Quincy would be admitted because he had studied under the eminent Mr. Pratt but he was afraid he'd be left with no one to sponsor him.

At last Mr. Gridley, who had been detained on business, arrived in the courtroom and began to whisper John Adams' name to the lawyers present. "He rose and bowed to his right Hand, 'Mr. Quincy,'—when Quincy rose up; then he bowed to me, 'Mr. Adams'—when I walked out."—Mr. Gridley bowed to the bewigged judges on the bench. " 'May it please your Honors, I have two young Gentlemen, Mr. Quincy and Mr. Adams to present for the Oath of an Attorney . . . Of Mr. Adams, as he is unknown to your Honors, it is necessary to say he has lived between two and three Years with Mr. Putnam of Worcester, has a good Character from him and all Others who know him, that he was with me the other Day several Hours, and I take it he is qualified to study the Law by his Scholarship . . . I therefore recommend him, with the Consent of the Bar, to your Honors for the Oath.' Then Mr. Pratt said two or three Words, and the Clerk was ordered to swear us; after the Oath Mr. Gridley took me by the Hand and wished me much Joy and recommended me to the Bar. I shook Hands with the Bar and received their Congratulations, and invited them over to Stone's to drink some Punch"—the tavern was across the street—"where most of us resorted, and had a very cheerful Chat."

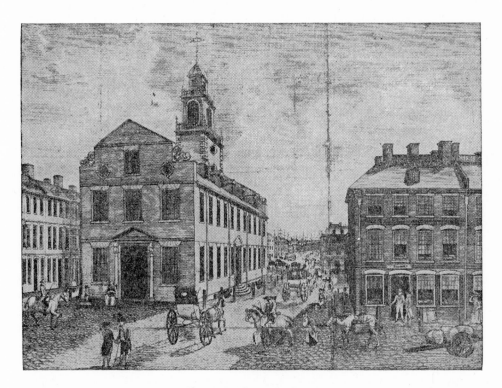

The State House in Boston.

John Adams's first case, back home in Braintree, was a spite case about a horse that had broken into a man's field and eaten some of his crop. The owner of the field had taken the owner of the horse into court for damages. He had lost because the owner had driven his horse home before it could be impounded, but he was still sore and wanted to bring fresh charges. John Adams drew a writ for him. In his greenness and excitement he drew it up wrong. The writ was thrown out of court. John Adams suffered agonies. He felt he was the laughing stock of the community.

"Let me see if Bob Paine don't pick up this Story to laugh at" he wrote ruefully in his journal. ". . . I should endeavor," he added "on first setting out, to possess the People with an Opinion of my Subtlety and Cunning. But this affair certainly looks like a strong Proof to the Contrary."

He consoled himself reading Cicero against Cataline aloud in his room: "The Sweetness and Grandeur of his Sounds, and the Harmony of his Numbers, give Pleasure enough to reward the Reading, if one understood none of the Meaning. Besides I find it a noble Exercise. It exercises my Lungs, raises my Spirits, opens my Pores, quickens the Circulations and so contributes much to Health."

Cases came slowly. He represented a man who claimed that a Boston hatter had done him on a hat. He was involved in an interminable suit about who should pay for the hay an old horse ate while he was being boarded during the past winter. The horse had died. That seemed enough to terminate the contract. Beaten again. Another dissatisfied client. John Adams was unlucky with horses. "What am I doing?" he wrote in his journal. "Shall I sleep away my whole seventy Years?"

He was ready to throw up the law. He was an active stocky young man. He was crazy about the girls. What he really enjoyed was chopping wood and pitching hay and walking through the fields. "No, by everything I swear I will renounce this contemplative, and betake myself to an active roving Life by Sea or Land," his feelings broke out in his journal.

He had hardly traced the words with his quill before his deep seated ambition took hold of him again . . . "or else I will attempt some uncommon, unexpected enterprize in Law; let me lay the Plan and arouse Spirit enough to push it boldly. I swear I will push myself into Business; I'll watch my Opportunity to speak in Court, and will strike with Surprise;—Bench, Bar, Jury, Auditors and all . . . I will not forgo the Pleasure of ranging the Woods, climbing Cliffs, walking in Fields, Meadows, by Rivers, Lakes &c for Nothing. I'll have some Boon in return, Fame, Fortune or Something."

He stuck to his work doggedly. He began to win cases. His reputation grew. By January of the following year he was able to write of a lawyer who had been his opponent in many petty cases . . . "I have come off pretty triumphantly every Time and he pretty foolishly."

"Yet I have managed Pettifoggers, more than I did."

These were the years of the elder Pitt's great victories. Every newspaper brought out from Boston to Braintree carried world-sweeping events. Quebec was taken from the French. George II's reign ended on a triumphant roll of drums. The Grand Banks were safe at last for New England fishermen. North America was secured to the Englishspeaking peoples. Ambitious young lawyers began to dream of playing parts on history's stage.

Meanwhile at home, in the time he could spare from his reading and his lawcases, John Adams was busy with reform. He was interested in the improvement of highways. He worried about the increase of drunkenness. He led a movement to reduce the number of taverns in Braintree.

Litigation was another vice of the Suffolk county farmers. Every cobbler and wig-maker and hog-caller could get himself admitted to practice before the county courts. John Adams was trying to induce his brethren of the bar to restrict practice to really competent individuals. The public interest was as engrained in him as his ambition to excel.

This was all townmeeting kind of business, the sort of controversies that had filled up his father's life during his many terms as selectman. In February 1761 John Adams rode into Boston to hear his friend James Otis argue before the Governor and Council a case that far transcended the limits of Massachusetts.

The new reign had brought in a new administration at Westminster. George III was a conscientious young man whose mother had raised him in horror of his grandfather's slack ways and easy morals. He intended to rule, in Bolingbroke's words, as a Patriot King. Laws were to be enforced, colonies to be reminded of their subservience to the home government, war debts paid off. The American colonies had profited mightily from the victory over the French: it was up to them to help pay for it. American shipmasters must be taught to obey the law. Smuggling must be suppressed. Chief among the laws that were to be enforced were the Navigation Acts.

The New England merchants groaned. Their most profitable business came from evading these same Navigation Acts and the regulations the Trade Lords made to enforce them. Customs officers in Boston seized a ship's cargo worth ten thousand pounds. They needed search warrants to trace goods smuggled ashore. A Salem official named Cockle applied to the General Court for a particularly virulent type of search warrant known as a Writ of Assistance. The merchants hired Oxenbridge Thacher and James Otis to plead against such writs. It was the greatest constitutional question to be argued in an American court in the memory of man.

John Adams tried to take notes,—and indeed our knowledge of Otis's famous speech is mostly based on his minutes—but he was too excited, so he wrote later, to get much down: "I was much more attentive to the Information and to the Eloquence of the Speaker than to my Minutes and too much alarmed at the Prospect that opened before me to care much about writing a Report on the Controversy . . . England proud of its Power, and holding us in Contempt, would never give up its Pretensions. The Americans, devoutly attached to their Liberties, would never submit . . . There was no Alternative left but to take the Side which seemed to be just, to march intrepidly forward in the right Path, to trust in Providence for the Protection of Truth and Right, and to die with a good Conscience and a decent Grace, if that Trial should become indispensible."

From the day he sat in the council chamber in the old state house trying to keep track of James Otis's eloquence he began to feel that perhaps he himself had a part to play. Worcester had been too far from the bustle of Boston. Even the cosy family farmhouse at Braintree was getting too small for him now.

"Now let me collect my Thoughts which have been long scattered among Girls, Father, Mother, Grandmother, Brothers, Matrimony, Hustling, Chat, Provisions, Clothing, Fuel, Servants for a family, and apply them with steady Resolution and an aspiring Spirit to the Prosecution of my Studies.

"Now let me form the great Habits of Thinking, Writing, Speaking."

John Adams was already a prosperous lawyer. He was buying his own land. Since his father's death his decisions were his own. He had been carrying on flirtations with all the eligible girls in the neighborhood. Now he was ready to marry and set up a family. When he was twentyseven he made up his mind.

"I passed the Summer of 1764 attending Courts and pursuing my Studies, with some Amusement on my little Farm, to which I was frequently making Additions, until the Fall when on the 25th of October I was married to Miss Smith, second daughter of the Rev. William Smith, Minister of Weymouth, Granddaughter of the Honorable John Quincy of Braintree, a Connection which has been the Source of all my Felicity."

It was a moment for some general reflections: "Here it may be proper to recollect"—he made this entry in his diary—"something which makes an Article of great Importance in the Life of every Man. I was of an amorous Disposition, and, very early, from ten or eleven Years of Age, was very fond of the Society of Females. I had my Favorites among the young Women and spent many of my Evenings in their Company . . . they were all modest and virtuous Girls . . . No Virgin or Maiden ever had Occasion to blush at the Sight of me, or to regret her Acquaintance with me . . . I presume I am indebted for this Blessing to my Education. This has been rendered the more precious to me, as I have seen enough of the Effects of a different Practice . . . The happiness of Life depends more on Innocence in this Respect, than upon all the Philosophy of Epicurus or of Zeno without it."

The first years of their marriage were busy for both Adamses. Children came fast. Though Abigail was a rather shy bookish girl when he married her she became an able housekeeper and a hostess quite able to match wits with any man he brought to the house. Through Abigail, furthermore, he became connected with the Quincy family so eminent in Suffolk County. It was a connection very useful to a rising young lawyer.

He was learning to know his Massachusetts and its citizens were learning

At 21 John Trumbull painted himself in the style Copley had made fashionable. In 1778 even a young man from one of Connecticut's first families was not ashamed to admit to being a painter

Ben Franklin as the successful young Phila-delphia business man. John Greenwood (?)

Paul Revere representative of the colonial crafts-men and mechanics who furnished so much of the brain and sinew of the young republic. Painted by John Singleton Copley at his best

Even John Adams who brooked no nonsense was glad to have C. W. Peale limn his likeness. "He is ingenious," he wrote of Peale. "He has vanity, loves finery, wears a sword, gold lace, speaks French, is capable of friendship, and strong family attachment and natural affections."

The Sons of Liberty gaily pulling down George III's equestrian statue in New York. William Walcutt

In Rome Copley painted the wealthy South Carolinian Ralph Izard and his wife looking a little uncomfortable amid all the trappings of the archaeological school just coming into style—the heavy gold furniture, the grecian urn, the antique sculptures. For good measure he included a distant view of the Colosseum

The Death of Chatham was financially one of Copley's most successful pictures in the journalistic vein made popular by West's "Death of Wolfe." The Morning Post *estimated that when it was exhibited in London at a private showing twenty thousand people paid more than £5000 to see it. Copley was said to have refused fifteen hundred guineas for the picture. He sold engravings of it by the thousands*

to know him. Clients poured into his study. Like his colleagues he rode the circuits, from Boston to Worcester and Springfield and north to Pownalboro in the extreme back woods up the Kennebec, and south to Taunton and the Cape and Martha's Vineyard. Court days were social gatherings where a respected attorney would meet all the leading lights of each community.

He held various town offices. During the Stamp Act agitation he prepared the resolutions of protest for Braintree. Next the town of Boston engaged him, along with his eminent patron Jeremiah Gridley and with James Otis, whose brilliant intelligence was already clouding into madness and melancholy, to argue Boston's case before the Governor and Council. He wrote for the newspapers. He was prominent in the Boston lawyers' political club. By the time little John Quincy Adams was a year old, John and Abigail had decided that they needed a town house. They moved into a white mansion on Brattle Square.

Westminster was trying to intimidate the Bostonians by quartering troops on them.

"On my return" (from the summer circuit), John Adams wrote in the fall of 1768, "I found the Town full of Troops, and as Dr. Byles of punning Memory, expressed it, our Grievances *red*-dressed. Through the whole succeeding Fall and Winter a Regiment was exercised by Major Small, in Brattle Square, directly in front of my House. The spirit-stirring Drum and the ear-piercing Fife aroused me and my Family early enough every Morning, and the Indignation they incited, though somewhat soothed, was not allayed by the sweet Songs, Violins and Flutes of the serenading Sons of Liberty under my Windows in the Evening."— already the colonists were organizing for resistance—"In this Way and a thousand others I had sufficient Intimations, that the Hopes and Confidence of the People were placed in me as one of their Friends; and I was determined that, so far as depended on me, they should not be disappointed."

Though in an effort to keep out of partisan politics, he refused several invitations to address Town Meeting, John Adams was becoming intimate with a namesake of his who was in politics up to his neck. Samuel Adams of the prominent Boston Adamses had inherited a bent for town politics from his father. He had been brought up in popular gatherings such as the group of shipwrights and ropewalk hands and sailmakers and small businessmen and artisans of the North End who were in the habit of meeting to plan how to put measures they wanted through Faneuil Hall. In the end he made this Calkers Club or Caucus Club the center of opposition to the Boston Tories and to the taxing operations of the home government.

"The Caucus Club meets, at certain Times," John Adams wrote, "in the Garret of Tom Dawes, the Adjutant of the Boston Regiment. He has a large House and he has a moveable Partition in his Garret which he takes down, and the whole Club meets in one Room. There they smoke Tobacco till you cannot see from one End of the Garret to the other. There they drink Flip, I suppose, and there they chose a Moderator who puts Questions to the Vote regularly; and Selectmen, Assessors, Collectors, Wardens, Firewards and Representatives are regularly chosen before they are chosen in the Town . . . They send Committees to wait on the Merchant's Club, and to propose and join in the Choice of Men and Measures."

Paul Revere celebrates John Hancock and Magna Carta.

Sam Adams was no writer. Neither was he an orator. He was an organizer. There was a deadly private earnestness about him that influenced men when he talked to them face to face. He had the knack of inducing diverse groups to work in harmony. From the Caucus Club his web of influence spread into Town Meeting and the merchants' club and the lawyers' club and permeated the groups of tough young men who liked to call themselves the Sons of Liberty. Through the committees of correspondence he was to become perhaps the chief architect of American unity.

No man had less sympathy with rowdyism than John Adams, but he found himself drawn into the social affairs organized by his indefatigable namesake: "On August 14, 1769," he noted, "dined with three hundred and fifty Sons of Liberty, at Robinson's the Sign of the Liberty Tree in Dorchester. We had two Tables laid in the open Field by the Barn, with between three and four hundred Plates, and an Awning of Sail-Cloth overhead, and should have spent a most agreeable Day, had not the Rain made some Abatement of our Pleasures . . .

There was a large Collection of good Company . . . To the Honor of the Sons, I did not see one Person intoxicated, or near it . . . Between four and five o'clock the Carriages were all got ready and the Company rode off in Procession—Mr. Hancock first in his Chariot . . ."

Ornate John Hancock, who if not the richest was certainly the most flamboyant of Boston merchants, was already a client of John Adams. On the theory that since he had no part in electing the parliaments that had voted the excise he should not be bound by their laws, he was defending that worthy in the High Court of Admiralty where Hancock was charged with smuggling a cargo of madeira wine ashore from his sloop *Liberty*.

It was impossible to practice law without getting deeper and deeper in the political controversy. John Adams successfully defended John Hancock. He defended four Marblehead seamen charged with murder for killing a naval lieutenant who led a pressgang aboard their brigantine. Impressment into the Royal Navy was one of the burning griefs of American seamen. It was the greatest day of his life when the court brought in the verdict of justifiable homicide. The two Adamses had become the Gracchi of the popular party in Massachusetts.

John Adams's next case was a severe test of that popularity. He defended the English soldiers held for murder for firing into a Boston mob, because he felt they had the right to a fair trial.

"The year 1770 was memorable enough in these little Annals of my Pilgrimage," he wrote in his autobiography. "The Evening of the fifth of March I spent at Mr. Henderson Inches's House, at the South End of Boston, in company with a Club with whom I had been associated for several Years. About nine o'clock we were alarmed with the Ringing of Bells, and, supposing it to be the Signal of Fire, we snatched our Hats and Cloaks, broke up the Club, and went out to assist in quenching the Fire, or aiding our Friends who might be in Danger. In the Street we were informed that the British soldiers had fired on the Inhabitants, killed some and wounded others, near the Town-House . . . The next Morning, I think it was, sitting in my Office, near the Steps of the Town-House Stairs, Mr. Forrest came in . . . With Tears streaming from his Eyes, he said, 'I am come with a very solemn Message from a very unfortunate Man, Captain Preston, in Prison. He wishes for Counsel, and can get none. I have waited on Mr. Quincy, who says he will engage, if you will give him your Assistance; without it, he positively will not.' . . . I had no hesitation in answering, that Counsel ought to be a very last Thing that an accused Person should want in a Free Country. Upon this, Forrest offered me a single Guinea as a retaining Fee, and I readily accepted it.

"The Trial of the Soldiers was continued for one Term," Adams's account continues "and in the mean time an Election came on for a Representative of

Boston . . . Notwithstanding the late Clamor against me (his taking the English officers' case had caused resentment among the Sons of Liberty), and although Mr. Ruddock (his opponent, a master shipwright) was very popular among all the Tradesmen and Mechanics in Town, I was chosen by a large Majority.

"I had never been at a Boston Town Meeting, and was not at this, until Messengers were sent to me to inform me that I was chosen. I went down to Faneuil Hall, and in a few Words expressive of my Sense of the Difficulty and Danger of the Times, of the Importance of the Trust, and of my own insufficiency to fulfill the Expectations of the People, I accepted the Choice. Many Congratulations were offered, which I received civilly, but they gave no Joy to me. I considered the Step as a Devotion of my Family to Ruin, and myself to Death; for I could scarce perceive a Possibility that I should ever go through the Thorns and leap all the Precipices before me and escape with my Life.

"At this time I had more business at the Bar than any Man in the Province. My Health was Feeble. I was throwing away as bright Prospects as any Man ever had before him, and I had devoted myself to endless Labor and Anxiety, if not to Infamy and to Death, and that for Nothing, except what indeed was and ought to be all in all, a Sense of Duty. In the Evening, I expressed to Mrs. Adams all my Apprehensions. That excellent Lady, who has always encouraged me, burst into a Flood of Tears, but said she was very sensible of all the Danger to her and to our Children, as well as to me, but she thought I had done as I ought; she was very willing to share in all that was to come, and to place her Trust in Providence."

The leadership had stood by him nobly, but thinskinned John Adams was tortured by the mutterings of the rank and file. He began to hate the dense town life. A few years before he had written: "Who can study in Boston streets? I am unable to observe the various Objects I meet with sufficient Precision. My Eyes are so diverted with Chimneysweepers, Sawyers of Wood, Merchants, Ladies, Priests, Carts, Horses, Oxen, Coaches, Market Men and Women, Soldiers, Sailors, and my Ears with the Rattle Gabble of them all, that I cannot think long enough in the Street, upon any one thing, to start and pursue a thought." In the 'rattle gabble' of the crowded streets he was hearing the clacking of tongues: "Tory," "turncoat."

His hurt feelings became physical symptoms, pains in the chest, an asthmatic difficulty in breathing. The continual demands on him to speak and to attend committee meetings coming on top of the incessant labor of his law practice were wearing him out. He packed up his family and moved home to his farm.

As always, a few months in Braintree brought him back to life. "The air of my native Spot" he was soon writing "and the fine Breezes from the Sea on one

Side, and of the rocky Mountains of Pine and Savin on the other, together with daily Rides on Horseback and the Amusements of Agriculture, always delightful to me, soon restored my Health."

It was not long before he had regained enough confidence in the future and in his career to build himself a new town house on Queen Street. His move back to Boston was triumphant. "I have now got through the Hurry of my Business" he wrote. "The Produce of my Farm is all collected-in; my own Family is re-moved and well settled in Boston; my Wood and Stores are laid in for the winter; my workmen are nearly all paid; I am disengaged from public Affairs and now have nothing to do but to mind my Office, my Clerks and my Children."

This tranquility was shortlived. The conflict between the colonies and the administration at Westminster could no longer be postponed. The Sons of Liberty were taking to direct action. On December 17, 1773 Adams wrote: "Last night three Cargoes of Bohea Tea were emptied into the Sea . . . This is the most mag-nificent Movement of all. There's a Dignity, a Majesty, a Sublimity, in this last Effort of the Patriots, that I greatly admire. The People should never rise without doing something to be remembered, something notable and striking. This De-struction of the Tea is so bold, so daring, so firm, intrepid and inflexible, and it must have so important Consequences, and so lasting, that I cannot but consider it an Epocha in History."

It was indeed an epoch in history. A few months later John Adams had to give up his law practice. He was called from the provincial affairs of Massachusetts to the affairs of the thirteen confederated colonies. The people's representatives assembled for the General Court in Boston in June 1774 appointed him to the Continental Congress about to meet in Philadelphia.

He hurried out to Braintree for a breath of sea air and a chance to walk through his farms and to cogitate. "Since the Court adjourned without day this Afternoon" he wrote in his journal "I have taken a long Walk through the Neck as they call it, a fine Tract of Land in a general Field. Corn, Rye, Grass inter-spersed in great Perfection this fine Season. I wander alone and ponder. I muse, I mope, I ruminate. I am often in Reveries and brown Studies. The Objects be-fore me are too grand and multifarious for my Comprehension. We have not Men fit for the Times. We are deficient in Genius, in Education, in Travel, in Fortune, in everything. I feel unutterable Anxiety. God grant us Wisdom and Fortitude. Should the Opposition be suppressed, should this Country submit, what Infamy and Ruin! God forbid! Death in any Form is less terrible!"

Election to the Continental Congress was an appalling challenge. "This will be an Assembly of the wisest Men upon the Continent," he wrote when the matter was first broached to him, "who are Americans in Principle, that is against the

Taxation of Americans by Authority of Parliament. I feel myself unequal to this Business."

He was leaving his practice he had worked so hard to build up, his farm he had bought field by field out of his savings, and the admiring circle at Braintree of relatives and friends, and Abigail and precocious John Quincy and the smaller children he loved so dearly. If the opposition should be suppressed, as well it might, he and the rest of the delegates stood a good chance of being hanged. If they succeeded they were ushering in a new epoch in the history of the English-speaking people.

This was the great stage of history where the Roman heroes trod: "There is a new and grand Scene, open before me, a Congress."

In Philadelphia his talents immediately placed John Adams among the pre-eminent group; it wasn't until the next session of the Continental Congress in the following summer that he met Jefferson, who was to be his political opponent and intellectual crony through so much of his life. The lanky Virginian was seven years his junior. Like the New Englander he was an eager student of the law; for both men the law was becoming more and more a means to an end. Their interest was turning to what Gouverneur Morris called "the sublime science" of state-building.

After his father's death young Thomas Jefferson had found the backwoods life of Albemarle as dull as John Adams had found Worcester. After completing a couple of years of schooling under the Reverend James Maury at the Mountain near Castle Hill he wrote his guardians suggesting it was time he went to college.

When Jefferson rode into Williamsburg splashing through the muddy ruts in the chilly spring weather of 1760, his seventeenth birthday was only a few days ahead. All the long ride down the valley of the James, his blood must have tingled with anticipation of city life; and the library full of books, and Hunter's printshop with new publications from England and gazettes fresh from the press with their dispatches announcing new victories for Mr. Pitt; and candlelit ballrooms rustling with pretty girls, and pleasant friends to gossip with round the punchbowl; and blooded horses to match on the racetrack.

The first large building he saw, riding in from the Falls of the James, most likely was the college. It was one of the largest brick buildings in the colony. The gold hands of the clock in the cupola over the central entrance gave it a metropolitan air.

Jefferson was arriving on the verge of one of the "public times" when Williamsburg was full of bustle and must have seemed to the colonists a tiny fragment of metropolitan London. The burgesses had met during the early part of March and the session of the General Court was coming in April. Some of the members of the governor's Council may well have already been lumbering about the rutted streets in their coaches.

Probably the young man's first duty, upon alighting from his horse, sore and bowlegged from hours in the saddle, after changing his clothes at whatever friends' house he was lodged in, was to wait upon the more eminent members of his family connection who happened to be in town: on Peyton Randolph, back from studying law in England, perhaps, or Peyton's father, Sir John Randolph, the Attorney General of the colony.

His next duty was to pay his respects to the president of the college, Mr. Dawson, and it is to be hoped he found him sober. Eventually he was ushered into one of those rooms with bare plaster walls which his mathematics teacher Dr. Small, looking back on them from the comfort of London a few years later, described, with evident restraint, as being "at first sight rather disgusting." Arrangements were made with the housekeeper for his laundry and for the mending of his stockings, and his name was entered for board and lodgings in the bursar's book. His first sensations must have been of disappointment. He was entering the college in one of its least flourishing moments as an institution of learning.

The faculty had been torn apart by the litigation over the Two Penny Act. The professors took sides violently with their Cloth in this controversy with the House of Burgesses, which had the backing of the great bulk of Virginia landowners, large and small, over the amount of clergymen's salaries. It had been the custom to pay the minister of a parish sixteen thousand pounds of tobacco a year. The French and Indian War had war's usual effect of raising prices and taxes and depreciating currency. The planters were feeling the pinch. Now that tobacco was high the Burgesses for two successive years passed acts to the effect that clergymen and other public officials should be paid their salaries in the depreciated currency of the colony at the rate of twopence a pound of tobacco. Governor Fauquier sided with the Burgesses and transmitted the acts to London with his approval.

No other public servants complained, but the clergy roared to high heaven that the acts were illegal. In a frenzy of litigation the professors at William and Mary quite forgot that it was their business to teach school. They brought out pamphlets. They banded together to finance suits. Three of the professors became so vehement they were removed by the Board of Visitors. Two of them set sail for England to cry for relief in the lobbies of Parliament and in the anterooms of the Bishop of London, from whose diocese the Virginia church depended.

Eventually they returned with an annulment of the acts. One of them, the Reverend John Camm, brandished the annulment so insolently under Governor Fauquier's nose that the governor rang for his Negro lackeys and told them never to let the Reverend Camm across his threshold again. Eventually juries were forced to find for the clergy, but, as in the famous Hanover case where Patrick Henry made his first appearance, they set merely nominal damages.

The result of all this litigation was to widen the breach between the gentry and the clergy in Virginia. The challenge to the right of the colonists to handle their own financial affairs had an effect on men's minds in Virginia very similar to the campaign in Massachusetts against writs of assistance in which James Otis was the popular champion.

The row demoralized the college faculty. The Reverend Thomas Dawson, the president, who as Commissary was representative of the Bishop of London and who was also Minister of Bruton Church, was so torn by conflicting sympathies that he took desperately to drink. He had spoken early in the controversy against the first Two Penny Act; but later veered around to the side of his parishioners and made an honest effort to allay the bitterness of the discussion; he was thoroughly reviled by his fellow clergymen for his pains. When he was indicted for drunkenness before a grand jury, he humbly confessed his fault and promised to mend his ways. Governor Fauquier was reported as saying no wonder the poor man had taken to drink, his colleagues had driven him to it because he wouldn't take their side. Dawson died not long after, a confirmed drunkard.

Luckily for Jefferson the one professor who kept his mind on his teaching during all this hubbub was neither a drunkard nor a clergyman. He was a thoroughly competent young Scot named William Small.

"It was my great good fortune, and what probably fixed the destinies of my life," Jefferson wrote in his autobiography when he was an old man, weighing each word as he put it down, "that Dr. William Small of Scotland was then Professor of Mathematics, a man profound in the most of the useful branches of the science, with a happy talent of communication, correct and gentlemanly manners, and an enlarged and liberal mind. He, most happily for me, became soon attached to me, and made me his daily companion when not engaged in the school; and from his conversation I got my first views of the expansion of science, and of the system of things in which we are placed. Fortunately, the philosophical chair became vacant soon after my arrival at college, and he was appointed to fill it per interim: and was the first who ever gave in that college, regular lectures on Ethics, Rhetoric and Belles Lettres."

Jefferson had reason to feel obliged to Dr. Small. He arrived in Williamsburg a lanky upcountry lad whose experience since he had grown up out of childhood had been limited to Shadwell and the raw plantations in the foothills. It was Small who first opened his mind to the philosopher's world. Jefferson had done a lot of reading but, unless he got some intimation of it from Joshua Fry as a small boy, he had never met a man who could speak with authority of the cosmopolitan empire of science which the investigative cast of thought, theoretical and applied, was bringing into being.

The inquiring thinkers of that day were members of a sect: the sect of philosophers. Their common religion was enlightenment. From Small, Jefferson caught a feeling of kinship with men speaking other languages in other countries. He learned the duties and privileges, the manners and ethics and the profound faith in man's intellect implicit for that generation in the word "philosopher."

"He returned to Europe . . ." Jefferson wrote of him, "having previously filled up the measure of his goodness to me, by procuring for me, from his most intimate friend, George Wythe, a reception as a student of law, under his direction, and introduced me to the acquaintance and familiar table of Governor Fauquier, the ablest man who had ever filled that office, with him and at his table, Dr. Small and Mr. Wythe, his *amici omnium horarum*, and myself, formed a *partie quarrée* and to the habitual conversations on these occasions I owed much instruction."

George Wythe at thirtyfive was a showpiece in the colony for his classical learning.

Andrew Burnaby, an Oxford man and one of the first of British tourists to look down their noses at the Americans, gave the Virginia planters a bad name in his book of travels. He accused them of indolence and lack of enterprise. He berated them as "entire strangers to that elegance of sentiment which is so particularly characteristic of refined and polished nations," but he remembered Wythe as he was correcting his proof and added in an apologetic footnote: "General characters are always liable to many exceptions. In Virginia I have had the pleasure to know several gentlemen adorned with many virtues and accomplishments, to whom the following description is by no means applicable. Amongst others I cannot resist the inclination of mentioning George Wythe, Esquire, who, to a perfect knowledge of the Greek language, which was taught him by his mother in the backwoods, and of the ancient, particularly the Platonic philosophy, had joined such a profound reverence for the Supreme Being, such respect for the divine laws, such philanthropy for mankind, such simplicity of manners and such inflexible rectitude and integrity of principle, as would have dignified a Roman senator, even in the most virtuous times of the republic!"

George Wythe became the teacher of a generation of Virginia lawyers. He was born and raised near Hampton in Elizabeth City, in the most thickly settled part of the colony which was hardly considered "the backwoods" by the Virginians. Though it seems likely that all the Greek his mother taught him was the alphabet, he combined the study of Greek and Latin authors with such a com-

pendious knowledge of the law that he came to be known as "the walking library." His notes on the comparative etymology of Latin and Greek words surely
interested Jefferson, whose mind had the same bent for grubbing down into roots
and origins.

At the time Jefferson first met him, Wythe was the familiar spirit of the
Capitol. He had been clerk of many committees. He had been elected Burgess for
Williamsburg. When Peyton Randolph went to England to represent the colonists
in the pistole tax dispute it was natural that Dinwiddie should appoint Wythe Attorney General in interim. Not being involved in any of the selfinterested groups
or family connections that pulled and hauled in the Governor's Council, he was
the man everyone turned to for impartial advice.

Whenever the burgesses found themselves entangled in a particularly tough
problem involving law or finance or procedure they put Mr. Wythe on the committee to deal with it. In his profession only Edmund Pendleton was considered
his peer. Already he was a revered figure among lawyers who practiced at the
bar of the General Court. He was the Jeremiah Gridley of Virginia, one of those
lawyers other lawyers look up to as a teacher. They somewhat feared him too
for the knotty quotations from classical authors that ornamented his pleadings
which often proved hard to parse for men trained only in the hasty hog Latin of
the law.

By the time young Jefferson had been two years in Williamsburg he decided
he had absorbed all the college had to offer. He owned a lot of land in his own
right and he managed some more for his mother, but land didn't mean cash. The
only professions that brought in cash in Virginia were surveying and the law. His
friendship with George Wythe offered him a marvelous opportunity to learn the
profession. While Jefferson, as a clerk in Wythe's office, was pursuing the principles of the Common Law through Coke and Littleton and into Bracton's black
letter and the Norman and Anglo-Saxon usages behind them, a contest was preparing in Parliament which would dramatize the whole theory of constitutional government. At the same time in Virginia, before Jefferson had finished working his
way through Coke's voluminous notes, the freeman's challenge to arbitrary authority—which was the root of the English constitution—began to take visible and
audible form in his own experience.

Among Jefferson's friends a sort of village Hampden appeared to make mani-
fest in an outburst of oratory the uprising of the upcountry planters, with whom
young Jefferson identified himself, against the provincial oligarchy of the tidewater families.

The winter before Jefferson started college at Williamsburg he had spent the
Christmas holidays, which the Virginians enthusiastically celebrated in the old

English style, at Colonel Dandridge's in Hanover County. There he had seen a lot of a sallowfaced young man of Scottish descent named Patrick Henry. Although Henry was several years Jefferson's senior, a married man who had signalized himself largely by having managed to fail at farming, at keeping store and even at tending bar at Hanover Court House, Jefferson was much taken by his gift of fluent speech. All his life he pleasantly remembered Patrick Henry at that early time as a good rough country fiddler and a great teller of stories and pleasantries round the campfire in the woods at night while the hunters sat on their heels waiting for the dogs to tree a coon or a possum.

Evidently Henry himself had cottoned to the spindly youth from Albemarle, who in spite of his bookishness loved fiddling and dancing and horseflesh, and who had a special knack for making friends of men older or younger than he was. Jefferson was hardly settled in Williamsburg when the gaunt backwoodsman appeared in his rooms at the college with the tall tale that he had read law for six weeks and was ready to take the bar examination.

Peyton and John Randolph were so carried away by Henry's gift of gab that upon his promising to do some more reading they signed his admission to practice before the General Court. According to Jefferson he never kept the promise! Henry, he used to say, was the laziest man for reading he had ever known. Finicky George Wythe refused to sign but Robert Carter Nicholas let himself be talked around. So Patrick Henry was admitted to the bar.

He promptly became the most successful jury lawyer in the colony. He spoke, said Jefferson, as Homer wrote. He didn't give up his hunting. "Whenever the courts were closed for the winter season," Jefferson wrote years later to William Wirt when Wirt was collecting material for Patrick Henry's biography, "he would make up a party of poor hunters of his neighborhood, would go off with them to the piney woods of Fluvanna, and pass weeks in hunting deer, of which he was passionately fond, sleeping under a tent, before a fire, wearing the same shirt the whole time, and covering all the dirt of his dress with a hunting shirt."

Henry's first important case was the Parson's Cause. According to Jefferson it was the only case he ever read up for in his life. Jefferson's old schoolmaster, James Maury, who became more contentious the older he got, was suing his vestry for back pay. He based his claim on the annulment of the Two Penny Acts by the Privy Council. Patrick Henry, arguing the vestry's case before a jury at Hanover Court House, took the high ground that the Crown had no right to annul acts of the colonial legislature.

"The jury seems to have been so completely bewildered," wrote Wirt, "that they lost sight not only of the act of 1748, but that of 1758 also; for thoughtless even of the admitted right of the plaintiff, they had scarcely left the bar, when they returned with a verdict of *one penny damages*. A motion was made for a new trial; but the court too, had now lost the equipoise of their judgment, and overruled the motion by a unanimous vote. The verdict and judgment overruling the motion were followed by redoubled acclamations, from within and without the house. The people, who had with difficulty kept their hands off their champion, from the moment of his closing his harangue, no sooner saw the fate of the cause finally sealed, than they seized him at the bar, and in spite of his own exertions, and the continued cry of 'order' from the sheriffs and the court, they bore him out of the court house, and raising him on their shoulders, carried him about the yard, in a kind of electioneering triumph."

Henry was the most popular lawyer in Virginia. He moved further up in the forest to a place called the Roundabout in Louisa. There the settlers took him to their hearts and returned him as a Burgess.

Jefferson himself was admitted to the bar early in 1767 in his twentyfourth year. He had found it hard at first to knuckle down to the lugubrious hairsplitting of the old commentators. Adolescent daydreams kept distracting him from his books. One Christmas day soon after he'd started work under the learned Wythe he wrote his friend John Page in serio-comic style about the loss of Becky Burwell's likeness which he carried in his watch. "And now although the picture be defaced there is so lively an image of her imprinted in my mind that I shall think of her too often I fear to get through old Cooke"—he should have written Coke —"this winter: for God knows I have not seen him since I packed him in my trunk in Williamsburg . . . well, Page I do wish the Devil had old Cooke, for I am sure I never was so tired of an old dull scoundrel in my life."

Serving an apprenticeship in George Wythe's office meant a great deal of drudgery, copying briefs, looking up authorities, clerical work. In spite of his affection for his patron and his reverence for the man's learning, the experience left him somewhat skeptical as to the value of the apprentice system.

When his uncle Thomas Turpin asked him to take his younger cousin Phill Turpin into his practice as an apprentice, he begged off: "I always was of opinion," he explained, "that the placing of a youth to study with an attorney was rather a prejudice than a help. We are all too apt by shifting on them our business, to encroach on that time which should be devoted to their studies. The only help a youth wants is to be directed what books to read and in what order to read them."

If the program he drew up for another young friend named Bernard Moore at about the same time is any indication of Jefferson's own studies while he worked in Wythe's office, he was indeed, as John Adams put it, "a rubber off of Dust."

First, he explained to young Moore, a student of the law needed a good grounding in French, Latin, mathematics, geography and natural philosophy. As "a great inequality is observable in the vigor of the mind at different periods of the day," he suggested that the early morning hours, before eight when presumably he ate his breakfast, be spent reading on agriculture, chemistry, anatomy, botany, ethics, natural religion, sectarian religion, and the law of nations. "From Eight to Twelve read Law," that "old dull scoundrell" Coke and his commentators, and Lord Kames for equity. "From Twelve to One read politics" Locke, Sydney, Montesquieu and many more. "In the Afternoon read history." Whether this was before or after dinner he does not say. "From Dark to Bedtime" you should relieve your fagged spirits "with belles lettres, criticism, oratory etc."

No wonder he wrote John Page from Shadwell one winter during his law studies that he had lost among other things the whites of his eyes, which were giving him such exquisite pain he had had to stop reading.

His commonplace book has survived, though the bulk of his legal papers were lost when his mother's house burned at Shadwell.

These notes, so he wrote Thomas Cooper fifty years later, "were written at a time of life when I was bold in the pursuit of knowledge, never fearing to follow truth and reason to whatever results they led, and bearding every authority which stood in their way."

When occasion demanded he even attempted to "beard" his esteemed mentor George Wythe. One of the few cases in which his pleading has come down is Howell vs. Netherland. Jefferson was trying to get a colored man his freedom. The plaintiff was a mulatto who claimed he was being illegally held in slavery.

The mulatto's grandmother was the daughter of a white woman by a Negro man. She had been bound by the churchwardens according to colonial law as a bondservant. During the period of her servitude she was delivered of the plaintiff and he was sold back to his grandmother's owner who now claimed his service until he should reach the age of 31.

Jefferson's pleading was that the purpose of the acts under which this man was held in bondage was to "deter women from confusion of the species, which the legislature seems to have considered as an evil." He claimed that once the first master had taken on obligations with the churchwardens to bring up the child he had no more the right to sell the child than the master of any other bondservant or apprentice had. He tried to draw a distinction between indenture and slavery.

In the course of his pleading he stated in unequivocal terms the conviction which was to be the heart of his thinking all his life long:

"I suppose it will not be pretended that the mother being a servant, the child would be a servant under the laws of nature . . . Under the law of nature all men are born free, everyone comes into the world with a right to his own person, which includes the right of moving and using it according to his own will. This is what is called personal liberty."

He claimed that the acts under which the defendant claimed ownership of the

plaintiff made the children of such mulattos bondservants but not slaves. "It remains for some future legislature, if any be found wicked enough, to extend it to
any grandchildren and other issue more remote."

The court seems to have heard him patiently. After all Thomas Jefferson was
a rich and well connected young man who already had a reputation for phenomenal
erudition. But before George Wythe could open his mouth to plead for the defendant the Court awarded their verdict in his favor. In 1770 the Governor's
council of the Virginia colony was tolerating no nonsense about freedom for
mulattos.

The word "Monticello" appears for the first time in Jefferson's account book
for 1767 which was the year of his admission to the bar. Under the heading "Work
to be done at Hermitage" he lists the planting of raspberries, gooseberries, strawberries, asparagus; wagoning wood and sand, and putting up a hen house. At some
point the word *Hermitage* was crossed out and *Monticello* written in its place. In
the first extant letter dated from Monticello he described his new home to a young
clergyman named Ogilvie: "I have lately removed to the mountain from whence
this is dated, and with which you are not unacquainted. I have here but one room,
which, like the cobbler's, serves me for parlor for kitchen and hall. I may add for
bedchamber and study too . . . I have hopes however of getting more elbow
room this summer."

He was planning to marry. He needed a mansion for his bride. By August the
building had proceeded so far he was able to write Robert Skipwith, who had just
married his intended's halfsister: "Come to the new Rowanty . . . Separated
from each other but a few paces, the possessions of each would be open to the
other, a spring, centrically located might be the scene of every evening's joy.
there we should talk over the lessons of the day or lose them in Musick, Chess, or
the merriments of our family companions. the heart thus lightened our pillows
would be soft, and health and long life would attend the happy scene. come then
and bring our dear Tibby with you: the first in your affections, the second in mine.
offer prayers for me too at that shrine to which, tho' absent, I pay continual devotion. in every scheme of happiness she is placed in the foreground of the picture, as the principal figure."

Dimly through the haze of years there rises from the scanty record the figure
of a small gentle highspirited eager young woman. To Jefferson and her sisters
she was known as Patty. "My sister Skelton," Skipwith wrote of her, "with the
greatest fund of good nature has all that sprightliness and sensibility which promises to ensure you the greatest happiness mortals are capable of enjoying. May
business and play, musick and the merriments of your family companions," he

added, echoing Jefferson's words to him, "lighten your hearts, soften your pillows and procure you health long life and every human felicity."

A pleasantly romantic tale came down in the Jefferson family about how the
young couple were married at Patty's father's house, The Forest, in Charles City
County, on New Year's Day; and how they traveled by carriage through snowy
roads as far as Blenheim, the empty seat of one of the Carters. They had to ride
horseback the last eight miles to Monticello because the snow was so deep on the
hills. They arrived late at night and found the slaves all gone to bed and slept in
the little building at the end of the south wing which Jefferson used as his law
office. There may be a spice of fable in the story but its essence rings true. Thomas
Jefferson and Martha Skelton were well suited and loved each other dearly until
she died.

These years of his early law practice were the happiest of Jefferson's life. It
was a time of warm friendships and affections. As if to make up for the loss of his
specially loved sister Jane—"longe longeque valeto," he'd written in her epitaph—
his sister Martha married Dabney Carr, the schoolmate from Maury's school who
had become the intimate companion of his young manhood. Carr was a lawyer
with a mind addicted like Jefferson's to basic political principles. He left the
reputation of being a brilliant speaker. He lived near enough so that they could
meet constantly. It was a repetition of the friendship between his father and
Joshua Fry that Jefferson used to tell of with so much sympathy.

It was a time of high spirits. Young Jefferson had a profitable practice; his
scholarship was the wonder of the countryside. He was happily married. He was
rich. His Patty was the heiress to an estate about as large as his own.

As a leading citizen of Albemarle his reputation was fast outrunning the
memory of his father's. In 1769 he was elected, along with his father's friend, Dr.
Walker, to the House of Burgesses. Governor Botetourt appointed him to his
father's post of County Lieutenant, which carried with it the honorary rank of
colonel. He was famous for his horsemanship.

The practice of the law in those days entailed a great deal of hard riding. On
the spring and autumn circuits judges and lawyers rode in a troop from courthouse to courthouse. When court was in session the ordinaries and law offices
round the county courthouses were a hive of sociability. Settlers rode in from
their lonely plantations to see their friends and hear the lawyers wrangle even if
they had no stake in the cases on trial. In these years as a trial lawyer Jefferson got
to know his Virginia and its people as intimately as his father had known them on
his rough and tumble surveying trips. His practice took him particularly into the

ruder northern and western counties, where present prosperity had not wiped out the memory of the warwhoops of raiding parties during the French war.

Jefferson's first term as a Burgess, the year he began to read Montesquieu's *Spirit of the Laws,* lasted only ten days. The Assembly had expressed its solidarity with the sister colony of Massachusetts with so much vigor that one of the new governor's first official acts was to dissolve it. This was regrettable because the Baron de Botetourt had been sent as a conciliator.

When Jefferson's friend Fauquier died it was decided at Buckingham House that it would flatter and possibly somewhat overawe the Virginians if a royal governor should appear among them in person. Fauquier had been merely a deputy. After a great deal of pulling and hauling; because, while a number of people wanted the emoluments, none of them wanted to live in Williamsburg, Norborne Berkeley was appointed.

A Tory who had sat in the Commons for Gloucestershire, he was one of the more raffish members of the inner circle round Buckingham House. The King had rewarded him for his vote by making him groom of the bedchamber and by help-ing him, on somewhat doubtful title, revive the obsolete barony of Botetourt. He had poured out his money on wine, women and the gaming table. In spite of the support of the King's Friends, his finances had reached a point where there was nothing for it but to put the ocean between him and his creditors.

"I saw nothing but the ruins of loo, Lady Herford's cribbage and Lord Botetourt, like patience on a monument smiling at grief. He is totally ruined," wrote old Walpole's finicky son Horace, to his friend Conway, in a letter of chit-chat about his doings in town during the summer of 1768. "And quite charmed. Yet I heartily pity him," he added. A fashionable nobleman of the period couldn't imagine anything more horrible than exile to the wilds of Virginia.

So long as Botetourt lived his tact and friendliness helped keep the conflict in suspense in Virginia though that bland gentleman must have been shocked again to see at one of his balls a hundred ladies prancing in local homespuns instead of in imported silks. When he succumbed to the climate and perhaps to the result of youthful indiscretions, the Burgesses commemorated his agreeable qualities by ordering the statue erected to him which stands to this day in front of William and Mary College.

The Earl of Dunmore who succeeded him was one of the hungry Scottish noblemen who had flocked down to the court at Westminster in the wake of the Earl of Bute. He too tried to be conciliatory. He invested in the Ohio company. He brought his family to the palace and the members of the Council of State found them charming. The new daughter born there he named Virginia. That

Smibert's portrait of Jeremiah Gridley, lawyer and journalist, the dean of the Massachusetts bar in John Adams's youth.

John Adams as a young man.

Abigail Adams in the early years of their marriage.

The Patriots in the Dumps.

Whig cartoonists gave no quarter to the lobsterbacks.

Town meeting.

BRITISH HEROISM.

The Continental Congress voting independence, by Robert Edge Pine.

William Small, the brilliant Scott whose teaching so influenced Jefferson. After returning home he became a member of Matthew Boulton's Soho circle in Birmingham and was the middleman in the formation of the famous Boulton-Watt partnership to build steam engines.

George Wythe.

Patrick Henry.

Edmund Pendleton.

American officer, 1778.

American soldier, 1778.

James Madison had still the air of a beardless boy when he first attended the Continental Congress. Painted in Philadelphia by C. W. Peale.

pleased the colonial ladies. He consulted young Mr. Jefferson, who already had some reputation as an architect, about improvements in the palace.

When his Assemblies showed fight he dissolved them. His idea was that the less he saw of the Burgesses the better. At first he didn't pay too much attention to the fact that the minute he dissolved the Burgesses they trooped up Duke of Gloucester Street to the Raleigh and there continued as a voluntary convention.

In March of 1773 Jefferson was one of a group of delegates who met at that tavern to discuss the need for establishing a committee of correspondence with the sister colonies. At about the same time, in the raw New England spring, Samuel Adams was shepherding his resolution to establish similar committees through town meeting in Boston. These committees of correspondence were the first links in the structure of union on which the Confederation was built.

The committees of correspondence of the various colonies were responsible for the organization of the Continental Congress. Appeals forwarded from one county to another called for the appointment of delegates "by assemblies, conventions or by committees of correspondence" to a meeting planned at some convenient spot for early September of 1774. Jefferson was absent, although he and Jack Walker had been duly elected for Albemarle, from the convention that sent the first batch of Virginia delegates to Philadelphia.

It was August. He was taken with a fit of dysentery on the road and forced to turn back to Monticello. In his place he sent a paper which was printed in Williamsburg under the title of *A Summary View of the Rights of British America* and reprinted in London. Thomas Jefferson became widely known as the author.

He was still a minor figure in Virginia politics. It was as a partisan of Lawyer Henry and of the radical upcountry party that he sat in the convention made up of lawyers, surveyors and country gentlemen which met in March of 1775 in St. John's Church in the little hamlet of Richmond. When he was appointed to the Continental Congress it was as Peyton Randolph's alternate.

Jefferson never was much of a speaker. He was never the courtroom lawyer. All his life his influence was exercised through the give and take of committee meetings round a table or through letters and writings. At this Richmond convention it was Patrick Henry's voice that made the chandeliers ring with "Gentlemen may say peace, peace, but there is no peace. . . . I know not what course others may take but as for me . . . give me liberty . . ."

"He stood like a Roman Senator defying Caesar," wrote a delegate, "while the unconquering spirit of Cato of Utica flashed from every feature, and then closed the grand appeal with the solemn words: 'Or give me death' which sounded with the awful cadence of a hero's dirge . . . and he suited the action to the word by a blow upon the left breast with the right hand which seemed to drive the dagger to the patriot's heart."

Jefferson was one of the members who listened with breathless approbation. The church was so crowded that many delegates could hear only by clinging to the windows from the outside. Edward Carrington, dangling from a window-frame to hear better, was so moved that he begged his friends, when he died, to see that he should be buried on that spot.

It was as the author of the *Summary View* that Jefferson was known to John Adams and his colleagues from the sister colonies when he drove his single-seated phaeton into Philadelphia in June of 1775 to take Peyton Randolph's place. Virginia's most seasoned frontier campaigner, whom John Adams, writing his wife Abigail, called "the modest and virtuous, the amiable, modest, and brave George Washington Esq." had just been elected generalissimo of the colonial forces now encamped behind Boston.

That city was in the hands of what the delegates still liked to call "the ministerial troops." The same day Washington wrote his brother Jack, "I am embarked on a wide ocean, boundless in its prospect and from whence perhaps no safe harbor is to be found."

The trampling of horses and the sound of fife and drum, as many of the delegates and a troop of light horse in uniform accompanied their new general on the first stage of his road to Massachusetts, had hardly died out when post riders brought into Philadelphia news of the bloodshed on Bunker Hill. Jefferson wrote Francis Eppes, his brotherinlaw at The Forest, "War is now heartily entered into."

In the published proceedings of the Virginia conventions the year 1775 appears under the heading INTERREGNO. With the beginning of 1776 the printer set up in brave type across the top of the page the words: ANNO REIPUBLICAE CONDITAE PRIMO.

The founding of a republic demanded a plan of government. The basic tradition was already there. The question was into what form it should be moulded. During the preceding fall the lawyers among the representatives assembled in Philadelphia had in the privacy of their lodgings done a good deal of talking about possible forms of government. "We ought to consider," John Adams wrote George Wythe, "what is the end of Government, before we determine which is the best Form. Upon this Point all speculative Politicians will agree, that the Happiness of Society is the end of Government as all Divines and moral Philosophers will agree that the Happiness of the Individual is the End of Man. From this Principle it will follow that the Form of Government which communicates Ease, Comfort, Security, or in one Word, Happiness, to the greatest Number of Persons and in the greatest Degree, is the best."

Tom Paine had brought these discussions out in the open with his sketch for a system of government in *Common Sense* published in the preceding winter. To counteract what he considered dangerous errors in Paine's plan John Adams rushed into print with the scheme he had been discussing with Richard Henry Lee and with George Wythe. Richard Henry Lee, in turn, started circulating his own version of Adams's scheme in the *Virginia Gazette*. Another published plan, attributed to Carter Braxton, one of "King" Carter's many grandsons, which perpetuated the life tenure of the Council of State, represented the opinion of the tidewater magnates of Virginia.

Patrick Henry, the mouthpiece of the upcountry party, told off the anonymous author as aristocratical in no uncertain terms. Meanwhile, George Mason, no lawyer but a great reader of Locke who was enjoying his customary ill health amid the fastidious elegance of his lovely paneled rooms at Gunston Hall, was bringing his fine mind to bear on John Adams's scheme and moulding it, in accord with his philosophy of free institutions, into a sketch for the Virginia constitution. It was in everybody's head that as Virginia was the most populous colony and as the feeling for independence was almost universal there, Virginia's should be the first trial constitution.

Jefferson hurried home over wintry trails from Congress at the end of 1775. As soon as he was settled at Monticello, he plunged into his library to do some research in constitutional law. In Congress and in the Virginia convention he had been insisting that the King's statement, in his speech from the throne, that the colonies had been planted and nursed at the expense of the British nation was a downright lie. He set out to prove his contention that the Crown had never invested a shilling in their establishment.

In February when his fat Yorktown friend Thomas Nelson Jr. sent him what he described as two shillings' worth of *Common Sense*, Paine's hearty phrasing stirred up his thoughts about a scheme of government he had been discussing with John Adams in Philadelphia.

His friendship with the New England lawyer dates from those long fall sessions at the Continental Congress when the slowness with which the evolving will of the more laggard colonies was being made known to their delegates seemed unbearable to men who, like Adams and himself, had already made up their minds.

In the fact that John Adams of Braintree and Thomas Jefferson of Monticello became warm friends from the first day they met we can find a hint of why, after all the hesitations of the timid, and the adjustments that had so painfully to be made to regional differences, and the plaguing difficulties of communication, this mixed bag of provincial lawyers, farmers, clergymen, merchants and doctors could find in themselves the common ground on which to found a republic. The similarities in their thinking were greater than the differences.

Virtue for John Adams, as for Thomas Jefferson, instead of being a matter of salvation in the next world, was a matter of civic duty in this. As a lawyer he took

very seriously his oath as officer of the court. Hadn't he appeared as counsel for
Captain Preston and his redcoats? He shared with Jefferson, as with so many of the
best minds of the age, a spontaneous pleasure in the working of selfgoverning
institutions.

Physically there was the greatest contrast between the two men. John Adams
was a stubby little man. Blue eyed and redfaced, downright and explosive, he
could have sat for a portrait of John Bull. The reticent Jefferson was tall raw-
boned and redhaired. Under all the polish of his education there remained a good
deal of the closemouthed frontiersman about him. Daily life in Albemarle County
demanded a different type of alertness from the urban existence of Braintree and
Boston. Jefferson was still a reluctant talker. He had no voice for public speaking.
"Though a silent Member in Congress," Adams wrote retrospectively to Pickering
years later, "he was so prompt, frank, explicit, and decisive upon Committees and
in Conversation, not even Samuel Adams was more so, that he soon seized upon
my Heart."

Jefferson was back in Philadelphia May 14, 1776. Congress had already
adopted John Adams's resolution urging each of the individual colonies to take
over all the powers of government. May 15 the Virginia convention, acting on its
own, recommended that Congress declare the colonies independent. A committee
was set up in Williamsburg to draft a constitution for that commonwealth. While
Thomas Nelson Jr. was riding posthaste to bring the Virginia resolutions to
Philadelphia, Jefferson was appointed along with John Adams, Dr. Franklin, and
Robert R. Livingston of Clermont to the committee to draw up the declaration.
Most of the work fell on Jefferson. While he sat at his traveling desk, expounding
in carefully cadenced phrases a set of principles already established as his belief,
in the upstairs parlor of bricklayer Graff's new house, a large part of his mind
was on the doings at Williamsburg.

The Declaration of Independence, though a magnificent state paper, was
after all merely the elegant expression of the common denominator of the political
beliefs of the American Whigs. There was never any doubt in Jefferson's mind
that the work of the Virginia convention was more important. There the delegates
were cutting out the pattern for a new society.

Sometime in May or early June he had found time to write out his own
outline for a state constitution. When he found there was no way of getting a
release from Congress to go home himself, he sent copies of his final draft to
George Wythe and to Edmund Pendleton who was presiding at Williamsburg.

His first principle was universal manhood suffrage. Jefferson's plan would
establish as electors "all male persons of full age and sane mind having a freehold

estate in one four of an acre of land in any town, or in 25 acres of land in the country, and all persons resident in the colony who shall have paid scot and lot to government the last two years shall have right to give their vote in the election of their respective representatives, and every person so qualified to elect shall be capable of being elected."

To make sure that no man would be excluded from voting by the property qualification, under the heading: "Rights Private & Public," he included a clause: "Every person of full age neither owning nor having owned 50 acres of land, shall be entitled to an appropriation of 50 acres, or to so much as shall make up what he owns or has owned: 50 acres in full & absolute dominion, and no other person shall be capable of taking an appropriation."

The acreage appears in brackets in each case. He intended that enough free land to make him a voter should be distributed to every present adult male inhabitant and to all future inhabitants, "persons who by their oath or affirmation, or by other testimony shall give satisfactory proof to any court of record in this colony that they propose to reside in the same 7 years at the least, and who subscribe the fundamental laws."

The second principle wiped out the aristocratic custom of entailing property and slaves. "Descents shall go according to the laws of Gavelkind, save only that females shall have equal rights with males," he wrote in his final draft. The wording of the first draft explains what he meant in layman's language. "Descents, instead of being to the eldest son, brother or other male cousin of the ancestor as directed by the laws heretofore, shall be to all the brothers & sisters of the said heir."

Jefferson wanted a community of small and medium landowners where every man would have enough land to establish him in the dignity of voter and citizen and where the more active and enterprising could amass as much wealth as they had a mind to without being allowed to hand down great aggregations to be held in mortmain for a succession of eldest sons.

The third principle established freedom of religion and disestablished the Episcopal Church: "All persons shall have free and full liberty of religious opinion: nor shall any be compelled to frequent or maintain any religious institution."

The fourth laid the foundation for the gradual elimination of slavery. "No person hereafter coming into this country shall be held within the same in slavery under any pretext whatever."

On a number of Jefferson's principles, such as freedom of the press, and the division of governmental powers into legislative, judicial and executive, the radical and conservative Whigs were in agreement.

The constitution which the Williamsburg convention established for Virginia was substantially George Mason's. It was preceded by his famous declaration of rights, which laid down the political axioms that all men were created free and independent, that political power was vested in the people, that the majority had the right to reform any government, and that no man should be taxed without his consent.

"When I came here," George Wythe wrote Jefferson from Williamsburg, "the Plan of Government had been committed to the whole House. To those who had the chief Hand in forming it the one you put into my Hands was shewn. Two or three Parts of this were, with little Alteration, inserted in that; but such was the Impatience of sitting long enough to discuss several important Points in which they differ, and so many other Matters were necessarily to be dispatched before the Adjournment that I was persuaded the Revision of a Subject the Members seemed tired of would at that Time have been unsuccessfully proposed. The system agreed to in my opinion requires Reformation. In October I hope you will effect it."

The struggle to accomplish the reformation Wythe spoke of was to take up Jefferson's political energies for the next five years.

Meanwhile, at the same time as a republic was being established, a war had to be fought. "We have a Constitution to form for a great Empire, a Country of fifteen hundred miles in extent to fortify, Millions to arm and train, a naval Power to begin, an extensive Commerce to regulate, numberless Tribes of Indians to negotiate with, a standing Army of twentyseven thousand Men to raise, pay, victual and officer," John Adams had written to Abigail from Congress the year before.

It was another hot summer in Philadelphia. Congress was endlessly in session and committees dragged on into the night. Rules had to be improvised to regulate debate. A great seal for the United States had to be designed. Plans had to be made to clear up the confusion of the various colonial currencies. A committee on military affairs had to listen to painful postmortems on the miscarriage of the expeditions to Canada. Great bales of paper money had to be printed and carted off to the paymasters. Discussion of principles kept being interrupted by the compelling need for salt, for lead, for gunpowder, for blankets for the troops. It was a period of much effort and little accomplishment. "We suffer inexpressibly for want of Men of Business," John Adams wrote home, "—Men acquainted with War by Sea or Land, Men who have no pleasure but in Business. If you have them send them along."

When Jefferson was elected to the Virginia House of Delegates George Wythe, who was taking Mrs. Wythe along on his tour of duty in Congress, thoughtfully offered Jefferson for the session his handsome house across from the palace in Williamsburg. For once Jefferson's dear Patty was well enough to travel. At last he could set himself, in full peace of mind, in the company of the woman he loved so tenderly, to a task he felt really suited him.

The public times Jefferson saw in Williamsburg in the fall of 1776 were very different from any of the public times he had known in the past. Gone were the royal chariots and the provincial pomp of old Speaker Robinson which Peyton Randolph had continued in the splendor of gold lace and a full wig. Now Patrick Henry, who on his elevation had given up hunting shirts and homespun for a black suit and the scarlet cloak of a Glasgow merchant, topped by a neat tie wig, was occupying the palace as governor, and Jefferson's personal friend and public opponent, Edmund Pendleton, was presiding as speaker in the Capitol.

Edmund Pendleton had the reputation of being the ablest lawyer in the Virginia colony. He had entered politics as a protégé of the Robinson tribe in the old days when genial John Robinson combined the offices of treasurer and speaker with a weighty voice on the governor's Council. Left a penniless orphan, Pendleton was apprenticed to the clerk of the court of Caroline County; it was to the credit of the Robinsons that they had appreciated the special quality of his mind when he was a mere boy.

"Mr. Pendleton," Jefferson wrote in his autobiography, ". . . zealously attached to ancient establishments . . . was the ablest man in debate I have ever met with. he had not indeed the poetical fancy of Mr. Henry, his sublime imagination, his lofty & overwhelming diction: but he was cool, smooth & persuasive: his language, flowing, chaste & embellished: his conceptions quick, acute and full of resource; never vanquished: for if he lost the main battle he returned upon you and regained so much of it to make it a drawn one by dextrous manoeuvres, skirmishes in detail, and the recovery of small advantages which, little singly, were important all together. you never knew when you were clear of him, but were harassed by his perseverance until the patience was worn down of all who had less of it than himself. add to this that he was the most virtuous and benevolent of men, the kindest friend, the most amiable and pleasant of companions, which ensured a favorable reception to whatever came from him."

The death of Peyton Randolph marked the end of the leisurely rural pomp of the old House of Burgesses. The House of Delegates Pendleton presided over was a very different body. The wigs and the hair powdered and dressed full over the ears and the frilled shirts and the lace cuffs of the tidewater planters were still in evidence, but among them could be seen fur caps, homespun greatcoats, leather jackets, deerskin leggings, militia uniforms. Lanky men from the Piedmont and from settlements west of the mountains predominated over the round and

There were a great many very young men. Edmund Randolph for example ceremonious tidewater magnates.

had been elected at only twentytwo to the office of Attorney General which his Tory father had vacated to retire to England. Their dress was as varied as their opinions. Some young bloods among the radical Whigs had taken up the fashion of wearing the conical felt hats affected by the republican Puritans of England at the time of the Long Parliament. One young man from Orange County, who instead of being tall was small and slight, had his conical hat stolen in the hallway of a friend's house in Williamsburg and made a funny story about it, because on account of non-importation he had no way of buying himself another.

This was James Madison, son and heir of the Montpelier Madisons. He had appeared in Williamsburg for the first time as delegate from Orange at the May convention, and had made such a name for himself for modest diligence that as soon as he reported to the House of Delegates that fall he was placed with Jefferson and Carter Braxton and Robert Carter Nicholas and a number of prominent men from both the conservative and radical Whigs on the highly contentious Committee on Religion. It was in the daily work on this committee, which was besieged with petitions for the repeal of the laws infringing on religious liberty, that Jefferson first recognized the younger man from Montpelier as an intellectual kinsman.

Jefferson had known the Madisons all his life. In his circuitriding days as a young lawyer he would occasionally enter in his account book small losses at the game of "pitcher" to a John Madison up in the Valley. When James Madison of Montpelier arrived in Williamsburg one of his first friendly meetings must have been with his cousin of the same name, whose father was this John Madison of the Valley branch of the family. This James had been a schoolmate of Jefferson's at Maury's, had studied law under George Wythe in Williamsburg and now taught Dr. Small's course in natural philosophy at the college. Though a Whig and a solid republican, he had recently returned from taking orders in England. He combined allegiance to the Episcopal Church with fervent enthusiasm for the natural sciences. Immediately he set to work with the help of Dr. Small's two other disciples, Jefferson and John Page, who both eventually became members of the Board of Visitors, to modernize and liberalize the curriculum at the college. When the Tory John Camm resigned the presidency, it was the Reverend Madison who took his place.

Both Madisons were warm friends and admirers of Jefferson. With one he started immediately to work for the reform of the curriculum at the college. The other, just launched on the career of statesmanship which would culminate in the *Federalist Papers* and in his collaboration in the Federal Constitution, became Jefferson's ablest assistant in the contest which began with that first session of the Assembly, to establish the commonwealth on a pattern they considered "truly republican."

By the time the session of a scant eight weeks ended in the middle of December, Jefferson had become the prime mover in legislation which would establish a selfgoverning commonwealth of landowners, based on the theory he had frankly put forward in a letter to the more conservative Pendleton that summer. "You have lived longer than I have & perhaps have formed a different judgment on better grounds," Jefferson wrote Pendleton from Philadelphia in August, "but my observations do not enable me to say I think integrity the characteristic of wealth. in general I believe the decisions of the people, in a body, will be more honest & more disinterested than those of wealthy men: and I can never doubt an attachment to his country in any man who has his family and peculium in it."

Looking back to these early days when he sat writing his autobiography at the end of his life, it seemed to Jefferson that the laws abolishing entail and primogeniture, disestablishing the Church and asserting complete freedom of religion, along with the measure he drafted, which was unfortunately never adopted, to set up a system of free public schools, were the most important accomplishments for which foundations were laid in that great session: "I considered these four bills passed or reported, as forming a system by which every fibre would be eradicated of past or future aristocracy; and a foundation laid for a government truly republican. the repeal of the laws of entail would prevent the accumulation or perpetuation of wealth, in select families, & preserve the soil of the country from being daily more and more absorbed in mortmain . . . The restoration of the rights of conscience relieved the people from taxation for the support of a religion not theirs; for the establishment was truly of a religion of the rich, the dissenting sects being composed entirely of the less wealthy people; and these, by the bill for a general education, would be qualified to understand their rights, to maintain them & to exercise with intelligence their parts in self-government."

Before that tremendous session of the first Virginia Assembly was over, Jefferson, as if he had not already taken on enough work to kill a mule, had accepted with alacrity a place on a committee which was set no lesser task than the modernizing and clarifying of the entire code of English law in use in Virginia. The committee promptly elected Jefferson chairman and decided to go to work in January at Fredericksburg.

They met January 13 in the quiet little wintry town at the head of navigation of the Rappahannock. It was a moment of mighty hopes. The day after Christmas Washington had brought his retreat across the Jerseys to a brilliant close by surprising the Hessians at Trenton and a few days later had checked the main British force at Princeton. For the first time it began to look as if the Continental Army could hold its own against British regulars.

Jefferson was sitting down, away from the pressure of parliamentary detail, with his revered friend and teacher, George Wythe; with subtle George Mason who took an amateur's pleasure in the machinery of selfgovernment; with Edmund Pendleton, a conservative whom he liked and whose workings he thoroughly understood, and with Thomas Ludwell Lee, the oldest surviving of the brilliant sons of old Thomas Lee, who, as an associate of George Mason's in the Ohio Company, was a western-minded man.

The task before them was something like old Coke's, or Bracton's, or the modern work of Blackstone then still fresh from the English press. Jefferson thoroughly understood that there were only certain times in the history of nations when fundamental reforms were possible. The iron was glowing and malleable. Now was the time to hammer it out. It was the work for which his training in the law, his Latin, his Anglo-Saxon, his close reading of old Norman French texts, his enthusiasm for John Locke and Algernon Sidney and for the great republicans of the English Commonwealth had long been preparing him.

In the end, like most such enterprises, the reform of the legal system of Virginia was left incomplete. Some of the most important measures failed to pass the legislature. It was ten years later, after Jefferson had virtually retired from the contest, that his young friend and disciple, little James Madison of Montpelier, established on the statute books the ruins of the great reform.

From the beginning the drudgery fell on Jefferson and Pendleton. George Mason, always an indolent man, begged off because he was no lawyer. Thomas Ludwell Lee retired to his home on the same pretext and soon after died. George Wythe remained the sympathetic consultant. In all one hundred and twentysix bills were presented to the House of Delegates. Jefferson worked on considerably more than half of them. In its inception it was one of the boldest enterprises in the history of laws. As the five men gathered round a table in the wintry quiet to settle to work the greatness of the task must have made their blood tingle. It was one of those times when everything seems possible.

The only copy of the memorandum they kept is in the handwriting of George Mason.

"The Common Law not to be meddled with," it begins, "except where alterations are necessary . . . The Statutes to be revised and digested, alterations proper for us to be made; the Diction, where obsolete or redundant, to be reformed . . . The Acts of the English Common-wealth to be examined. The Laws of the other Colonies to be examined, and any good ones to be adopted . . . Bills to be short, not to include Matters of different Natures: not to insert an unnecessary word, nor to omit an useful one."

Part *2*

GEORGE WASHINGTON:
PATER PATRIAE

George Washington:
Pater Patriae

THE GREATEST SKILL OF ALL
WAS WASHINGTON'S:
statesmanship, leadership, a sense of the whole, the skillful self-restraint of a leader who knew how to lead just so far and no further.

His beginnings were not particularly auspicious.

As a surveyor he early learned the ways of the western settlements and the halfbreeds and the hunting Indians of the hills. He had a knack for sizing up frontier land. After four years of surveying, before he'd had any military training at all, he was appointed, through the influence of his in-laws the Fairfaxes, a Major in the Virginia Regiment.

War was brewing with the French. He volunteered for a hazardous winter reconnaissance of their posts among the upper tributaries of the Ohio. The pretext was an embassy.

Washington as a young man kept a meticulous journal. He enjoyed keeping a record as much as Jefferson did. Back in Williamsburg he copied out the journal of his icy journey for Governor Dinwiddie to read. The Governor thought so highly of it he had it printed. In London the young Virginia officer's spirited narrative was enthusiastically read. It was as a travel writer that George Washington had his first fame.

Next spring as second in command and then as commanding officer he returned to reconnoitering the trails beyond Wills Creek. He saw his first skirmish. "I heard the Bullets whistle and, believe me, there is something charming in the Sound." He ambushed a party of French his Indians said were coming in to attack. Their leader the Sieur de Jumonville was killed. A few weeks later Jumonville's brother had his revenge when, advancing with a large force of French and Indians, he surrounded Washington's detachment at Great Meadows.

It was raining, their powder was low, their food was gone, every horse and mule was killed. The French let the Virginians walk out of their hasty stockade which Washington characteristically had named Fort Necessity. They retired with the honors of war but not before their commander had signed his name to a paper.

Washington knew no French. Huddled over a candle in the middle of the night in the driving rain an interpreter hurriedly spelled out the capitulation. The document read that Washington regretted not the accidental death, which he did regret, but the murder of Jumonville.

The French found his fresh journal in the baggage he had to abandon. They hurried it to France and published it in garbled translation along with his admission that the attack on Jumonville had been unprovoked. Their claim was that Jumonville was bound on an embassy like Washington the year before. In the war of words that accompanied the shooting war they denounced George Washington as a murderer. Washington's second diary had a very different fame from the first. Even in Virginia his reputation suffered. He threw up his commission in chagrin.

This was enough to ruin any young officer's career.

But somehow George Washington grew in stature through misfortune.

He was induced to go along with Braddock. He was thought indispensable to any expedition into the western country. Again a defeat. After he'd buried Braddock under that unlucky road through Great Meadows and arrived home half dead with dysentery and despair, he summed up his military career in a letter:

"I was employed to go on a journey in the Winter (when I believe few or none would have undertaken it) and what did I get by it? My expenses paid. I was then employed with trifling pay to conduct a Handful of Men to the Ohio. What did I get by this? Why after putting myself to considerable expense equipping and providing Necessaries for the campaigns, I went out, was soundly beaten, and had my Commission taken from me. . . . I then went out as a Volunteer with Gen'l Braddock and lost all my Horses and many other things . . . I should not have mentioned it was it not to show that I have been on the losing order ever since I entered the Service."

On the slippery trails from Will's Creek to the Ohio Washington got his schooling in the uses of war; he grew in stature through misfortune.

He was a good business man, an excellent farm manager. As a dealer in western lands he was successful. He built up his holdings, made a good marriage, took over his dead halfbrother's estate at Mt. Vernon. His judgment in Western matters was prized in the House of Burgesses and the Governor's Council and in the Ohio Company.

The Continental Congress appointed him to command the recruits massing in front of Boston to oppose the ministerial troops. He was John Adams's choice.

Long Island,

White Plains,

the retreat across the Jerseys,

Valley Forge: George Washington grew in stature through misfortune. For six years he was "on the losing order" until in 1781 for just one month the tides of war ran in his favor.

The American commander in chief was painfully aware that his marches and countermarches were part of a wider war between rival empires that covered half the globe. Sitting in his headquarters in what he called "his dreary station" at New Windsor on the Hudson he learned in the spring of 1781 that a great French fleet was sailing out of Brest.

This was a year of disaster for the Tory cause. King George's ministers had managed to array all the maritime powers of the world against them. Besides the Bourbon alliance, they were at war with the hardheaded Dutch. The Baltic powers were arrayed against them under the guise of armed neutrality.

The mission of De Grasse's fleet was to undo the mischief gouty old Rodney had been doing the French and Spanish in the West Indies. When the hurricane season threatened the admiral might cruise to the northward and take a hand in the American campaign.

All summer, while Cornwallis, the Hannibal of the Southern Department, ravaged Virginia, Washington kept the British in New York guessing as to his

intentions. "Matters now having come to a crisis and a decisive Plan to be determined on" he noted in his diary for August 14, he was obliged "from the
shortness of Count de Grasse's promised stay on this Coast, the apparent disin-
clination of his naval Officers to force the harbour of New York," to seek a decision in Virginia.

Cornwallis was finding his victories expensive. His troops were sick with
ague and camp fever. He needed a salt water harbor to refit the army he had
dragged through the wilderness of the Carolinas. Sir Henry Clinton in New York
ordered him to Yorktown.

Meanwhile on the west bank of the Hudson Washington was assembling
his ragged army and Rochambeau's handsomely uniformed battalions. To keep
Clinton guessing he was having the French build bakeovens and make a great
show of getting ready an encampment opposite Staten Island. The British fleet
was deployed to defend New York.

His agents' skill at intercepting dispatches proved Sir Henry Clinton's un-
doing. All Washington's dispatches spoke of a joint French and American attack
on New York.

Meanwhile Washington's army was on the move. August 30 he wrote in
his diary he hoped to conceal his intention for one more day's march . . . "Under
the idea of marching to Sandy Hook to facilitate the entrance of the French fleet
within the Bay the whole army was put in motion, in three columns." One of these
columns was detached to make a feint towards the Jersey shore.

With their baggage and their artillery and their flatboats mounted on wheels
Washington's two columns and Rochambeau's one converged on Trenton. They
marched unbelievably fast. Washington ordered the cattle and horses swum
across the Delaware to save time.

By September 5 he was south of Philadelphia.

Every man who saw him on the march that day remembered the look of
joy that came over his face when a rider caught up with him on the road out of
Chester with the news that De Grasse's fleet was safe at anchor inside the Virginia Capes. Some said he shouted and waved his threecornered hat like a boy.

"I hope you will keep Lord Cornwallis safe, without provisions or forage
till we arrive" he wrote his favorite Frenchman, who in command of the cavalry
had been showing the skill of a seasoned campaigner in keeping his small force
out of Cornwallis's reach. In fact young Lafayette had managed to turn the noble
earl's triumphal progress through ruined tidewater plantations into something that
began to look like a retreat.

The siege of Yorktown became one of the great battlepieces of the century.
The press of onlookers was so great Washington was forced to bar them by a
general order: "The Commander in Chief having observed that the Trenches are

PATRIÆ PATER

Washington

Rembrandt Peale's portrait that hangs in
the Vice President's office in the capitol.

An unknown woodcarver's idea of Washington.

John Trumbull's set piece to celebrate Washington as Commander in Chief. As son of a Connecticut governor, Trumbull served for a while as one of Washington's aides; personal recollections must have entered into even so formal a composition.

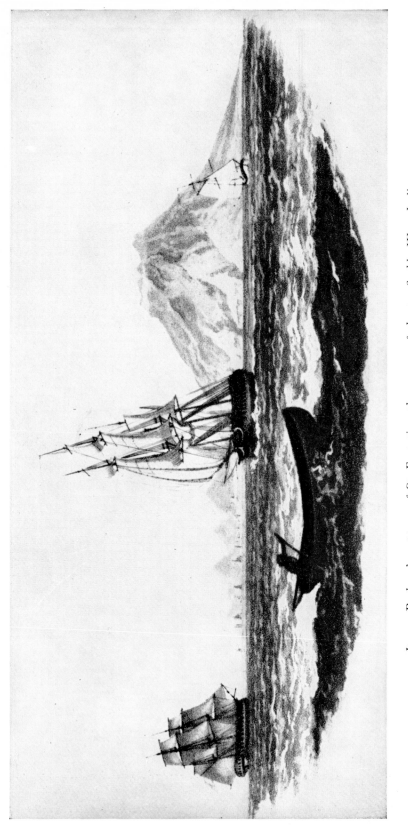

It was Rodney's capture of St. Eustatius, the center of the profitable West Indies trade, that caused the French to send de Grasse's great fleet overseas.

Houdon's life mask of the general.

The French fleet in one of its famous formations.

Engravings glorifying the modern Cincinnatus were hung in every home in the thirteen states.

This portrait of George Washington as a Mason is attributed to a William Williams, a different Williams from Benjamin West's teacher. To a fervent reader of his letters and diaries it seems the closest we come to seeing the man as his Virginia neighbors saw him.

*George and Martha Washington sitting at home with the Custis grand-
children; the Potomac River in the background and a map of some of the
general's landholdings on the table: by Edward Savage.*

constantly crowded by Spectators, who by passing and repassing, prevent the
men from working and thereby greatly impede the operations of the Siege; He
therefore orders that . . . no inhabitant or person not belonging to the Army
be suffered to enter the Trenches at any time without permission . . ."

Before the wining and the dining of the defeated British and of the French
allies that followed Cornwallis's surrender was over, before the bloated carcasses
of the horses the British had killed and thrown into the river had been washed
away by the tide, or the bodies of Negroes dead of smallpox and camp fever
had been properly buried among the ruins of the tiny town of York, Washington
was at his travellingdesk writing apprehensive letters. He feared, he wrote Governor Nelson of Virginia, "lest the late important success, instead of exciting our
exertions as it ought to, should produce such a relaxation in the prosecution of the
war, as will prolong the calamities of it."

His apprehensions were justified. De Grasse refused to remain on the American coast long enough to help in the expeditions to relieve Wilmington and
Charleston which Washington had set his heart on. In fact he showed so little
interest in the American campaign he stayed cooped up on his magnificent flag-
ship *Ville de Paris* throughout the siege. He wasn't even tempted by the great
show of the capitulation, but allowed himself to be represented by a subordinate.
His chief interest seemed to be to get his table furnished with fresh vegetables before sailing south to the more lucrative battlefields of the sugar islands of the
Caribbean. The Chesapeake was left open to the British again.

By early November Washington had finished despatching the prisoners inland and reviewing the courtmartials of deserters captured with the British, and
set off for Mt. Vernon for a few days repose before travelling to Philadelphia.
At this stage of the war he deemed it more important to watch Congress than to
watch the British.

At Colonel Bassett's house near Ruffin's ferry he found his wife Martha's
son sick with camp fever. Jack Custis though no soldier had come down from
Mt. Vernon to see Yorktown's fall. Though he seems to have been a spoiled
young fellow not fit for much except foxhunting and country dancing he was
the nearest thing to a son George Washington had. Martha and Jack's wife and
his small daughter and a couple of helpless physicians were at his bedside. Next
day he died.

George Washington hid his grief behind his stony leader's mask. He arranged for the funeral and the settlement of the young man's estate in his usual
businesslike way and escorted the bereaved ladies to Mt. Vernon. There he al-

lowed Martha a week of mourning before he packed her into her chaise for Philadelphia.

The dinners and the toasts and the addresses of welcome and the recitations by schoolgirls in white dresses that greeted the General's party at every turn of the road seem to have had an appreciable effect on Mrs. Washington's spirits. By Christmas the General was writing from Philadelphia that his wife was better than he could have expected after her heavy loss.

It wasn't until the end of March that Washington resumed direct command of the army on the Hudson. Since his wife came with him he set up new head-quarters at a pleasant stone house in Newburgh.

Since the day he had taken command at Wadsworth house in Cambridge he had strained every nerve to raise an army and to keep it under arms; now, while peace negotiations dragged on in Paris, it was his painful business to get his troops safely scattered to their homes again. Winter quarters had always been a period of cabals and quarrels. The army seethed with contention. As enemy pressure subsided every smoldering gripe came to the surface. Most of them were justified.

For years officers and men had served without proper clothing or equipment. Their pay was in certificates with a merely nominal value which soon sank to zero in the all-encompassing inflation. With the war nearly won the soldiers began to ask for their arrears in pay in some form they could use for money.

Their griefs were summarized in a memorial written in Colonel Lewis Ni-cola's careful hand and laid on the general's desk. Colonel Nicola was no firebrand. He was one of the most respected older officers in the army. When he announced himself to be convinced "of the weakness of republicks," Washington caught his breath. The memorial went much further than to state the grievances of the troops. It suggested that the army secede from the Confederation and form a new nation in the virgin lands to the westward with George Washington as their king.

Washington was brought up a Whig. As staunchly as any English country gentleman he believed the military should be subordinate to the civil power. In his mind the cause of independence was indissolubly associated with the cause of representative government. Nicola's memorial shocked him to the marrow.

He answered in his own hand . . . "I am much at a loss to conceive what part of my conduct," he wrote "would have given encouragement to an address which to me seems big with the greatest mischiefs that can attend my country."

Colonel Nicola was so aghast at the indignant tone of his Commander in Chief's reply that he wrote three separate letters of apology.

Months dragged on. Washington was writing daily letters to members of Congress or to his friends in Philadelphia. The troops must be paid. "The patience, the fortitude, the long and great sufferings of this Army is unexampled in history: but there is an end to all things and I fear we are very near one . . ." "The situation of the officers," he wrote again ". . . distressing beyond description . . . a large part have no other prospect before them than a Gaol if they are turned loose without liquidation of accounts." According to the crude legal procedure of the day, having had to borrow money to feed their families and buy equipment during the war, most of them were in danger of being arrested as defaulting debtors the moment they stepped out of uniform.

The army seethed. Nicola's plan was revived in more seditious form. An anonymous address called on the continental soldiers to take the law into their own hands.

Washington had been keeping his troops busy building themselves barracks during the winter. Among them was a handsome edifice to use as a church and dancing academy which the soldiers had nicknamed "The Temple". There one Saturday afternoon the Commander in Chief called his officers together. He strode into the hall wearing his buff and blue. He was visibly agitated as he stepped up to the lectern. He tore into the reasoning behind the addresses. He said he doubted the motives of their author: "My God! What can this writer have in view, by recommending such measure? Can he be a friend of the Army? Can he be a friend of this Country? Is he not an insidious Foe?"

He begged them to be patient, not to sully the magnificent reputation they had made themselves in the world: "And you will, by the dignity of your Conduct, afford occasion for posterity to say, when speaking of the glorious example you have exhibited to Mankind, 'had this day been wanting the World had never seen the last stage of perfection to which human nature is capable of attaining!' "

It was the most moving speech of Washington's career.

At the end he pulled a letter from a friend in Congress out of his pocket, which he tried to read to back up his statement that Congress was working with desperate haste on the problem of finding funds for the army. He read a few words haltingly and then fumbled in his pocket for the reading glasses Rittenhouse had recently ground for him. "Gentlemen," he said, "I have grown gray in your service and now I find myself growing blind."

Many a man had tears in his eyes. Washington abruptly turned the meeting over to the senior officer present, who happened to be his old enemy Horatio Gates, and walked out of the hall.

It turned out later that the addresses had been concocted by young John Armstrong who was a member of Gates's staff, whether with Gates's knowledge or not was never surely known.

At the meeting in the Temple no man dared say a word in favor of the addresses. There was no more talk of monarchy in America. Washington was able to forward a set of resolutions to Congress and to report that "the proceedings on the part of the Army had terminated with perfect unanimity and in a manner entirely consonant with my wishes."

Spring brought good news. A parliamentary pact had been signed with Britain. Better terms than anyone could have imagined. "The news" wrote Washington "has filled my mind with inexpressible satisfaction."

The day the news of peace came the Paymaster-general opened an office in Newburgh to settle the accounts of the army.

For password that morning the Commander in Chief chose "America", for countersigns "Triumphant", "Happy".

When the British evacuated New York, General Washington announced that the day of his retirement had come. Leaving Horatio Gates, whose ambition to become Commander in Chief was at last fulfilled, in charge of the dwindling army he rode into the city. At Fraunces' Tavern he toasted his officers with a last glass of wine. With tears rolling down his face he kissed every man on the cheek and took his leave. As the oarsmen rowed him across the bay past the British ships preparing to set sail he stood in the barge's stern waving his three-cornered hat. Through misfortune he had grown in stature till he overshadowed any man in America.

Farewells, addresses of adulation, celebrations of esteem followed on each other's heels until at last in Annapolis the long awaited day came when he could resign his commission. The members of Congress had moist eyes. The ladies in the galleries wept. The General's hand shook as he held out the paper under his eyes: "Having now finished the work assigned to me, I retire from the great theatre of action; and bidding an Affectionate farewell to this August body under whose orders I have so long acted, I here offer my commission and take my leave of all the employments of public life."

George Washington resigned his commission at noon on December 23, 1783. Always a hard rider, in spite of a slow blustery crossing of the Potomac ferry, he was in Mt. Vernon Christmas Eve and next day ate Christmas dinner in front of his own fire with his wife Martha and her grandchildren.

Part 3

THE RISING GLORY OF
AMERICA

Masthead of Pennsylvania Packet.

A People of the Pen
and the Press

CHAPTER 1   ✧

THE EIGHTEENTH CENTURY SAW THE BIRTH OF THE DAILY NEWS-paper, the monthly magazine, the popular novel, and of that proliferation of presses by which phrases were brought, fresh from the pensman's fingers, to the plain man's breakfast table before the ink had time to dry on them.

Not too long after the success of such novel ventures as *The Gentleman's Magazine* (for which Samuel Johnson reported on Parliament), in London, similar ventures were undertaken in Boston and Philadelphia. Every young colonial who aspired to letters tried to model his English on the elegant journalism of Addison and Steele. Benjamin Franklin wrote his first pieces for his brother's newspaper in Boston.

It was his knowledge of the printer's trade that gave him a chance to scrounge himself up an education, and to roam the cosmopolitan world from Boston to Philadelphia and Philadelphia to London and back again in search of his fortune.

It was to buy types and presses to set up a publishing house for Sir William

Keith, then Governor of Pennsylvania, that Franklin first set sail for England on the ship *London Hope* in the fall of 1724. As he supposed, and as the Governor had assured him, letters of recommendation to literary men and friends of that somewhat crackbrained functionary's were in the ship's mailbag when she sailed. They were to establish young Ben's credit, and to put him on the road to preferment and place.

The London the young American saw and smelt and heard about him when he first stretched his legs, that still felt light from the straining and heaving of the ship, on the muddy cobbles, was already the great capital, the *urbs et orbis* of eighteenth century England. It was a foggy crowded city of clattering lanes and narrow streets, opening here and there into smoothpaved courts and pumpyards and into the new great squares flanked by facades in the very personal style which Sir Christopher Wren had a generation before worked up out of memories of Palladio and Vitruvius for the rebuilding after the great fire of 1666. Although the population of England was only something like eight millions, nearly one tenth of it was crowded into the great seaport city.

The streets were full of racket of hugewheeled carts and coaches, and rang with the cries of hucksters, fishwives, oysterwomen, applesellers, boys yelling papers and almanacs and running after gentlemen to shine their shoes. There were few sidewalks as yet, but in the better streets big stone posts protected those on foot from the wheels that squdged through mud and streaming gutters, and from the jostling of porters bowed under heavy loads or of strapping fellows in livery carrying people of means around in sedan chairs. Fops and elegants when they walked carried long canes with silver pommels to help them over the uneven pavements. Women covered their dresses with hoods and cloaks to protect them from the spattering mud and clattered along on wooden pattens.

At night the watchmen with their pikes and long cloaks went through the streets gingerly in groups and shook their lanterns from corner to corner to call for help when they needed it. Around the waterfront dives, pressgangs were often busy kidnaping seamen for the Royal Navy. It was a raw tough city where dog eat dog was the law.

Young Franklin took lodgings with a friend at three and sixpence a week in the anthill's very center, in Little Britain, and began to look about him. When it dawned on him that Governor Keith's backing had been all talk and that he had sent him no letters of recommendation at all, he got himself a job as a compositor at Palmer's famous print shop in Bartholemew Close.

To a curious young man from the colonies, avid for discussion, information and discovery, the coffeehouses and taverns were the great attraction. There men of wit and reputation, indeed all kinds of men, went to meet their friends and to talk. The clubs of the London coffeehouses were like the *tertulias* that survived up into our own time in the cafés of Madrid. Men went there to show themselves and to look at the bigwigs and to expound and to listen. While they waited for their friends they read the reviews and the newsletters.

The great men Franklin saw were the great of a second generation. The Augustans were gone. Addison had obtained preferment and place and the Countess of Warwick and had died. Steele was coming to the end of his gay career paralyzed and broke in a Welsh farmhouse. Swift was living in bitter exile in his Dublin deanery. Pope, the little sickly spidershaped man whose sting was always ready for friend or foe, still lurked in his garden at Twickenham, undisputed master of the realms of gold, but was rarely seen in London.

Franklin went often to Batson's Coffeehouse in the hope of someday seeing Sir Isaac Newton, who was spending his last years in the quiet post of Master of the Mint, but never got a glimpse of him. He did meet Dr. Mandeville, a Dutch physician who was the Mencken of the day and whose *Fable of the Bees* was immensely popular at the time, and Sir Hans Sloane, the explorer and botanist and popularizer of quinine. He sold Sir Hans a purse made of asbestos he'd brought with him from America, and went to his house in Bloomsbury Square to see his collection of curios.

But mostly young Ben associated with printers, mechanics, old ladies in lodginghouses, chance acquaintances of the street and tavern. Ready as a sponge to soak up everything essential he touched, he did not need to sit across the table from the great masters themselves. The style they had invented was everywhere; their neat jocular verse, their cool prose based on the cadences of conversation pervaded the smoky air of the city.

The streets Ben walked in were the streets of Gay's *Trivia*. The groups in the coffeehouses were the Club out of *The Spectator*. Events in the world of power were flavored with the sharp partisan bitterness of Swift's pamphlets. The Augustan pomposities out of the classical past that Dryden had set up like stage scenery at the end of every vista were focused sharp and clear and small by the diminishing lens of Pope's precise and narrow mind. It is not surprising that in these eighteen months Franklin's writing lost the routine provincial sound of his boyish journalism and that he went home to Philadelphia with one of the simplest and most direct-from-the-lips English styles ever written.

From the Augustans he had caught the habit of taking for granted a republic of letters, universal brotherhood of brains, curiosity and discovery, which was implicit in the best works of the age. It was an attitude which gave scope to that unfenced openness of mind he was to transmit, in his long career of influencing all classes and types of men, to a generation of Americans.

The all too brief journal Franklin kept of his trip home on the *Berkshire* is the first example we have of the style of writing that is the making of the *Auto-*

biography and of his letters. Instead of the raw youth who had wangled his way into the cabin on the *London Hope,* the Ben Franklin who came back from London on the *Berkshire* was the Franklin the world was gradually to get to know: Mr. Franklin, the sharp man of business so canny in the ways of the world, who understood the uses of money and respectability without ever being quite won by them; Dr. Franklin the philosopher and mechanic, the ingenious amateur who loved to tinker with scientific appliances and with metaphysical notions and droll rhymes and sayings, who out of his keen inspection of the men and women around him, and of the weather, and of the ocean and its currents, and of drafts and thunder clouds managed through his long life to build himself up into an epic figure of his time, the *bourgeois gentilhomme* who set his stamp on the whole American nation.

In the quarter century before the Declaration of Independence bright young printer's devils, impatient of restrictions in Britain, kept making their way to America to set themselves up as printers and publishers. Free speech was far from assured in the colonies but there was a great deal more leeway than in England. Many a publisher found himself shut up in jail for an article that displeased the authorities, but John Peter Zenger of the *New York Weekly Journal* had won his famous case, and as the century advanced men of wealth and property began to lend a certain respectability to journalism.

In New York William Livingston, of the great manorial clan of Livingstons, was regularly turning out flippant essays for *The Independent Reflector.* In Philadelphia Provost Smith of the Philadelphia College was encouraging his pupils, Francis Hopkinson and Thomas Godfrey, to write for the magazines that started up in competition with Franklin's various ventures. In Boston, John Adams's mentor, the austere Jeremiah Gridley, the leader of the bar, condescended to edit a magazine.

As the war of words between the Whigs and the King's Friends became acute throughout the English speaking world the Whigs in America became more and more outspoken. John Wilkes and the elder Pitt were their universal heroes. Young men in the colleges embraced Whig doctrines with enthusiasm.

Princeton was a dangerous hot bed, so the Tories put it, of American whiggism. The Reverend John Witherspoon had infected the college of New Jersey with the intellectual ferment he had brought with him from Scotland.

In the late seventeen sixties while Jefferson was taking up the practice of the law in Virginia, and being swept off his feet by Patrick Henry's oratory, little James Madison from Orange County, whom Jefferson had not yet met, and Philip Freneau, the poetical Huguenot, and the impecunious Scottish tutor Hugh Henry Brackenridge were encouraging each other's Whiggish convictions at

Nassau Hall. In the debates between student factions they excoriated the Tories with bawdy doggerel.

Ardent young colonials of the generation of 1776 were intoxicated by Bishop Berkeley's verses on America written a generation before:

> There shall be sung another golden Age,
> The rise of Empire and of Arts;
> The Good and Great inspiring epic Rage,
> The wisest Heads and noblest Hearts;
>
> Not such as Europe breeds in her Decay:
> Such as she bred when great and young,
> When heavenly Flame did animate her Clay,
> By future Poets shall be sung.
>
> Westward the Course of Empire takes its Way
> The four first Acts already past:—
> The fifth shall close the Drama with the Day:
> Time's noblest Offspring is the last!

That rhapsodic theme found echoes in all the class poems and commencement day versifyings of the time. At the graduation exercises at Princeton in 1771 Madison's two cronies Freneau and Brackenridge intoned antiphonally an ode they had composed on *The Rising Glory of America*.

> ". . . . I see, I see,
> A thousand kingdoms raised, cities and men
> Numerous as sand upon the ocean shore;
> Th' Ohio then shall glide by many a town
> Of note: and where the Mississippi stream
> By forests shaded now runs weeping on,
> Cities shall grow and states not less in fame
> than Greece and Rome,"
>
> declaimed one young man;
>
> "And thou Patowmack, navigable stream
> Rolling thy waters through Virginia's groves
> Shall vie with Thames," the other answered.

Every heart beat faster when they reached their preoration:

"And here fair freedom shall forever reign.
I see a train, a glorious train appear
Of Patriots plac'd in equal fame with those
Who nobly fell for Athens or for Rome.
The sons of Boston resolute and brave,
The firm supporters of our injured rights
Shall lose their splendors in the brighter beams
Of Patriots fam'd and heroes yet unborn.

'Tis but the morning of the world with us . . ."

In those same years, and under the same inspiration another clutch of versi-
fiers and journalists was hatching at Yale. At the tiny college on the New Haven
common John Trumbull (the cousin of the painter John Trumbull) who was
about to import the Hudibrastic style of satirical doggerel into America, and
David Humphreys, who was to become one of George Washington's secretaries,
and Timothy Dwight and Noah Webster, the first proponent of an American
language, were lashing each other into a froth of patriot ardor. It was among this
group of young men that Joel Barlow first sprouted his poetical pinfeathers.

Barlow was born on Redding Ridge in the township of Fairfield. His father
Samuel Barlow had raised two families and some pretty fair crops off his hundred
and seventyodd acres of stony land. One of the last acts of his life was to take
young Joel, a strapping chubbyfaced hobbledehoy of nineteen, out into the wilderness to Hanover in New Hampshire, where the Reverend Eleazer Wheelock
had recently founded Dartmouth College as a seminary to prepare young Indians
and whites for carrying the gospel among the heathen to the northward.

The Reverend Eleazer Wheelock believed in the dignity of labor as well
as of study. Manual work on the farm and in the gristmill was part of his curriculum. Samuel Barlow arranged that Joel should work his way waiting on table and
running errands. In return Joel was to be provided with "eating, drinking, wash-
ing, firewood, candles, study room and tuition."

Samuel Barlow wanted this boy to have a college education. He directed in
his will that Joel's portion of the estate should be paid him in installments for that
purpose without waiting for him to come of age.

In spite of all Eleazer Wheelock's labor in the vineyard of the Lord the
young men of Joel's generation couldn't keep their minds on carrying the gospel
to the heathen. The students at Hanover were troublesome; they complained about
the food, they showed a worldly spirit and a lack of enthusiasm for manual labor.

The year before Joel went to Hanover, John Ledyard, another promising
young Connecticut Yankee, had set the institution in an uproar by his worldshak-
ing restlessness. He had fomented the putting on of a stage play, Addison's *Cato*,

had induced the boys to climb mountains in the dead of winter, and had taken the study of Indian affairs so literally that he was absent without leave three months in the lodges of the Iroquois to the northward. His final exploit was to build himself a dugout canoe and to paddle off in it down the Connecticut River with nothing but a Greek Testament, a volume of Ovid and an old bearskin for baggage, so beginning the travels which were to take him round the world with Captain Cook and to his death in Cairo far from the gentle landscape of his native state.

Joel Barlow didn't like Dartmouth any better than Ledyard did. After his father's death he told President Wheelock that it would be better for him to attend college nearer home; so he was sent off to New Haven with a letter recommending him to President Daggett of Yale as "a good genius and a middling scholar."

At New Haven he got along very well. He had a sense of humor and a knack for composing plausible verses in the rhapsodic manner of the day. He studied under Ezra Stiles and the learned Timothy Dwight, then a recent graduate and a tutor, and was admitted into a literary society known as "Brothers in Unity."

Among the tutors who struggled to hammer some learning into the undergraduates' heads was Abraham Baldwin, an ambitious young man about Joel's age. With him and his brother Dudley, Joel formed one of the close associations that were a part of his easy gregarious way of living.

Joel's formal education, in spite of his father's tender care for it, turned out scrappy. He was hardly settled at New Haven when the news came of the fighting at Lexington and Concord. College was suspended and the undergraduates set to drilling. When college opened again after Bunker Hill, the students were already formed into a trainband sufficiently exercised to escort George Washington across town with fife and drum when he went through New Haven on his way to take command of the Continental forces at Cambridge. Noah Webster was the sergeant and snapped out the commands. The smart appearance of the students was noticed in the newspapers.

These were times that "tried men's souls." It was hard for college students to keep their minds on their work. For one thing they were too busy reading *Common Sense*.

Published in Philadelphia on January 10, 1775, the pamphlet set the country on fire. Its author was a disgruntled English exciseman, who arrived in America carrying one of those letters of introduction from Benjamin Franklin which proved passports to fortune to so many young men of parts.

Born in Thetford, a moldy little river town in Lincolnshire, Tom Paine was the son of a Quaker corsetmaker. He suffered a cramping childhood. Dissenters in England still lived in a sort of ghetto cut off from the splendors and emoluments of the great world of the landed gentry. "If the taste of a Quaker had been consulted at the creation," Paine wrote in later life "what a silent and drab-colored world it would have been." His father's business never flourished. Due to Quaker disapproval of the lusts and battles set forth in the Roman classics, or more likely because of lack of funds, young Tom was not allowed to study Latin in school. He showed a taste for reading but without a classical education no man could expect preferment in the world of letters. At thirteen his father put him to work cutting whalebone on oak boards in his corsetmaker's shop.

He stuck to the trade for four years, then he broke with the whole constricted world of provincial poverty and Quaker meeting by running away to sea. The legend had it that he sailed on a privateer. He was hardly built for a seaman's life. He soon found himself cutting whalebone again. Essentially a man of letters, like Franklin he picked himself up an education in the coffeehouses and the public lecture halls. He earned his way as a journeyman staymaker. The talk in alehouses over the gazettes was his university.

He drifted from job to job through southern England. He set himself up as master staymaker on borrowed money in Sandwich, married, failed. His first wife died. With his father's help he got himself a government job as an exciseman. He was discharged for laxity in carrying out his inspections. He taught English grammar and syntax in private schools. Managing to get himself reinstated in the excise, he moved to Lewes in Sussex. There he lived several years, lodging with a Quaker tobacconist whose daughter he married and whose business he inherited.

In Lewes he became the lion of the radical Whigs who gathered evenings at the White Hart Tavern. They nicknamed him the Commodore. Paine was the barroom philosopher. He composed songs to his friend Richman's music. His ballad on the death of Wolfe became very popular. As the only man of literary talents among them he became the leader of the local excisemen. When they tried to bring their grievances, low pay and bad working conditions to the attention of Parliament he wrote a memorial for them and carried it to London.

He spent a city winter lobbying in the coffeehouses. He made the acquaintance of silent Oliver Goldsmith and of the ubiquitous Dr. Franklin. His memorial was printed. His espousal of the exciseman's cause earned him a final discharge from the service.

His wife's business had been neglected. Back from London, he found that his creditors were putting the tobaccomill and furniture up at auction. His wife demanded a separation. He deeded back to her all that was left of her father's property, and lived single from then on.

"Go to America," Dr. Franklin told him. He sailed from London a ruined man on a feverridden emigrant ship the year before Lexington and Concord and

Bunker Hill. Landing sick and penniless in Philadelphia, with only a bundle of essays in his wallet, he rapidly made a name for himself as editor of *The Pennsylvania Magazine*. He found tutoring the sons of well to do merchants quite profitable. He had prospects of opening a school. In later life he used to claim that the revolutionary war interrupted a promising literary career:

"Scarcely had I set foot into the Country but it was set on fire about my ears. All the plans and prospects of a private life . . . were immediately disconcerted . . . From a principle devoted to the love of liberty, and a disposition to assist injured and suffering people, I felt a pleasure in sharing their fate without even troubling myself about consequences."

He proved himself the greatest journalist of his age. *Common Sense* put the case of the American provincials against the British crown into terms every man could understand. The success of Paine's pamphlets filled the heads of the young men of Barlow's generation with ambitions for literary glory. Indeed the pen was mightier than the sword.

Yale College kept its sessions going fitfully throughout the war, occasionally suspended on account of an epidemic of "camp distemper" or by the shortage of victuals for commons. The students' wits were woolgathering. In March 1777 President Daggett announced with chagrin in chapel one morning that college would have to be dismissed. He cited the difficulty of procuring provisions and announced that furthermore he was going to resign. The students scattered until the following spring, when Ezra Stiles accepted the presidency. Thereafter there was better order in the academic groves.

The senior class was graduated, after some hurried cramming under the learned president, in July of that year. Barlow read the class poem, *The Prospect of Peace*, which began:

> The closing scenes of Tyrants' fruitless rage,
> The opening prospects of a golden age,
> The dread events that crown th' important year
> Wake the glad song and claim th' attentive ear.

"Westward the course of Empire . . ." He was graduating into a world giddy with prospects of a golden age.

After graduation Barlow went through a painful period of doldrums. The *Prospect of Peace* had been universally admired. Its author decided he would be not only a poet but a great poet. Right away he set to work on another patriotic poem to be called *The Vision of Columbus*, which he hoped and his friends hoped would be the epic of the young American republic, as the *Aeneid* had been the epic of the new empire of Augustus. The trouble was how to make a living meanwhile.

He applied for the job of tutor at Yale, but the trustees didn't feel that a knack for tossing off couplets was enough qualification, or that patriotic ardor was a sufficient substitute for that profound devotion to Calvinist theology and solid learning they demanded in their instructors.

Barlow scraped up a little cash teaching school at New Haven and by borrowing from his older brothers. They seem to have felt, as his father and mother had felt, that they should make any sacrifice they could to further the young poet's career.

He lived on as best he could in New Haven, boarding with his friends the Baldwins and very much the center and pet of a group of clever young people. Elizabeth Whitman and Betsy Stiles, the president's daughter, and other girls set their caps for him, but there was no doubt in anybody's mind that he was in love with Abraham Baldwin's sister Ruth. Old Michael Baldwin blew up and ordered Joel out of the house and sent his daughter away to Guilford.

Joel had warm friends in college and out. Timothy Dwight invited him to Northampton, where he could pay for his keep by helping him out with the school Dwight kept there. Buckminster revised his couplets for him and wrote him encouraging letters. Noah Webster and the Wolcotts tried to find him a position tutoring in some wealthy family. David Humphreys wrote letters to his friends in search of a patron for the great poem. Soon after meeting Barlow Humphreys wrote that he considered him "one of the most considerable geniuses in poetry which we have ever had rise up amongst us."

Meanwhile Joel rode around Connecticut from one hospitable friend's house to another, having a good time wherever he went, but gnawed within by the knowledge that his small stock of money was running out and that there was no more where that came from. The price of living kept rising. Nobody had any hard cash. The whole economic life of the thirteen states had been thrown out of kilter by the war. What with the British raids, and the difficulty of getting farm products to market, and with continental paper and the emissions of the states swirling up into hopeless inflation, Joel couldn't ask his brothers to help him any more.

He and Ruth Baldwin were crazy in love with each other. Since her father and stepmother had set themselves against the match she was no longer happy at home. It was time they got married. He had to find some way of making a living.

Brother Abraham, "Prom" as they called him, was serving in the Continental Army as a chaplain. In spite of Joel's distaste for preaching a doctrine he only vaguely believed and in spite of the suspicions of the Connecticut Association of

Ministers, who felt that his views were far from orthodox, an appointment as chaplain to the Fourth Massachusetts Brigade was managed for him. He hurriedly boned up on his theology and was licensed as a candidate for the ministry in New Haven in August 1780. His friendly innocence of manner and his patriotic couplets won the day even with the Connecticut clergy.

With considerable misgivings, the Reverend Cleremont, as in his letters to Ruth he called himself in his clerical form, in contradistinction to Quamminy the poetic sprite who polished up the couplets, set off to join his regiment at Hackensack.

After the horrors of preaching his first sermon were over he began to enjoy the life of an army chaplain. Prom was stationed near him and they found themselves a billet together in a Dutchman's neat stone house. At the funeral of General Poor he met Nathanael Greene, to whom he had already been recommended by Humphreys, and a number of other high ranking officers. His pleasant country manners and the humorous straightforwardness of his talk immediately won him friends. His songs caught on among the soldiery and increased his reputation as patriot and poet.

He received an invitation to dine at headquarters with General Washington. "How do you think," he wrote Ruth, "I felt when the greatest man on earth placed me at his right hand with Lord Stirling on his left?"

When he went on leave he was very much the lion at Redding Ridge and preached a sermon from the pulpit of his old schoolteacher, the Reverend Bartlett. His brothers felt that young Joel was a credit to the family. Joel had discovered that patriotism was a good substitute for religion in a sermon. He no longer complained of a hollow feeling of sham when he got up to call on the name of the Lord. For the first time in his life he had a regular salary.

On the strength of it he and Ruth were married. On account of old Baldwin's opposition they had decided to keep their marriage secret for a while.

During the following summer he was sent up to Vermont on army business and came back with a violent fever. His friends nursed him back to health. While he was recovering at a stone house on the Hudson he made up a song for Ruth:

> Soon my charmer soon returning
> That impatient hour shall come
> When, my soul with rapture burning,
> Peace and Love shall call me home.

He was up and about in time to attend the Yale Commencement in September 1781. It was the first public Commencement in seven years. Relief and jubilation were beginning to run through the thirteen states. Although the war wasn't over yet, there was a feeling abroad that it was won. A friend shepherded Ruth round the ceremonies while Barlow delivered a sermon in chapel and at the exercises recited at President Styles's invitation a poem entitled *The Genius of Literature*. Such sentiments as

> . . . New arts ascend
> New manners rise, newwealth and power extend,
> Allure the hero, feed th' enquiring sage,
> Enlarge the genius, dignify the age,
> Till laws and empires swell the rising reign
> And their own navies whiten on the main

thrilled the audience with a premonition of Yorktown. It was announced that the verses were a sample of *The Vision of Columbus*. To crown his successes the corporation elected him tutor. He was already making better money as an army chaplain. He declined the honor with thanks.

When the army went into winter quarters he got leave and settled down for several months in his brother Aaron's house at West Redding. There he worked like a beaver piling up couplet on couplet, counting out the invariable pentameters on his fingers. It was a thoroughly national production, and, from that viewpoint, it is possible even now to understand the endearing qualities that Barlow's friends and contemporaries felt in the work.

By the following fall *The Vision of Columbus* was far enough along to justify Barlow's trying to find a publisher. The only way possible to publish such a poem in America at the time was to collect the cost of printing ahead by subscription. In the company of General Lincoln and the Paymaster General, Mr. Pierce, Barlow left camp, where his wife had been visiting him at the stone house on the Hudson, to ride across the Jerseys through the brilliant October countryside to Philadelphia.

It had been suggested that the poem should be dedicated to Louis XVI, the birth of whose son and heir had lately been celebrated at West Point by an elaborate ball for the French officers. General Lincoln was going to introduce Barlow to the French ambassador, through whom he was to secure His Most Christian Majesty's permission for the dedication; and friends were writing Dr. Franklin in Paris to interest him in the book. Good patriots felt it was fitting that their victory and the peace should be celebrated by a poem in the heroic style.

After seven years of war it was not without emotion that army officers in buff and blue and periwigged members of Congress read Barlow's *Hymn to Peace:*

> . . . From scenes of blood, these beauteous shores that stain
> From gasping friends that press the sanguine plain,

From fields, long taught in vain thy flight to mourn,
I rise, delightful Power, and greet thy glad return.
Too long the groans of death, and battle's bray
Have rung discordant through th' unpleasing lay;
Let pity's tear its balmy fragrance shed,
O'er heroes' wounds and patriot warriors dead;
Accept, departed shades, these grateful sighs
Your fond attendants to th' approving skies . . .

When they met Joel and found him a modest and unassuming young man, a comical talker and tablecompanion over the wine after dinner, they took him to their hearts and vowed that along with the greatest commander and the wisest statesmen of all time, America had produced a poet.

Full of hopes for the future Joel went back to Hartford to start housekeeping with Ruth. His friend John Trumbull who practiced law there, was a neighbor. Trumbull had already published the first cantos of *M'Fingal* and was considered the main literary light of the state. He had the distinction of having studied law in the office of John Adams in Boston.

One of Trumbull's intimates was a physician named Lemuel Hopkins, a gentleman of literary tastes who had great enthusiasm for satiric and mock heroic verses. As Hartford was the state capital, Barlow's college friend, Oliver Wolcott, Jr., son of the Governor, already making his way in politics in his own right, was often there. Noah Webster, too, busy with his *Grammatical Institute*, came in and out of town and was invited to the first meeting of their literary club. It was this group of highly diverse friends who were lumped together by literary gossip under the name of "The Hartford Wits."

Joel had to find some way of making a living. His army pay wouldn't last forever. No patron appeared for the heroic poem. He started a printing, stationery and bookselling business in partnership with a certain Elisha Babcock. Between them they published a weekly paper called *The American Mercury*, which proposed "to furnish a useful and elegant entertainment for the different classes of customers," as well as to print in installments the London account of Captain Cook's last voyage.

As publishers Barlow and Babcock brought out Timothy Dwight's *The Conquest of Canaan* and a new edition of the Psalms of the famous Dr. Watts, revised by Barlow, and Part III of Noah Webster's *Grammatical Institute*, in which were cited, as examples of stylistic felicity, a number of passages from the not yet published *Vision of Columbus*, as well as quotations from Dwight's *Conquest of Canaan* and *M'Fingal*. They also plagiarized an almanac and almost got themselves into a lawsuit over it.

Plagiarism was something that was beginning to hit home at Barlow and Trumbull. One of the first things the Hartford Wits needed, if independent writing were to be possible at all, was the passage of a copyright law. Barlow wrote to various influential friends urging them to put such a law through the state legisalture and the federal Congress. No such thing as literary property existed in America. Poor Trumbull whose *M'Fingal* had sold very well was never able to make a cent out of the book, and what was worse he saw all sorts of scurrilous doggerel published under his name without being able to do anything about it.

T H E

[C O N N E C T i C U T.]		[V O L. I.———N U M B. 19.]
A M E R I C A N		M E R C U R Y,
M O N D A Y		*NOVEMBER* 15, 1784.
H A R T F O R D: By		BARLOW AND BABCOCK.

Masthead of American Mercury.

As a publisher Barlow wasn't much of a success. After a year his partnership with Babcock was dissolved, on a friendly basis, by the publication of the following notice in *The American Mercury* for December 5, 1785:

Joel Barlow & Elisha Babcock

HAVING by mutual consent dissolved their partnership, request those who have accounts open with the late firm of BARLOW & BABCOCK to forward them for settlement as soon as convenient. Those who are indebted to them may depend on having their payment made easy provided it is made soon.

Said BABCOCK will carry on the printing business and attempt to please every body.

Said BARLOW has opened a store of BOOKS and other Goods at the house of the late Doctor Jepson near the South Meeting House; where may be had the new Edition of Psalms and hymns,

LIKEWISE,

RUM, Molasses, Hyson and Bohea Teas, Alspice, Ginger, Broad Cloths, Coatings, Camblets, Chintzes, Callicoes, Gauzes, Ribons, &c. ** Any kind of Public Securities or Country Produce taken in Payment.

It was a restless time. The honeymoon period of the North American confederacy was over. Up to Yorktown all sections and classes had been united by the exigencies of battle. A man was a patriot or he was a Tory, and the Tories had been pushed off the map. But now that the war was over problems left unsolved for the duration came flocking home. All the latent local antagonisms, the sectional jealousies, the class divergences that had been anaesthetized by the need to unite against the redcoats, began to make themselves felt. Business was paralyzed by the worthlessness of the paper money and certificates of debt the Continental Congress kept printing. New England farmers were going back to barter for the exchange of goods. Speculators were buying up every conceivable commodity from "indents" to potatoes. Producers of goods felt everywhere at a disadvantage. Farmers couldn't sell their produce for any money that was worth anything and felt that the men of the counting house were to blame. As the Continental Army disbanded, and Washington went back to his own agricultural problems at Mt. Vernon, men feared that the union was falling apart. "A hoop for the barrel" began to be the toast in the taverns.

When George Washington's friend, the great Philadelphia merchant, Robert Morris was appointed to the finance office just before Yorktown, he called in as assistant a young New York lawyer who bore the same name as he did but who came from a very different family background.

Gouverneur Morris was the son of the Second Lord of the Manor at Morrisania. His father died an embittered eccentric while Gouverneur was still a small boy. "My Actions have been so inconsiderable in the World," the elder Morris wrote in his will, "that the most durable Monument will but perpetuate my Folly while it lasts. My Desire is that nothing be mentioned about me, not so much as a Line in a Newspaper to tell the World I am dead. That I have lived to very little Purpose my Children will remember with Concern when they see the small Pittance I have left them."

Gouverneur Morris grew up an eccentric but not an embittered one. "I have naturally a taste for pleasure," he wrote with the frankness that endeared him to his friends and was considered impious cynicism by his enemies. From early in life he had to contend with pain. An accidental scalding as a child left him with a crippled arm.

He took his bachelor's degree at King's College. The boon companions of his youth were John Jay, the Westchester Aristides, and Robert R. Livingston, who was to head the Livingston clan. In their company he became a serious student of constitutional law. With them, though he was already outspoken in his fear of the mob, he took the revolutionary side in 1775. He helped draft the New York State constitution and led the fight for religious toleration. He worked hard to get through measures abolishing slavery. All his life he was an abolitionist.

Well read, highspirited, witty, sarcastic, not a man to suffer fools gladly, he aroused considerable hostility when he appeared in Congress to represent New York. In spite of his disability he had a commanding presence. Years later in Paris he was to pose for George Washington when Houdon was working on the statue Congress had ordered. His gaiety was irrepressible. Too whimsical, men said. There was a self assurance about his language in debate that threw older men off. The delegates called him "the tall boy."

Gouverneur Morris.

The ladies doted on him. Scandal hung round his name. He had the reputation of a headlong lover pushing himself into bedrooms where others feared to tread. He was a free spender, fond of the best in food and drink. Since what little revenue he had in his own right was cut off by the war, he did some speculating on the side to keep himself in cash. It was Gouverneur's keen nose for moneymaking, combined with a congenial taste for women and wine and sprightly conversation after dinner, that first endeared him to Robert Morris. Perhaps the selfmade man took some pleasure in associating with someone of his own name who belonged so unequivocally to the rich and well born.

Gouverneur served two years in Congress. Appointed to the liaison committee that visited the army during the winter of Valley Forge, he formed there a warm unshakable affection for George Washington. Their friendship was mutual. The commander in chief had a ready appreciation of young men with brains. He enjoyed youthful high spirits.

Washington and Gouverneur agreed in putting the nation before anything.

Possibly because Gouverneur refused to follow Governor Clinton of New York in his stubborn insistence on New York's claims to the region east of Lake Champlain where the Green Mountain settlers had already formed themselves into the independent state of Vermont, the New York Assembly failed to reelect him. The tall boy's speeches punctured too many complacencies.

He returned to Philadelphia and was admitted to the Pennsylvania bar. There was not much for him in New York at that point in his career. The New York Assembly under George Clinton was fanatically partisan. Gouverneur's mother was known to be at least a passive Tory. One of his half brothers was a major general in the British Army. His home was occupied by the British. He was a man of metropolitan tastes. Philadelphia at that point in the war was definitely the American metropolis.

It is not at all impossible, besides, that the attractions of a certain Mrs. Plater had a good deal to do with his settling in that city. Gossips linked that lady's name with an accident Gouverneur suffered the winter before he took up his duties at the Finance Office. In a hurry to be gone before the unexpected arrival of the injured husband, so the story went round Philadelphia, he let a pair of wild horses he was driving get out of hand. His phaeton turned over and his leg, caught in a wheel, was so badly shattered that the doctors insisted on an amputation below the knee. His friends were filled with admiration at his "becoming fortitude" during the agony of the operation but they could not help teasing him about the tender cause. Even the sober John Jay wrote "I have heard that a certain married woman after much use of your legs was the occasion of your losing one."

Of one fact there was no doubt. It was into the Platers' house that he was carried after the accident. For the rest of his life Gouverneur Morris stumped about on a wooden peg.

Statebuilding remained his hobby. The minds of the young men he had grown up with in New York were saturated with political speculation. Eating and drinking, sleeping and waking, the young men of their circle, like the rising lawyers who frequented townmeeting in Massachusetts, and the Virginians arguing in the ordinaries round the backwoods courthouses of the Old Dominion, were entranced with the problem of how man should govern himself. Politics in the broad sense of the word was their hobby and their vocation. They read all the books ancient and modern; they sat up nights discussing them. They needed to convince others of the truth of their deductions. They wrote in the newspapers.

The press had found real freedom for the first time since the peace. All through the later days of the war an argument on what form the federation should take had raged through the gazettes. When Gouverneur Morris failed of reelection to Congress he turned to the press as a pulpit from which to continue his plea for a strong continental government. He based his argument on economic grounds. The existence of thirteen disparate governments, all regulating trade, was ruinous business. His articles signed "An American" came out in *The Pennsylvania Packet* and were reprinted up and down the coast.

The discussion was already under way when he entered it. His ideas had been stimulated by an essay that a certain Pelatiah Webster, whom James Madison, alert as Morris to every fresh formulation of the relationship between finance and government, immediately described as "an obscure but able citizen", had published in the same paper during the preceding year.

Pelatiah Webster wrote a clear and homely style. He repeated the arguments of plain wayfaring men around the deep tavern fireplaces. An unsuccessful merchant, he had suffered in his own hide the tribulations of wartime. He had felt the tyranny of what Dr. Rush called "the spirit of town meetings and porter shops." As a small trader he had suffered from wartime legislation regulating prices, making the use of paper money mandatory as legal tender, controlling imports and exports. He had suffered in his pocketbook from the impediments that stood in the way of trade between the states.

"Let trade be free as air," he wrote in 1779. "Let every man make the most of his goods and in his own way and then he will be satisfied. Let every man taste and enjoy the fruits of that liberty of person and property which was highly expected under an independent government. 'Tis a sad omen to find among the first efforts of independence, greater restraints and abridgements of natural liberty than ever we felt under the government we have lately renounced and shaken off."

He pointed out that freedom of trade could be attained only under a strong general government. His articles elicited praise and abuse.

This *Pennsylvania Packet* in which Gouverneur Morris's and Webster's articles appeared, edited by John Dunlap under an attractive masthead of a ship in full sail, was the center of the controversy. Letters to the editor echoed rumors of the debates in Congress which were still unreported. Classical pseudonyms masked the identity of citizens who were carrying on the discussion in markets and in hairdressers' shops, on wharves and waiting for ferries or for the blacksmith to shoe the horses, or at mealtime in ordinaries and taverns.

Adam Smith's *Wealth of Nations* was stirring fresh ideas; free trade was still an untried and radical doctrine. From the Philadelphia newspapers the discussion spread as fast as the postriders could carry it into the rapidly proliferating press of the thirteen states.

Pelatiah Webster launched a theory of credit. Gouverneur Morris riposted with a disquisition on the nature of money. He explained how inflation produced a scarcity of goods. He demolished the theory that depreciation served a pur-

pose by acting as a tax or capital levy. Throughout the "An American" series
he developed the notion, which was to run like a thread through the long debate
which would culminate ten years later in Hamilton's funding and assumption acts,
that public finance could be the cement which would bind the thirteen states
together as a nation.

Alexander Hamilton was already writing. The moment he freed himself
from the routine of headquarters paperwork by resigning as Washington's secretary, his thoughts turned to the problems which had delighted him ever since
his college days in New York. The summer after his break with the commander in chief, during the first transports of his marriage with his doting dark-
eyed Elizabeth, for the first time enjoying family life with the congenial Schuy-
lers in their great square yellow brick mansion in Albany where he was the
family pet; while wires were being pulled to procure for him that "handsome
command in the light infantry" which would enable him to cut such a dashing
figure at the siege of Yorktown, he found time to write a series of articles.

They came out in the patriot edition of *The New York Packet,* printed in
those days at Fishkill on the Hudson. He took up the argument where Gouverneur Morris left it in his "An American" series. Hamilton signed himself "The
Continentalist."

Writing some of the best and plainest prose of his career, he put his great
gift of clarifying issues to work to discuss the establishment of a federated government. He pointed out that the blunders and failures in the conduct of the war
had resulted not from the disaffection of the people, who were ready to do
everything for "the glorious Cause", but from the mismanagement of their government. When the members of a federation were more powerful than the head,
a stable and unified command was impossible. The cure was to enlarge the
powers of Congress.

Hamilton's contentions jibed completely with Robert Morris's profound
convictions. "The inhabitants of a little hamlet," the Financier explained, "may feel
pride in the sense of separate independence. But if there be not one government
which can draw forth and direct the combined effort of United America, our independence is but a name, our freedom a shadow, and our dignity a dream."

Already Morris had noted down Washington's retired aide-de-camp as a
young man who would fit into his plans. By inducing him to serve as collector
of taxes for New York, he gave Hamilton a scrap of personal experience in fiscal
administration which he was to make good use of later on.

Reading law in Albany the year Elizabeth's first baby was born, a boy they
named Philip after her father, Hamilton continued his essays. At the same time he

served in the Assembly. A seat in the Assembly was a prerogative of the great New York families.

In spite of the fact that his time was taken up, so he wrote Lafayette, "rocking the cradle and studying the art of fleecing my neighbors"—that is, reading law; and that he was preoccupied with the uphill work of trying to induce the New Yorkers to pay their assessment to Congress, he found time to sketch out a plan for a rational system of continental taxation. Congress had to have the power to tax directly.

Before adjourning, the New York legislature elected young Hamilton one of its delegates to Congress. That suspended for a while his career as a journalist. "I am now a grave counsellor at law, and shall soon be a grave member of Congress," he boasted lightheartedly in a letter to Lafayette in France. "The Legislature, at their last session, took it into their heads to name me, pretty unanimously, as one of their delegates." Philip Schuyler was responsible for his election; he stepped aside to allow the nomination of his favorite soninlaw. "I am going to throw away a few months more in public life," Hamilton went on in toplofty vein;—he was twentyseven, though he only confessed to twentyfive; who could blame him for being a little giddy with all these honors?—"and then retire a simple citizen and good paterfamilias." Then he added, referring, enviously perhaps, to Lafayette's dazzling position at the French court, "You are condemned to run the race of ambition all your life. I am already tired of the career and dare leave it."

One of his many occupations during that summer's session of the legislature was putting through a resolution calling for a convention to frame a new constitution for the general government of the confederation. In Philadelphia he set to work to steer a similar resolution through Congress. In this he was complying with the dearest wishes of his old commander in chief.

Pelatiah Webster expressed some of the ideas which were eventually to prevail in a lucid little essay on *The political Union and Constitution of the Thirteen United States of North-America* he published in *The Pennsylvania Packet* in February of 1783. There he laid down three basic propositions: "The supreme power must have power enough to effect the ends of its appointment. . . . The supreme authority ought to be so limited and checked, if possible, as to prevent the abuse of power, or the exercise of powers that are not necessary to the ends of its appointment. . . . A number of sovereign states uniting into one commonwealth . . . do necessarily and unavoidably part with and transfer over to such supreme power so much of their own sovereignty as is necessary to render the ends of the union effectual, otherwise their confederation will be a union without bands of union, like a cask without hoops."

The phrase "a hoop for the barrel" was suddenly in every man's mouth. It appeared in the army's addresses to Congress. It was a favorite toast at public dinners. Writers for the newspapers repeated it lovingly.

"Your people is a great beast" Hamilton was accused of saying. One of the aims of the advocates of a federal constitution was to curb what they called "mobocracy".

It was inevitable that people of wealth and position should blame the rabble and that people without wealth and position should blame the rich for the weaknesses of the confederation. Joel Barlow didn't have wealth or position but his Hartford friends did. He was to some extent carried away by their side of the story. In that confused struggle between the advocates of hard and paper money, and between the rank and file Revolutionary veterans and the retired officers of means grouped round the Society of the Cincinnati, which came to a head in Shays's "rebellion" in Massachusetts, Barlow took the side of law and order.

David Humphreys had just come back to Connecticut after a brilliant official career. He had been one of Washington's aides-de-camp along with Hamilton. He had been voted a sword by Congress for gallantry at Yorktown. He had gone abroad as secretary to the legation in Paris and London and had learned to dress and strut according to the style of high society and had come back, not exactly full of Toryism, but full of fashionable English Whiggery on the model of Brookes's gambling club and the Prince of Wales's set in London. Immediately he took his place among the Hartford wits.

He lashed up Dr. Hopkins and Trumbull and their crowd to enter the fray against the rebellious rabble with a series of mock heroic verses which they pub-

During the first decade of the federal government the struggle between the popular, Jeffersonian or republican party and the conservatives who called themselves Federalists became more and more bitter. It finally flared up into fist fights on the floor of Congress such as this famous battle between Griswold of Connecticut and Lyon of Vermont.

lished in *The New Haven Gazette and Connecticut Magazine* under the title of *The Anarchiad.*

The twelve installments of *The Anarchiad* ranged from Humphreys's song, *The Genius of America,* through some effective lampoons on the Connecticut antifederalists, to the campaign verse of the *Speech of Hesper,* an invocation to the Constitutional Convention, that ends

> But know ye favored race one potent head
> Must rule your States and strike your foes with dread,

The finance regulate, the trade control,
Live through the empire and accord the whole.

Ere death invades, and night's deep curtain falls,
Through ruined realms the voice of UNION calls
Loud as the trump of heaven through darkness roars,
When gyral gusts entomb Caribbean towers—
When nature trembles, through the deeps convuls'd,
And ocean foams from craggy cliffs repuls'd
On you she calls! Attend the warning cry:
YE LIVE UNITED OR DIVIDED DIE!

These verses went through the *Gazettes* and *Posts* and *Advertizers* like wild-
fire and possibly did as much as Hamilton's and Gouverneur Morris's and Pelatiah
Webster's articles and the close reasoning of the *Federalist* papers to convince
Americans that a federal constitution was needed and that any constitution was
better than no constitution.

The "Hartford Wits" were fanatical Federalists. They were young and full
of high spirits and even managed to see the humor of their own bombast. One
number of the *Echo* series which followed *The Anarchiad* was a tremendous
piece of mockheroic spoofing describing the burning of a barn; and Trumbull was
heard to remark about his friend Timothy Dwight's *The Conquest of Canaan* that
the poem had so many thunderstorms in it the printer ought to furnish a lightning
rod with every copy.

Meanwhile the great wish of Joel Barlow's life was coming to pass. The sub-
scriptions had come in, the proofsheets had been corrected. On May 14, 1787
Hudson and Goodwin, printers of Hartford, published *The Vision of Columbus*.
The book appeared in time to get some copies to Philadelphia and into the hands
of the delegates to the Constitutional Convention. Even before it had its constitution the young republic had its epic poem.

Lewis and Clark were as successful diplomats as they were explorers. They got through with a minimum of this sort of thing.

A People of Travelers
and Explorers

CHAPTER **2**   ☼

WITH THE COMING OF THE PEACE AMERICANS STARTED TO MOVE around the world again.

The most enthusiastic American was a Frenchman. Arriving in Versailles breathless from Cornwallis's surrender, Lafayette brought a breeze of victory into the stale antechambers of the Bourbon regime. The king stayed away from his hunting long enough to drape the ribbon of the order of St. Louis round his neck. The marshals of France celebrated his homecoming with a dinner. He found himself upgraded in the army, over the heads of many older men, who took it far from kindly, to the rank of Maréchal du Camp. The envious began to dub him scornfully *le Vassington français.*

The Marquis had a gift for impressing other men with the brilliance of his coming destiny. He was enormously rich. The income that poured in from the diligence of intendants and hommes d'affaires, without his lifting a finger, amounted to considerably more than the equivalent of a hundred thousand dollars a year. No man in Europe had greater prospects.

Lafayette was incapable of idleness. He'd learned from Washington to be an early riser. He was always ready to leap on a horse or to throw himself into his carriage to be off at a gallop on some noble enterprise.

After the free and easy life of the American countryside Lafayette found he had lost his taste for Paris drawingrooms and the mummery and frustrations of the court. His heart was set on revisiting the land of his achievements. He was delayed by fruitless efforts to get some official glamor thrown about his journey but at last in the spring of 1784 he was able to announce to Washington: "Yes my dear General before the month of June is over you will see a vessel coming up the Pottomack, and out of the vessel will your friend jump with a panting heart and all the feelings of perfect happiness."

Landing in New York the Marquis set out eagerly for Virginia. Wherever he stopped to rest his horses he was greeted by the hugs and handclasps of old comrades-in-arms, by salutes from the militia and the ringing of churchbells and candles in the windows at night and toasts at public dinners in the taverns. The words liberty, republicanism, independence and glory rang in his ears from every welcoming address. In Baltimore a society of Irish exiles celebrated his services to the cause of oppressed humanity. At Mt. Vernon he threw himself into the arms of his adoptive father.

Lafayette had wanted his old commander in chief to accompany him on his triumphant tour but Washington instead invited him to come along on a hard crosscountry ride he was planning over the mountains and out to the Ohio to visit his western lands. The Marquis, who was familiar enough with American geography to know that there would be no public demonstrations along those shaggy and sparsely settled trails, pled other engagements.

Back in Philadelphia he fell in with James Madison who invited him on a trip which was more to his taste. Madison had been stimulated by Jefferson to interest himself in Indian languages. He was on his way to a great Indian powwow convoked at Fort Schuyler. The little Virginian immediately saw that Lafayette would be a trump in the hands of the American commissioners.

Many of the Indians still regretted the fatherly French rule. Lafayette's name had spread to their tepees, where he was known as Kayewlaah.

The trip appealed to all the Marquis's romantic aspirations. The long ride in the rain through the drenched forests of upper New York State gave Madison an opportunity to talk the Marquis into offering to use his good offices with the Bourbons of Spain to convince them that they should open the navigation of the Mississippi to the Americans.

The sly Madison noted with some amusement in a letter to Jefferson that the newfangled cloak of gummed taffeta Lafayette wore to protect him from the rain had been wrapped, when his baggage was packed, in newspapers that still stuck to it, so that his companions could read snatches of Parisian news off his back as they rode. Lafayette delighted everybody by his carelessness of civilized comforts and by his ingratiating manner with the savages.

A scene from back country America. Block house and mill.

To the dismay of the British agents on the scene, he immediately became the leading figure in the negotiations for a peaceful withdrawal by the Indians from frontier lands inside the state boundaries. Beside a crackling campfire in the cold October night, in declamatory French worthy of Chateaubriand, he addressed a group of chiefs of the Six Nations while the tobacco smoldered in the peace pipes.

Lafayette's American tour revived the celebrations of the peace. In Hartford the whole town turned out to do him honor at Bull's Tavern. As far out as Watertown he was greeted by a delegation of continental officers to escort him into Boston. Amid cannonading from the forts and from French warships in the harbor he was regaled with a banquet at Fanueil Hall on the anniversary of

Yorktown. He was made a citizen of three states and freeman of a number of cities. For the crowds who cheered him on his prancing stallion he was the living symbol of the French assistance that had won the war for independence.

Back in France Lafayette found that these fresh American triumphs had indeed, as Madison wrote Jefferson, formed "a bright column in the gazettes of Europe." Jefferson as American minister saw to it that the fulsome accounts of the Marquis's triumphant progress in the American gazettes which, Madison regularly forwarded to him, should come to the attention of the European editors. As Lafayette settled back into his routine at his palatial hôtel on the rue de Bourbon with his wife Adrienne and children whom he somewhat ostentatiously loved, in the American style, he set to weaving about himself the legend of the American Cincinnatus.

He was the adopted son and disciple of the great liberator. "In everything I do," he wrote back to Washington at Mt. Vernon, "I first consider what your opinion would be had I an opportunity to consult it." To add a touch of authentic American color to the domestic scene, an Oneida halfbreed he had met at Fort Schuyler and an Onondaga Indian boy he had induced to follow him to Europe attended him in costume. In full Iroquois regalia they ran errands for him. At the evening parties of the philosophic set they demonstrated the war dances of the noble savages.

Lafayette and Jefferson, who was now Minister to France, were becoming fast friends. Lafayette was twentyeight. Jefferson was fortyone. Perpetually in search of a father, Lafayette missed Washington's paternal advice. Jefferson liked nothing better than to tutor young men in the art of statebuilding. What started as a hospitable gesture on Lafayette's part became a firm collaboration.

In France as in America 1787 proved a landmark year. A few months before some forty Americans met in the Philadelphia statehouse to write a national constitution. Lafayette found himself engaging in the ceremony of the opening of an assembly of notables in the Hall of Fugitive Pleasures at Versailles. He was determined to take his part in the debates in a way that Jefferson and Washington would approve. Although the fluid society of the American frontier had little in common with the stratified society of France the immediate causes that brought the two assemblies together were the same: ruined finances and restraint of trade. The government at Versailles was nearly as bankrupt as the Continental Congress. The Assembly of Notables was called to raise money.

Jefferson was present at the opening sessions. He saw in the Assembly of Notables the opportunity for a gradual reform of Bourbon autocracy into something like the constitutional monarchy of England. While the notables wrangled public business would be at a standstill. Jefferson's negotiations, in which Lafayette had been very helpful, had been pretty successful. After three years under the leaden Parisian sky he felt starved for sunlight. His youthful plans for travel had time and again been postponed. Now was the time for a vacation.

During the preceding year Jefferson had been seeing a great deal of John Ledyard. The only Yankee on Captain Cook's last expedition to the South Seas, Ledyard's account of the discoveries had been published in Hartford and had done a great deal to stimulate the merchants in Boston and New York to finance the beginnings of the China trade.

Captain Cook had set out on his last circumnavigation just at the moment when the strained relations between the colonies and the Crown were breaking into violence. Franklin from Paris saw to it that this scientific expedition should not be interfered with by French fleets or American privateers. Ledyard spent the years of the Revolutionary War exploring the Pacific as a member of His Majesty's armed forces.

He was immensely stirred by the sight of the west coast of his own America. When he landed on Vancouver Island he immediately recognized that there was much in common between the cultures of the Nootka Sound Indians and of the Iroquois he had come to know so well. He made friends with Russian traders in the Aleutians. He was in the party with Cook on the volcanic shore the day the Hawaiians rose up against the explorer and killed him, and was among the men who saved their lives by swimming out to the ship.

Now he had turned up in Paris, broke as usual, trying to promote, along with dapper little John Paul Jones, whom he was hoping to induce to finance the expedition with his prize money, a fur-buying voyage to Nootka Sound which would plant the striped flag with its circle of stars on the western brink of America.

Ever since Jefferson as a boy had heard James Maury holding forth on the subject at school on the Mountain, Jefferson had been preoccupied with the idea of exploration westward. The December before leaving for France, while attending Congress at Annapolis, he wrote anxiously to George Rogers Clark of a rumor that a British expedition was being fitted out for that purpose: "I find they have subscribed a very large sum of money in England for exploring the country from the Mississippi to California. they pretend it is only to promote knoledge. I am afraid they have thoughts of colonizing into that quarter. some of us have been talking here in a feeble way of making the attempt to search that country, but I doubt whether we have enough of that kind of spirit to raise the money."

In John Ledyard, Jefferson met a man chockfull to his fingertips of "that kind of spirit." He took to the stocky towheaded Yankee at once and helped him with handouts from time to time. Jefferson and Ledyard between them cooked up the harebrained plan of traversing all Russia to the Bering Strait, crossing those narrow waters the way the Indian peoples had crossed them out of Asia in prehistoric times, and then walking across the continent to the English speaking settlements. Ledyard was the man to do it. He'd do it alone. He'd do it without money.

The Empress Catherine turned out as reluctant as later Russian rulers to have a foreigner poking his nose into her dominions. She refused formal consent though she did sugar the refusal by a present of six hundred francs. Ledyard announced he'd cross Russia with or without Catherine's consent. Egged on by Colonel Smith, the Adamses' romantic-minded soninlaw, who offered to finance the journey himself, and assisted by some small contributions collected in London by Sir Joseph Banks of the Royal Society and his friends, Ledyard set out for the Baltic.

Before he left he wrote Jefferson from England: "My friend, my brother, my Father—I know not by what title to address you. You are very very dear to me. Embrace the dear Marquis de la Fayette for me. He has all the virtues of his country without any of its little foibles. I am indeed a very plain man, but do not think that mountains or oceans shall oppose my passage to glory while I have such friends in remembrance."

Ledyard started on his journey through Copenhagen. There he promptly spent the ten guineas he had left in his pocket after buying his equipment in bailing out another American wanderer whom he found cooped up in a room at the inn because he had pawned all his clothes. By that time severe weather had come on. Nothing daunted, Ledyard walked all the way round the Gulf of Bothnia, which he'd planned to cross on the ice but which unluckily was open that winter, and across Lapland and Finland to the Russian capital.

Jefferson, who took pleasure in Ledyard's fantastic doings, wrote his friend John Bannister of Petersburg, Virginia, who had also known the errant Yankee in Paris: "I had a letter from Ledyard lately, dated at St. Petersburg. he had but two shirts & yet more shirts than shillings. still he was determined to obtain the palm of being the first circumambulator of the earth. he says that having no money they kick him from place to place & thus he expects to be kicked round the globe."

Jefferson was a great walker himself. In Paris his five or six miles a day really showed him the life of the streets as well as the parklike woodlands of the Bois de Boulogne. Under the man of letters and conferences, ever since he'd been stirred by boyish readings of Anson's exploits in the South Sea, there had always been a touch of the frustrated traveler.

Now, since walking around Paris with Ledyard, discussing the Asiatic origin of the American Indians, hearing his extravagant plans for exploring the enormous green northwestern slopes of the continent, he felt that a small segment of himself was headed with Ledyard east towards the American West.

There was a new element in Ledyard's approach to strange peoples, something quite different from the bland incomprehension that caused the death of the great Captain Cook, something based on "the lovely equality the poor enjoy with the rich" that Jefferson liked to boast about when he contrasted American society with that of Europe, which struck in Jefferson an immediately responsive chord. It was his particularly American knack for taking all sorts and conditions of men at their face value, unclassified, considering them by their nature free and equal creatures on the face of the earth, that enabled Ledyard to crawl into a Laplander's hut without knowing a word of the language, and instead of being beaten off with a club, to be fed and equipped with moccasins of reindeer hide and set on his way with affection. It was something that had a great deal to do with the mutation of the Christian doctrine of the brotherhood of man and the fatherhood of God into the selfevident truths of the Declaration of Independence.

Ledyard was confident he could meet any man in the world as an equal. He felt the same way about the elements. His life was a link in a chain that led from St. Francis to Thoreau.

When he got too lonely on his incredible hike across Lapland, he talked French out loud. "It is a most extraordinary language," he wrote Jefferson. "I believe wolves, rocks, woods and snow understand it, for I have addressed them all in it and they have all been very complaisant to me."

For his tour of the Midi Jefferson was determined to leave the minister plenipotentiary behind. He made his devoted maître d'hôtel, Petit, stay home. "I think one travels more usefully alone because he reflects more," he told Bannister. Having a servant at all, he wrote back to young William Short whom he'd left in charge of the legation, "is a sacrifice to opinion, and that without answering any one purpose worth a moment's consideration, they only serve to insulate me from the people among whom I am."

This time he was bound he would act according to the advice he gave other American travelers: "Take every possible occasion for entering the houses of the laborers, & especially at the moments of their repast; see what they eat, how they are clothed, whether they are obliged to work too hard; whether the government or their landlord takes from them an unjust proportion of their labor; on what footing stands the property they call their own, their personal liberty &c &c."

His letters from the road were brimful of delight. From Lyons he wrote Short that in spite of the rain, hail and snow that had followed him down from Paris, he had investigated the wine country. Unlike most connoisseurs, he was more interested in the people who tended the vineyards than in their product. "I mounted a bidet (a pony), put a peasant on another & rambled through their most celebrated vineyards, going into the houses of the laborers, cellars of the Vignerons & mixing & conversing with them as much as I could."

Somewhere below Lyons in the deep valley of the Rhone he came out into the sunshine. The almonds were in bloom. There was a pale yellow green on the willows. "I am now in the land of corn, vine, oil & sunshine," he wrote Short. "What more can a man ask of heaven? if I should happen to die in Paris I should beg you to send me here, and have me exposed to the sun. I am sure it will bring me to life again." This was from Aix-en-Provence, a clean little redtiled white-walled resort town where the doctors had instructed him to bathe his wrist in the warm springs.

He found out what the peasants ate: "Their bread is half wheat, half rye, made once in three or four weeks to prevent too great consumption. in the morning they eat bread with an anchovy or an onion. their dinner in the middle of the day is bread, soup and vegetables. their supper the same. with their vege-tables they always have oil & vinegar. the oil costs about eight sous the pound. they drink what is called piquette. this is made after the grapes are pressed by pouring hot water on the pumice. on Sunday they have meat and wine."

Wherever he went, he wrote Madame de Tessé, the great hostess of the philosophic set, he was "nourished with the remains of Roman grandeur." Already under the gray sky of Lyons he'd seen "some feeble Roman remains." At Vienne there was a palace and a sepulchral pyramid—he measured the columns; at Orange an amphitheatre and an arch of Marius; and at Nîmes the long waited for ex-quisite morsel of architecture, the maison carrée he'd studied with so much care.

He was so utterly happy sitting among the silkspinners and stockingweavers in the marketplace, who took him, so he wrote, for "a hypochondriac Englishman about to write with a pistol the last chapter of his history," gazing up at the goldtinted fluting of the columns crowned with acanthus:—"like a lover at his mistress," that in later life he used to tell people he'd spent a whole ten days there doing nothing else.

"The plan of my journey, as well as my life"—he was still in the mood of Ledyard when he wrote Madame de Tott, another Parisian blue stocking, from Marseilles—"being to take things by the smooth handle, few occur which have not something good to offer me. the Auberge for instance in which I am obliged to take refuge for the night, presents, in the first moment, nothing but noise, dirt & disorder. but the Auberge has been too much abused. a traveller, said I, retired at night to his chamber in an inn, all his effects contained in a single portmanteau, all his cares circumscribed by the walls of his apartment, unknown to all, unheeded and undisturbed, writes, reads, reads, thinks, sleeps, just in the moments when nature & the movements of his body & mind require. . . . I should go on Madam detailing to you my dreams & speculations, but that my present situation is most unfriendly to speculation. 4350 market women (I've counted them) brawling, squabbling, jabbering patois. 300 asses braying & bewailing to each other & to the world their cruel oppressions, 4 files of mule carts passing in constant succession, with as many bells to every mule as can be hung about him, all this in the street under my window & the weather too hot to shut it. judge whether in such a situation it is easy to hang one's ideas together."

At Marseilles Jefferson decided to push on into Italy. One of the aims of his journey was to find out why Piedmont rice brought a better price on the market than Carolina rice. He wanted to study its cultivation at first hand.

The further he advanced the more distant seemed the goal. The passes, they told him, were still filled with snow. Remembering Ledyard, he determined to push on anyway. "Tomorrow," he wrote Short from Nice, "I set out for my passage over the Alps . . . I am now in the act of putting my baggage into portable form for my bat-mule."

He noted the belts of climate in which the various fruits grew as the mules climbed up and down over the spurs of the mountains. "This is their order from the tenderest to the hardiest. caper, orange, palm, aloe, olive, pomegranate, walnut, fig, almond . . ." The highest point in the road was the Col de Tende. "In passing on towards Tende, olives fail us ultimately at the village of Fontan & there the chestnut trees begin in good quantity. He was impressed by the sight of olive trees growing out of mere masses of rock in the mountains.

Immediately he guessed the immense importance of the olive in the economy of the Mediterranean peoples, and began to wonder whether it could be of use in America. "Wherever there happens to be a little soil there are a number of olive trees & a village supported by them. take away these trees & the same ground in corn would not support a single family," he wrote. In Turin he heard his first nightingale and found the Nebiolo "a singular, a stringent and a pleasing wine."

He was a week out of Nice before he got a chance to ride round the dykes that enclosed the rice fields of the Lombard plain. He carefully noted the construction of the machine that beat off the husks, decided that the Lombard rice was a special variety and arranged to have a bag of the unhusked seed smuggled back to Nice for him by a stout muleskinner named Poggi who claimed he would do it although it meant his death if the customs men caught him.

In Milan, Jefferson was struck with the scenes painted alfresco on the outside walls of the houses. He took up his part of minister plenipotentiary long enough to try to induce the merchants there to import American whale oil. The cathedral, he told his friends, was "a worthy object of philosophical contemplation; to be placed among the rarest instances of the misuse of money."

He found the cheese factory at Rozzano much more interesting than the flamboyant Gothic. Parmesan cheese, like the machine for husking rice, was something you could use back home. Meticulously he noted down the entire process. They made ice cream there too. Snow, he noted, gave the creams a better flavor than ice.

In Pavia he ate green peas and admired the Certosa. In the dry grounds he found them planting Indian corn. With a pang of homesickness he watched the peasants cover the yellow grains with a pointed hoe. He was as far from the cornfields of Albemarle as he'd ever be in his life again. Before he left the rice lands he stuffed the pockets of his greatcoat with the famous seed rice which he later sent over for trial to the Agricultural Association in Charleston.

He was delighted with the sheltered valleys, the shingly beaches, the tiny harbors, the continually changing combinations of steep green land with blue sea of the Italian Riviera; "If any person wished to retire from his acquaintance to live absolutely unknown, & yet in the midst of physical enjoyments, it should be in some of the little villages of this coast, where air, water and earth concur to offer what each has most precious. here are nightingales, beccaficas, ortolans, pheasants, partridges, quails, a superb climate & the power of changing it from summer to winter at any moment, by ascending the mountains. the earth furnishes wine, oil, figs, oranges, & every production of the garden in every season. the sea yeilds lobsters, crabs, oysters, thunny, sardines, anchovies &c." May first he was in Nice again.

On the way back to Paris he gave himself a rest from the chafing of worn saddles on hardgaited mules and the jouncing of the carriage over stony roads. He travelled by the Languedoc canal.

"I dismounted my carriage from its wheels, placed it on the deck of a light bark & was thus towed on the canal instead of the post road," he wrote Short. "Of all the methods of travel I have ever tried, this is the pleasantest. I walked the greater part of the way along the banks of the canal, level and lined with a double row of trees which furnish shade. when fatigued I take seat in my carriage, where, as much at ease as in my study I read, write and observe. my carriage being of glass all round admits a full view of all the varying scenes through which I am shifted, olives, figs, mulberries, wines, corn & pasture, villages & farms. I have had some days of superb weather enjoying two parts of the Indian's wish, cloudless skies & limpid waters: I have had another luxury which he could not wish since we have driven him from the country of Mockingbirds, a double row of nightingales along the banks of the canal in full song . . . What a bird the nightingale would be in the climates of America! we must colonize him thither."

As he glided along the canal on a bark drawn by a single horse while a woman handled the rudder, he ruminated, as he usually did when he had a moment's leisure, on the lives of the people. It offended him to see women working the locks and handling the heavy sweeps. The work was too laborious for them. Meanwhile "the men are shoemakers, tailors, upholsterers, stay-makers, mantua-makers, cooks, house-cleaners, bedmakers; they coiffe the ladies & bring them to bed: the women therefore to live have to undertake the offices which they abandon . . . Can we wonder if such of them as have a little beauty, prefer easier courses to get their livelihood as long as that beauty lasts?"

He continued jotting down his notes as his barge slid gently through the early summer landscape. In the distance the Pyrenees were still snowy to the left. To the right red hills unfolded terraced with vineyards. "The canal yeilds abundance of carp and eel. I see small fish resembling our perch and chub. some plants of white clover and some of yellow on the banks of the canal near Capestan: santolina also & a great deal of yellow iris. the extensive & numerous fields of St. foin in general bloom are beautiful."

He drifted through Marseillette and Carcassonne and Castelnaudary. At Naureuze he took a long ride into the Montagnes Noires to see the aqueducts that kept the higher parts of the canal in water. He studied the locks. As soon as he reached Paris his notes on their construction were to be forwarded to Washington to use in planning the Ohio canal. At Toulouse his carriage was hoisted on its wheels again.

He drove into Paris through the porte d'Orléans and, climbing out of his carriage in front of the hôtel de Langeac into the welcoming arms of young Short, was greeted by a circle of countenances beaming and bowing: Petit, his maître d'hôtel, and Espagnol, his valet; and the flashing teeth of the slaves from Monticello, and the suisse and the porter and the cook and the gardener and the frotteur and the footmen and perhaps the mysterious "poor old woman" who bobs up from time to time as the recipient of gratuities in his account book. When he and Short retired upstairs to the study to take up official business the minister plenipotentiary found himself confronted by staggering great packets of mail, piled high on the Louis XVI tables.

We don't know if Jefferson found any news of Ledyard in that mail but towards the end of the year he did receive a cheerful letter from him from a place about half way between St. Petersburg and the Russian Pacific port of Okotsk. Ledyard was reporting that he was certain that the Siberian aborigines and the American Indians were one and the same people. He had found bones of mammoths in the river banks. A mere six thousand more versts would bring him to "that ocean which I hope will bear me on its bosom to the coast of America". He was in perfect health. "But notwithstanding all the vigor of my body, my mind keeps the start of me and anticipates my future fate with the most sublimated ardour . . . Pity it is that in such a career one should be subjected like a horse to the beggarly impediments of sleep and hunger."

It wasn't long after reading this letter that Jefferson was hearing the unhappy tale of Ledyard's expulsion from the Empress Catherine's dominions and of his arrival, broke and despondent and sick at Sir Joseph Banks's house on Soho Square in London. Dogged as ever Ledyard was trying again to stir up the English geographers to finance an exploration of the American northwest. He had no luck. Other men would carry out his plans.

In America the project Ledyard had suggested to Robert Morris soon after he came back from Captain Cook's last voyage was at last beginning to attract the merchants and shipowners. Morris invested in it. On Washington's Birthday, 1784 the *Empress of China* a ship of three hundred and fifty tons sailed loaded with gensing from New York for Canton. Another easterly voyage was made by the grand old *Alliance*, another by the *United States* out of Philadelphia. Soon Boston and Salem were joining in, inaugurating the triangular run from Massachusetts to Nootka Sound to buy sea otter furs and thence to Canton to exchange them for tea and Chinese luxuries. The Pacific trade which Ledyard had urged on his countrymen became a reality.

Meanwhile Ledyard himself was forced by lack of money and sheer disgruntlement to settle for an assignment Banks offered him to explore Africa. The plan was incredibly foolhardy. It was to travel up the Nile and across the interior of Africa to the headwaters of the Niger and to follow that legendary river to the sea. The Niger had become an obsession with Sir Joseph Banks and his friends of the Royal Society. Many a British explorer was to leave his bones on that quest.

In September of 1788 he was writing Jefferson from Cairo "I made the journey from Alexandria by water and entered the western branch of the mouths of the River Nile . . . it is a mere mud puddle compared with the accounts we have of it . . . Do you know the river Connecticut—of all the rivers I have seen it most resembles it in size . . . With regard to my Voyage I can only tell you with any certainty that I shall be able to pass as far as the western boundaries of what is called Turkish Nubia, and at a town called Sennar . . . I expect to get there with some surety—but afterwards all is dark before me: my design and wishes are to pass in that parallel across the continent . . . Cairo is a wretched hole, and a nest of vagabonds . . . Who is not ravished with gums, balms, dates, figgs, pomegranates, with the circassia and sycamores without knowing that amidst these ones eyes ears mouth nose is filled with dust eternal, hot fainting winds, lice bugs musquetes spiders flies—pox itch leprosy fevers and almost universal blindness."

Two months later he wrote again ". . . it is within a few days only that I have had any certainty of being able to succeed in the prosecution of my

voyage . . . I am now doing up my baggage—and most curious baggage it is—
for my journey . . . I travel from here SW about 300 leagues to a Black King:
there my present conductors leave me to my fate—beyond, I suppose, I go
alone . . . I shall write you if possible from the Kingdom of this Black gentleman.
If not, do not forget me . . . I shall not forget you. Indeed it would be a consolation to think of you in my last moments. Be happy . . ."

Within a few days after writing this letter to Jefferson John Ledyard
was dead.

The Grand Cairo.

For a long time Jefferson would not believe the rumor. It was Tom Paine
who finally convinced him that his Yankee friend had succumbed to some un-
named pestilence in the Grand Cairo.

Another boisterous young Yankee soon appeared in Paris to arouse the
American Minister's enthusiastic interest. *The Vision of Columbus* had established
Joel Barlow as the leading American poet but he still hadn't found any way of
making a living. In the winter of 1787–88 a proposition was made to him to go
to Europe to represent one of William Duer's land companies. That rash speculator had the idea that the patriotic poet, whose verses were inflaming the enthusiasm
of the lettered of Europe, was just the man to sell his Scioto Company's Ohio
lands for him. The fact that Duer hadn't yet taken title to the land he was selling
was a detail to be remedied later.

Joel, whose head was still full of couplets about the revolution of the world and the parliament of man, jumped at the idea. This was his chance to see with his own eyes how the great phrases out of the Declaration of Independence were revolutionizing France.

So, having left his wife Ruth with her brother Dudley, and being furnished with letters from all the bigwigs of young America to all the liberal bigwigs of Europe, with a power of attorney from Colonel Duer and a certificate of ownership of some shares of the Scioto stock in his pocket, he set out from New York on the French packet.

Joel had never been to sea before. The packet was an English sixteengun frigate which had been captured by the French during the war. A few crude partitions had been slapped up for the mail and passenger service. She had hardly poked her nose outside the Narrows before he began to feel qualms. When he crawled into his bunk he found it a miserable little pen lined with dirty calico, the home of an active group of fleas and a regiment of bedbugs. He was so sick that it was days after the ship made port before he could get his innards working properly.

Writing in his diary from his refuge, in what he describes as the fourth loft of the Hôtel de l'Aigle d'Or in Havre, where he lay in bed waiting to get his land legs back, he was drearily jocose about an argument he'd had with a fellow passenger concerning that absurd notion of Buffon's, which had so annoyed Jefferson, about the respective sizes of European and American animals. Buffon, Joel argued, undoubtedly based his theory on the greater size and ferocity of the European flea, which he claimed was heavier by a grain than his American cousin. The population of his lodgings in Havre, he went on, bore him out only too well in this contention.

As he walked about the cobbled streets of his first French seaport he could still feel the hideous heave and lurch of the packet. Everything in Havre was gray and strange and ancient. He was taken with the Hôtel de Ville which he found much handsomer than the City Hall in New York. Little complicated odds and ends of Gothic interested him because they were so different from any architecture he had ever seen or imagined. He was hospitably dined by the Swedish consul and, in company of the Swedes he met at the consulate and a young son of General Greene's who was going to Paris to be educated, whom he'd been asked to keep an eye on, he set out in a carriage for Paris.

In Paris Joel called on Jefferson and was invited to dine with him in the company of Lafayette, Duer's European agent Dan Parker, and an Italian gentleman whose name he couldn't catch.

Jefferson was completing his fifth and last year as American minister to the French court. His house on the route des Champs Elysées, then a country road leading out to the suburban villages of Boulogne and Neuilly, had taken the place of Dr. Franklin's house at Passy as the center of the American vogue.

Jefferson was a dryer man than Franklin. He hated to waste his time with the parties and the sexy repartee that the old philosopher in the coonskin cap had so revelled in. He was not so much the fashionable rage as Franklin but the full current of European ideas, political, philosophical and scientific flowed across his dinner table.

That afternoon in the fall of 1788 when Joel Barlow first went to dinner at Jefferson's, and for the first time put his fork into the light and tasty dishes, served with an abundance of green vegetables, for which the American minister's table was famous; and then sat, after the cloth had been taken away, Virginia style, drinking the light Beaujolais and listening to his tall redheaded host's explanation of the political situation in France; glancing from time to time across the table at Lafayette's narrow face, that had an intent lean blooded racehorse look above his frilled neckband, he must have felt, behind the amenities of polite conversation, in the background of every word, the roar of the floodwaters of history like the roar of a distant waterfall.

Joel was successful in selling Scioto land. By the middle of winter the first shipload of French immigrants arrived in Alexandria. He wrote Duer to impress on him "the immense undertaking" this colonization was "to the poor creatures who adventure in it, a situation in which all the passions are alive to the slightest impressions. They who lead the way trust their lives and fortunes to the representations that I make to them." He begged Duer to send a suitable agent to Alexandria to meet them and make the trip out to the Ohio easy.

Little did Joel know that by the time the unlucky Frenchmen landed in the busy brick town on the Potomac, the whole scheme would have blown up sky high. Duer failed to raise enough money to take up his options with Congress. His creditors closed in on him. He went bankrupt like poor Robert Morris a few years later, and died in the precincts of the jail.

For Joel the situation was epitomized in a draft which Duer in his last desperate struggle drew on him for a hundred thousand livres. Wherever Joel went in Europe that draft turned up to make life miserable. In London the bankers threatened jail if he didn't pay.

Joel had been writing Ruth passionate loveletters to get her to make up her mind to follow him to Europe. The idea scared her. She wrote him that she was too much the simple country girl to do him credit. He answered that she would be more "disgusted with the folly than awed at the splendor of this decrepit old world." Finally she consented and, with her heart in her mouth, sailed from New York for England on the vessel of a Captain Wolsey. When she reached

London she went to the address he'd indicated. There she found loving letters but no Joel.

At last Joel, who no longer dared set foot in England on account of the protested note that howled like a wolf after him down every London street, prevailed on Ruth to push farther into the unknown, in the company of his friends the Blackdens, and to come across to France.

During the next three years, while they oscillated between London and Paris Joel had to be all the time wooing her like a lover to keep her from going back home in a huff. Only gradually did he induce her to put her mind on learning the French and Italian languages he'd fallen in love with; and to enjoy meeting the odd and illassorted people that the restless life of the time churned up about them; and to feel the savor he felt in the crack of the postillion's whip and the merry grind of the postchaise's wheels over the gravel; and the accidents of the road and the ancient walls and spires of the villages; the *sole frite* eaten in seaside inns waiting for the packet; and even the sleety wind and the queazy huddle in the lurching cabin during Channel crossings; and the newspapers and the pamphlets and the neverending dinnertable talk; talk about wars breaking out, ministries falling, speeches in Parliament and in the National Assembly, the "decrepit old world" crumbling under the "prospects of a Golden Age."

Perhaps Ruth even began to feel, as Joel now felt it tingling in his blood to his fingertips, the excitement in the toast to which Joel's political friends lifted their wineglasses after dinner: "To the Revolution of the World." In France that revolution was advancing with breakneck speed.

There were times when it seemed like a stage play to American observers. Their own Lafayette had become the leading actor. His popularity reached its climax in the great Festival of the Federations held on the Champs de Mars on the first anniversary of the taking of the Bastille. The Constituent Assembly had completed its work. Lafayette headed the federation of national guardsmen who were to assure the stability of the new regime. Every unit sent its representatives to Paris to swear allegiance to the constitution. The channel packets were crowded with English radicals and reforming Whigs hastening to take part in the triumph of enlightened liberty. Revolutionists from every European nation pressed into Paris. Tom Paine arrived in time to carry an American flag in the parade.

There were many Americans in the enormous concourse of people drawn up in a hollow square to hear the constitution read. The King swore to support it. Assisted by four hundred priests with red white and blue sashes thrown over their white vestments, clubfooted Talleyrand, the Bishop of Autun performed High Mass on the towering altar of the fatherland. He blessed the banners of the eightythree departments.

With tears streaming down their faces his guardsmen shouted: *Je le jure.*
Cannon roared. There were discharges of musketry. At dusk fireworks filled
the sky.

Like the Americans the French had a written constitution but it was no
sooner sworn to than they started picking it to pieces. Everybody had a notion
of how to improve it. Lafayette was its sole defender.

Mirabeau's death left the wealthy Marquis the lone voice of authority in
France. When Louis bolted from the Tuileries disguised as a footman and fled
north to join the emigration it was Lafayette as commander of the national guard
who ordered his recapture.

The Fourth of July after the royal family's return to their emprisonment,
Gouverneur Morris, who had come to Europe like Barlow to sell western lands,
dined with Short the chargé d'affaires and a group of Americans at the legation.
Jefferson had long since returned home to serve as secretary of state. The guest of
honor as usual was Lafayette, who Gouverneur wrote had come near being hanged
for letting the King escape from the Tuileries. Paine was among them. Though
he knew no French he was editing a republican newspaper. His advice to the
French was to treat the King's attempt to escape as an abdication, and to set up
a republic. Gouverneur, who was becoming more conservative and sceptical with
each succeeding crisis, by this time loathed Paine. "Payne is here," he noted
scornfully in his diary, "inflated to the eyes and big with a litter of revolutions."

Able operators had discovered that immense things could be accomplished
by skillful use of the armed mob. Moderate minded Americans were shocked as
one bloody explosion followed another. In the abandoned convents and in the
gardens of the Palais Royale orators called for blood in the name of Tom Paine's
principles of liberty and reason. Treasons and plots became the morning fare of
the newspapers. To be a revolutionary meant to demand the death of traitors.
The great phrases from the Declaration of Independence hovered like birds of
prey over the Paris streets.

Lafayette wanted to behave as Washington would have behaved. He set
himself desperately to stem the torrent. He spent all the money he could raise
from his estates to bolster his constitutionalist party. He threatened and complained. He sought military appointments and resigned them. He retired for a
while to sulk in his château in Auvergne.

When the Declaration of Pilnitz seemed to threaten an emigré invasion
backed by the despots of Germany, the Assembly appointed Lafayette to command one of the northern armies. He threw himself in his carriage and drove off
at top speed to Metz. "I will send you an exact return of my Army when it is
finally arranged," he wrote Washington "for I always consider myself, my dear
General, as one of your lieutenants on a detached command."

The Constituent Assembly gave place to the Legislative Assembly. The seating of the new deputies in their redecorated hall suddenly became significant. On the right were Lafayette's constitutionalists, on the left the new shrill voices that hailed from the Gironde, from the Jacobins, from the Cordeliers, from the municipality of Paris. The madmen crowded in the extreme top benches to the left; they became known as the Mountain.

Old abuses and old vested interests were legislated away, but the strife and hatred between factions made orderly government impossible. Ambitions flared on every streetcorner. Ministry followed ministry. The armies of the Coalition of Kings were advancing from the north. Fear of retribution by the triumphant reaction filled the streets of Paris with madness. Behind every shuttered window republicans saw an avenging aristocrat.

The Assembly where Lafayette's constitutional party still had a thin majority was helpless before the ambitious men who had learned the dangerous science of evoking the mob. Only war to the death would unify the nation. War was declared on Austria. A month later the mob, goaded by news of defeats of the national armies, attacked the Tuileries.

Louis calmly walked out on a balcony wearing a liberty cap on his head and carrying a glass of wine in his hand, and stood looking stolidly down on the waving pikes and the red caps. This time his fumbling quiet demeanor quelled the insurrection. The Bourbon did not lack courage.

"The Constitution," Gouverneur Morris, who had just received the news of his appointment to succeed Jefferson as American Minister to France, noted in his diary, "has this Day I think given its last groan."

The moment Lafayette heard the news of a fresh uprising, abandoning his military command in the north, he set off post haste for Paris. He appeared at the bar of the assembly and by a passionate speech staved off a vote of censure. He tried to call out the National Guard to support the constitution. He would protect the person of the King and the liberty of the citizens. The time had come for the Washington of France to show himself on his white horse. He ordered the National Guard to gather on the Champs-Elysées and to discipline the Parisians.

Only a hundred men showed up.

Lafayette threw himself in his carriage and drove off to rejoin his army.

By August 10, 1792 the extremists were ready for their coup d'état. They were better prepared this time. The mob stormed the Tuileries again. The King told his Swiss guards not to fire. The Swiss were massacred almost to a man.

In a safe in the royal study documents were found to incriminate half the moderates in France, among them letters that purported to prove that Lafayette had been trying to arrange the King's escape from Paris.

The hour of the republic had come. A provisional government was set up with Danton as Minister of Justice. The jails were filled with liberals and monarchists. The King was deposed and confined in the Temple. Commissioners were sent off to the armies to announce the new regime that would complete the revolution.

Lafayette took three of them in custody and mustered his troops on the famous plain of Sedan. When he objured his soldiers to defend the King and the Constitution murmurings and mutterings were the only reply. On a sudden impulse he threw up his career as the Washington of France and rode off into the gathering dusk.

About twenty of his staff officers followed him. "Je me suis abandonné à mon sort," he wrote. The little troupe rode vaguely northward in search of neutral soil. There was no neutral soil in Europe. Near a Belgian village they stumbled on an Austrian detachment. When the officer in charge arrested him, Lafayette haughtily announced that since he had resigned from the French service he was an American citizen. He demanded to be taken to the American legation at the Hague. Instead he was hustled off to a dungeon in Magdeburg.

In a fit of republican enthusiasm the National Assembly, during the last weeks of its career, had conferred French citizenship on Washington, Madison, Hamilton, Paine and on a group of members of the British Society for Constitutional Information. On this second list appeared the name of the American poet, Joel Barlow. The younger Pitt's new anti-revolutionary policy was making England a dangerous place for American radicals. Paine, already under indictment for sedition, found himself elected to the new Convention by four French departments. He sailed out of Dover just one jump ahead of the sheriff's deputies and crossed to Calais. There he was received with tricolor delirium. Joel Barlow followed him to France a couple of months later, leaving Ruth worried and dismayed at their lodgings on Great Litchfield Street.

The day he reached Paris there was a dinner at White's Hotel on the passage des Petits Pères to celebrate the victories of the French armies over the Coalition. Paine was there, among deputies to the convention, a delegation of the military and visiting English and Irish reformers. Speeches were made, toasts were drunk to the revolutionary societies of England and Ireland and to Joel Barlow himself. Ten days later Joel accompanied John Frost, an English radical lawyer who had travelled to France with him, to the Tuileries to read from the bar of the Convention a message of congratulation from the Society for Constitutional Information of England, and to express the hopeful conviction that soon the French would have an opportunity to send a message in return to a similar constitutional convention in England. Adding deeds to words like practical Anglo-Saxons, they informed

*The earliest portrait of Jefferson, painted as a diplomat
by Mather Brown in London in 1786.*

Tom Paine as painted by Romney.

Ezra Stiles.

John Trumbull's portrait of David Humphreys, one of Washington's aides who so idolized the general he was said to have come to resemble him.

Noah Webster, the first man to recognize an American language: by James Sharples.

Mr Neilson's Battle, with the Royalist Club

Clubs literary and social were popular and rowdy. This sketch dates back to colonial times, from the minutes of the Tuesday Club of Annapolis.

Dr. Lemuel Hopkins by John Trumbull.

*During the first years of the young republic Philadelphia was in
every sense its metropolis.*

Brant, halfbreed chief of the Ojibbeways, painted in London by Benjamin West.

Inn sign celebrating union.

"*Here I am, Madam*," *Jefferson wrote Mme de Tessé,* "*gazing whole hours at the Maison quarrèe, like a lover at his mistress. the stocking weavers and silk spinners around it consider me an hypochondriac Englishman, about to write with a pistol the last chapter of his history.*"

"From Lyons to Nismes I have been nourished with the remains of Roman grandeur," wrote Jefferson to friends at Versailles.

"I am immersed in antiquities from morning to night. For me the city of Rome is still existing in all the splendor of its empire," wrote Jefferson.

The Grille de Chaillot. Jefferson's legation was in the two story house on the left.

Joel Barlow as he appeared, painted by his friend Fulton, on the title page of the Columbiad.

Ruth Barlow, painted by a Parisian acquaintance.

The Storming of the Tuileries.

The Execution of Louis XVI, from Monet's Les Principales Tournées de la Revolution.

U.S.S. Constitution. *During these years American ship designers had made notable improvements in shaping their hulls. United States ships were getting the reputation of being the fastest on the seven seas.*

A typical American brig.

*The last decade of the eighteenth century was a busy,
brilliant era for American shipyards.*

The Federal City of Washington seen from Georgetown.

Great Falls of the Potomac.

Frontispiece of Robert Adam's Palace
of Diocletian.

Illustration, from Clérisseau's Anti-
quités de France.

the Convention that their society was presenting the French nation with six thousand pairs of shoes.

About that time somebody suggested that Joel, like Paine, ought to be a member of the Convention. Savoy, recently liberated by the armies of the Republic, was a likely place to get elected. Joel was a man who never turned down a trip if he could help it. Delighted at the prospect of seeing some new country, he immediately set off for Savoy.

He took to the Savoyards; he enjoyed the mountains; he liked the inn at Chambery. He wrote letters urging the Piedmontese to throw off the yoke of the oppressor. Savoy made him think of Connecticut. He was snug as a bug in a rug there. But instead of getting himself elected to the Convention, he spent his time working on *Hasty-Pudding*, the best poem he ever wrote in his life.

Luckily for him Joel failed to be elected to the Convention. Back in Paris he found the political stage again transformed. It was the sixth month of the Year One of the Republic, One and Indivisible. In spite of Gouverneur Morris's undercover work to get poor Louis spirited out of the country and Tom Paine's courageous efforts from the floor of the Convention to save his life, the Bourbon was tried and found guilty.

His poor addled head was hacked off his body after two tries by the guillotine. This ingenious invention wasn't working so cleanly that day.

The Mountain had won over the Gironde. With Marat denouncing strangers every day in *L'Ami du Peuple* it was mortally dangerous for foreigners to try to meddle in French politics.

Joel induced Ruth to come back trembling across the Channel to bloody Paris. Philosophically he rented a pleasant little house at Meudon. He had gone into a shipbrokerage business with a Massachusetts colonel. Since he believed the republic had come to stay, he invested his profits in the national debt and in Paris real estate, as a good republican should.

Among other military men of brains a sawedoff Corsican who spoke French with a dreadful Italian accent, a certain Buonaparte, had begun to rise in the service of the Convention. Eventually it was the Little Corporal's victories that sent French consols up on the exchanges and made Joel Barlow a rich man.

Americans in Paris lived like people in a stormcellar during a tornado. There was no room for Anglo-Saxon liberals like Tom Paine and Joel Barlow. Establishing a republic was to them a day-to-day business of adjustment of men's rights; the means were allimportant. For the French who followed Robespierre the means didn't matter: the republic was a mystic and bloody ritual; the end was some mysterious, intellectual conception of unity.

Like so many Americans after him, who have tried to become citizens of

Europe, Joel suddenly found himself at a point where he could go no further. He set quietly to work to make two dollars grow where one grew before.

Already Joel's political exploits in France had been exaggerated at home in Connecticut. It must have been with a bitter laugh that he read a letter brought to him in the summer of '93 by a young man from New Haven. President Ezra Stiles of Yale, his old friend, wrote Joel in his ornate strangely illegible cuneiform handwriting, which was the result perhaps of too much study of oriental tongues:

> "I congratulate you upon the celebrity and fame which your poetical and political writings have justly merited and acquired to you, partly in pro-curing your conspicuous elevation and seat in the National Convention in France, one of the most important and illustrious assemblies that ever sat on this terraqueous globe; an assembly charged with the highest bestowments, and coming up from the people with the express power and authority for the accomplishment of three great works: the form of a Constitution, the taking into their hands the public administration and national government in the interim, and sitting as the judiciary tribunal on the life of a king—works great and arduous, momentous and of great consequence to the cause of public liberty, the rights of sovereignty and the indefeasible rights of man."

Joel must have laughed indeed. Dabbling in English politics had almost landed him in jail. He had already given up the idea of playing any part in France. He was thanking his stars that the good Savoyards he'd liked so much hadn't elected him as their deputy.

Paris that summer was full of American seacaptains. Pitt, largely to save the old order at home, had shoved England into the war on the side of the Coalition. The Convention in totalitarian mood had declared an embargo on all shipping and the French fleet had captured ninetytwo American ships and had brought them into Havre, Brest and Bordeaux.

White's Hotel was the center of negotiations of the American captains to get their cargoes freed of the embargo. From there they joggled packed angrily into cabs between Gouverneur Morris's official legation at Sainport, and Paine's lodgings in a dilapidated mansion that had once belonged to la Pompadour far out on the rue du Faubourg St. Denis.

For a while it looked as if the United States had two ministers. The split between Federalists and anti-Federalists at home—part of the worldwide cleavage between republicans and conservatives—was reflected in Paris by the strained re-lations between Morris, who like Burke was every day more appalled by the bloody follies of the revolution, and Paine, who still represented the spirit of '76.

Paine and Morris were both men who tended to have a chip on the shoulder. They had been acquaintances for years on account of Paine's friendship with

Gouverneur's elder brother Lewis, but as politics grew more and more bitter
mutual tolerance broke down into spiteful enmity. Morris thought Paine was intriguing to get his job as minister away from him, and Paine believed to his dying
day that Morris tried to cause his death by not claiming him as an American
citizen when Robespierre ordered his arrest and sent him to the Luxembourg.

His appeal for clemency for the Bourbon had marked Paine for execution.
He was arrested the night of December 27th, 1793. When the gendarmes came
for him at White's where he was dining as usual, he asked, on the pretext that he
spoke no French, to be taken to Joel Barlow's. Joel by this time wrote and spoke
French fluently. He and Ruth had moved into town for the winter to the hôtel
de la Grande Bretagne on the rue Jacob.

Joel went with Paine and the gendarmes to Paine's lodgings to interpret for
him while they searched his papers. The search took all night and most of the next
day. Joel convinced the agents that there was nothing antirevolutionary to be
found in Paine's writings.

They even let him take off to the printers the first part of *The Age of Reason*,
which Paine had been working on feverishly in the hope of setting up a reason-
able belief in God, the First Cause, against the hysterical atheism that was part of
the popular creed of revolutionary Paris. He had finished the pamphlet that
morning.

Paine escaped the guillotine by a miracle. He remained during the rest of the
Terror in the Luxembourg, and almost died there of prison fever.

Joel and the American seacaptains got up a petition to the National Convention asking for Paine's release as a fellow citizen. The seacaptains offered to
take him back to America.

Arguing with the Convention was like arguing with a Bengal tiger. Paris had
become so dangerous that Joel thought it wise to move his Ruth to Amsterdam.

He was on a business trip to Altona, across the river from Hamburg, when
he heard of Robespierre's last desperate speech before the Convention, and of his
arrest and execution. The sun seemed to shine again.

The Paris the Barlows went back to was more like the old pleasant city of
the early days of the National Assembly. The nobility had gone. The clergy had
gone. The revolutionists had gone. Outside of the army the businessman was
supreme.

The American colony was less torn by dissention since Gouverneur Morris
had packed off to Switzerland to follow his odd destiny among the noble ladies of
the Bourbon emigration. James Monroe, Jefferson's neighbor and devoted friend
and follower, had arrived as American minister. One of his first acts was to get
Paine out of jail. Monroe and his wife nursed him back to health at the legation.
While they waited for the French funds to rise enough to make it worth while to

sell out and go home, the Barlows settled down in a pleasant apartment on the rue du Bac.

Instead of going home Joel went to Algiers.

Joel was a man who never turned down a trip if he could help it. Now, through his old poetical crony David Humphreys, who for several years had held the post of minister to Portugal, the State Department asked him to represent the United States in its negotiations with a pirate state that was holding a hundred and thirty Americans as slaves.

Before Joel knew what he was doing he had said he would go. It would be an interesting trip, he pointed out to Ruth. He'd written and talked a lot about liberty, hadn't he? Well, freeing Americans from slavery was a practical way of working for liberty.

The survival in the year of enlightenment 1796 of Barbary pirates was a tribute to the sublime ineptitude of that old order in Europe which Joel Barlow had seen crumple before his eyes.

For over a century the empire of the Ottoman Turks had been largely held together by the fact that the courts of Europe were too busy fighting among themselves to put an end to it. The most prosperous dependencies of the Sublime Porte were the ports of North Africa, which were run by groups of Turkish soldiers, who had gone west to make their fortunes, each town under the leader-ship of whatever Pasha by skill of swordplay and poisoning managed to hack his way to the top. This gentleman, in return for a certain amount of specie and slaves, was recognized as regent by the Grand Signor in Constantinople. As they had long ago exhausted the resources of the country and the wealth of the local Moors and Berbers, the only way these soldier-states could live was by piracy.

The British seem to have felt that the Barbary pirates were useful to cut down competition in the carrying trade; it was rumored that the Admiralty was not at all displeased when the Dey of Algiers, having discovered that a new nation of unbelievers had sprung up across the western ocean, gave orders to his men to bring in American ships. The Algerines cruised far to sea and captured several American vessels off Portugal; their cargoes were seized and their crews made slaves by the Dey.

The United States government had been paying protection and ransom money through the religious order of the Mathurins, and had sent agents to negotiate with the Algerines without accomplishing more than the occasional release of an individual. At last Humphreys induced the State Department to appoint Joel Barlow to go to Algiers to talk to the leading ruffians and make a treaty with them no matter what it cost.

The assignment was made somewhat tougher by the fact that Algiers was a leading focus for bubonic plague. The lives of the Americans held there, already made hideous by the slavery of the Turks, were in danger from the plague every day that negotiations dragged.

So before dawn one raw January morning Joel found himself giving Ruth, still warm and intimate in her frilled dressinggown, a last hug and kiss; and leaving his comfortable apartment on the rue du Bac with its high rooms hung with lace curtains and damask portieres that smelt of Paris must and furniture polish; and saying goodbye to the bonne and to his little dog named Mignon, and setting off for the Midi.

Strapped to the caved creaking roof of his travelling carriage, and a great strain on the axle and on the springs and on Joel's nerves, was a huge portmanteau known in France at that time as a *vache*, stuffed with jewelry and gewgaws to the value of almost two hundred thousand livres as presents to the Dey of Algiers and his mamelukes.

Joel sailed from Marseille into the teeth of a gale and was driven, after several days tossing seasick and miserable in the Gulf of Lyons, into the shelter of the Bay of Rosas. At Rosas, after a day of arguments in the customshouse, he was allowed ashore. He hired a little twowheeled muledrawn chaise. He was all for taking any possible leg of a journey by land to avoid the horrible seasickness that never left hm aboard ship.

He enjoyed the drive south. The mule jingled along slowly and cheerfully over the bad roads. The Spanish drivers, who walked ahead urging on the mule with shouts of "*arré!*" were honest selfrespecting and polite.

Spring was beginning. Almond trees in bloom stood out against the dry blue distant mountains.

He went through the crumbling fortress towns of Figueras and Gerona, admired the prosperity of the shops along the well-laid stone streets of Barcelona, where there was an air of neatness and industry that contrasted with the misery of the countryside. To his relief the Spanish inns weren't so bad as he'd been told; it was true that you slept over the stables and that little pigs and all the barnyard poultry ran in and out of the kitchen, but the beds were fairly clean and although fleas were numerous and active he reported to Ruth that there were no bedbugs.

In Alicante he got news that Donaldson, the previous American agent on the Barbary Coast, had already signed a treaty with the Dey. All that Joel would need to do was to pay over the tribute and ransom money and to confirm the arrangement. Joel wrote Ruth he would be back home in a few weeks. Humphreys was sending the money by sea from Lisbon.

He reached Algiers four days later in another howling March gale. The sea was so rough that it was twentyfour hours before a boat could get him into the inner harbor behind the mole to set him ashore.

Algiers in those days consisted entirely of what's now called the Kasbah, a maze of narrow whitewashed streets zigzagging in steps up a steep hill. There was no street wide enough for a cart or carriage. Baggage was transported on the backs of porters or burros. Women were veiled to the eyes. The streets were full of filth and beggary.

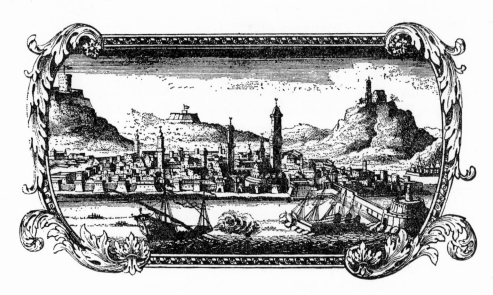

Algiers in the 18th Century *from Chatelain's* Atlas Historique

Hassan Pasha the Dey lorded it over the enslaved multitudes with scimitar and bastinado. For part of every season the plague was the town's real ruler. The Dey's bankers, whose fingers were in every pie, were the members of the Jewish family house of Bacry.

The dim light of the Dey's palace, the carpeted rooms without furniture, the salaamliks and the taking off of shoes and the squatting and the insolence of the Turks and the affability of the Jews and the silence and grumpiness of the big bearded brute who was absolute master of this strange world made a deep impression on Joel. He couldn't help remembering that behind every dark ferocious face, in every veiled mealbag of a woman, in the ulcerous filth of every beggar, and in every porter's glistening sweat, the plague waited silent and allpowerful, and wondering whether he was going to leave his carcase there in Algiers like poor Ledyard in Cairo.

One hopeful sign he noted. Slaves as they were, the Americans in Algiers had managed to make themselves more respected by the Turks than the other Europeans.

A few days after arriving he wrote Ruth, almost with relief, that there was nothing he could do in Algiers, the money supposed to be shipped from Lisbon hadn't come, the Dey wouldn't wait, the treaty was off. There was nothing to it but to go home. In eight days the Dey would send the American agents away and in thirty days more the Algerines would start raiding American commerce again.

The captives, who had been crazy with joy when Joel arrived, sank back into despair. It seemed that nothing was left to them but to wear out their lives there till the plague reached out for them or till their Turkish owner, feeling peevish some fine morning, would hack off their heads.

This business of American citizens being held as slaves was bad enough in the abstract; but now that Joel knew them himself, personally, for a fine bunch of young men, most of them New Englanders, he couldn't stand it. He had to do something for them.

Gradually he began to make out how Algiers worked. The real power in the regency was in the hands of the Jewish bankers. The Bacry had complete ascendancy over the Dey and when he was in a good humor could talk him into anything. Although a peevish and bloody despot the Dey was at bottom a fairly simpleminded fellow and anxious to do right according to his lights.

As the Barbary pirates were able sailors they admired the trim American vessels and the seamanship of their crews. Barlow got the idea of offering the Dey, through the Bacry of course, a present as a consolation for having had to wait so long for his money. If he would wait patiently for another six months Barlow pledged that the United States would send him a new fullrigged ship of twenty-four guns as a gift to his daughter.

The Dey raised the ante to thirtysix guns, but Joel could see that the ship appealed to him. He made more promises. He offered the Bacry ten thousand sequins to spread round the town where it would do the most good, with the understanding that a good deal of it would remain with the house of Bacry, where much good had been done already.

Meanwhile Donaldson sailed off to Leghorn to try to raise cash on American credit, leaving Joel alone in Algiers with his worries and his paperwork. In his letters to Ruth he took to cursing out his old friend Humphreys whose dumbness had caused all this mess . . . "If we had a good bankers' clerk in a certain place for a minister . . ." But the Dey was letting himself be thawed. He presented Consul Barlow with a horse.

Joel borrowed a saddle and bridle and took to riding out in the country round the town. He made pleasant acquaintances among the French and the Swedes. Everything delighted him: the landscape, the fruit, the gardens. Only man was vile.

"I remain alone and I work like a slave," he wrote Ruth; "I sent today a large packet for Lisbon and for Philadelphia. If Donaldson comes with the money to finish here, he will go to Tunis and I can fly to your arms. If he does not come I shall be driven from here, so I shall be free soon in any case. I shall have now very little to do after the departure of the ship which carries this. Then I shall try to amuse myself in my garden—for I have taken a country house here for the sake of appearances, as they believe me a fixed consul, and will think when I go, it is to bring my wife and other necessities for a long residence. Ah well! I shall bring her whenever she and I consent to bury ourselves in Barbary."

He wasn't telling Ruth quite all the truth. The real use of a country house was to keep away from the city while the plague made its annual flareup. The last day of May Joel wrote Monroe: "I have now to add the frightful news that the plague has broken out at Algiers. . . . It usually commences in February and begins to go off in June. The hot dry weather kills it in this country, so we hope it will not be severe nor last long. One of our poor fellows is attacked and will probably die."

All summer he tried to get the Dey to let him take the American slaves awaiting ransom out to his house in the country. For some who were so sick as to be useless to their masters he seems to have managed it. But in June he wrote Humphreys in despair: "Two of our finest young fellows, Nicholas Hartford of Portsmouth and Abraham Simmonds of Cape Anne, have already fallen . . . Since my last Joseph Keith, a native of Newfoundland, one of our mates, has died of the plague. Lunt is still in the hospital and John Thomas, a black man from Massachusetts. The contagion rages with greater severity than was expected."

The night of July 8th, at his wits' end, he sat down in his airy gardenhouse to write a farewell letter to his wife. He'd made up his mind that he would never get out of Africa alive. Tomorrow he was going back to Algiers to work on a scheme he'd thought up as the last chance of ransoming the Americans before they all died. He wrote:

"My dearest Life and only Love: I run no risk in alarming your extreme sensibility by writing this letter, since it is not my intention that it shall come into your hands unless and until, through some other channel, you shall have been informed of the event which it anticipates as possible . . . A pressing duty of humanity requires me to expose myself more than other considerations would justify, in endeavoring to save as many of our unhappy citizens as possible . . . and to embark them at this cruel moment for their country . . . I certainly hope to escape from this place, and return to your beloved arms. No man has stronger inducements to wish to live than I have. I have no quarrel with the world; it has used me as well as could be expected. I have valuable friends in every country where I have put my foot, not excepting this abominable sink of wickedness, pestilence and folly,—the city of Algiers. I have a pretty extensive and dear-bought knowledge of mankind; a most valuable collection of books; a pure and undivided taste for domestic tranquility; the social intercourse of friends; study; and the exercise of charity. I have a moderate but sufficient income; perfect health; an unimpaired constitution; and to give relish to all enjoyments and smooth away the asperities that might arise from unforeseen calamities, I have the wife that my youth chose . . . I will use every precaution for my safety, as well for your sake as mine. But if you should see me no more, my dearest friend, you will not forget that I loved you . . ."

The scheme Joel had thought up to pay the ransom of the slaves was a pure Yankee trick that did him credit as a son of the Nutmeg State.

He explained it in a letter to Jefferson which he sent along with the captives when he shipped them home. "I have the pleasure at last to announce the liberation of our citizens from slavery at this place . . . My being able to secure the liberation of the captives at this time has been owing to an accident. Money has been extremely scarce here for some months back. The Jew house who serve as our brokers and who do the greater part of the business here, have had their funds for some time in the hands of the French government to the amount of half a million dollars. Though I had so far gained the confidence of the Jews that they declared to me that they would advance the money to the amount of the redemption if it could be raised, I had little faith in these professions because I believed they said so under the idea that the money could not be had in the town. The plague broke out in the latter end of May, & very much increased my anxiety for the fate of our people. Some time in June a new French Consul arrived & by some brilliant presents revived the influence of the Republic with the Dey, so as to borrow from the public treasury about $200,000, which he paid into their Jew house. I immediately insisted that they should prove the sincerity of their friendship by lending me this sum, & as much more as the redemption would amount to, for which I would give them my bills on Mr. Donaldson at Leghorn."

The Bacrys, stimulated by esteem for Joel, by philanthropy, by a desire to continue to do business with the new nation in the west, and perhaps by the fact that discounts on bills drawn on Leghorn were unusually high, delivered the money. The Dey, whose mind was not built to follow these financial intricacies, saw his own cash counted out in front of him and accepted the ransom.

Joel immediately packed such of the American seafaring men as had survived the plague on board the ship *Fortune*, which belonged to the house of Bacry, and to which he gave American registry for the trip. An American skipper, Captain Calder, was put in command.

They set sail for home. Joel himself had to stay on as a sort of living promissory note of the United States government. He wrote Ruth in September that he was the only American slave left in Algiers.

Letters had come from Humphreys announcing that the amount had been shipped in gold from Lisbon early in July on Captain O'Brien's brig. But where the devil was the brig? Even with the worst of winds a vessel couldn't take three months between Lisbon and Algiers. Day followed day. Joel was in despair at the thought that she'd been lost.

The Dey made up his mind that he'd been had. He got into such a pet that not even the Bacry could put in a word for the American. The Dey's pets tended to be dangerous to the bystanders. The slaves had been his security. Here he'd let this unbelieving dog trick him into letting them slip through his fingers. He began muttering that he'd have the smooth Americano's head.

To make matters worse the British blockaded the Mediterranean, thus cutting off Donaldson who was trying to get bills of exchange through the Leghorn bankers. Joel was at the end of his tether. There was nothing to do but keep out of sight. He let his mustaches grow long and interested himself in getting ready for the vintage at his gardenhouse in the country.

All the while American ships, since Humphreys was announcing to all and sundry that he had settled the treaty with the Barbary states a year ago, were pouring into the Mediterranean. During the early days of September Joel was busy writing to American consuls at Gibraltar and Marseille and Alicante and Lisbon to do everything in their power to stop them. The skippers were keen for business and fretted at consular formalities. The American flag had been seen as far east as Smyrna.

What was worse, the supercargo of a vessel from Ragusa told of having spoken a Tripolitan pirate on her way into Tripoli with two prizes that had a Yankee rake to them. One was a twomaster and one a threemaster. They'd been captured in the Atlantic off the Portuguese coast by an unusually enterprising corsair that was captained by a British renegade. Gradually news seeped into Algiers that one of the American boats that had been taken into Tripoli was Captain O'Brien's brig with the tribute on board.

When everything seemed blackest, a brig came unexpectedly to anchor off the port of Algiers. The skipper was rowed ashore in the longboat. It was O'Brien.

Immediately Joel's luck changed. The Dey's ill temper blew off in the direction of Tripoli. He'd have that Bey's head off for molesting a ship that had his passport. On board the brig were two ambassadors from Tripoli to beg the Dey's pardon. Now that that potentate had somebody else to pick on Barlow Effendi, father of all the consuls, was in highest favor. The Dey even broached the idea that the Americans were hardly unbelievers or Christian dogs at all.

They didn't bow down to graven images, and they worshiped one God, like the Moslems, and they kept their word like good Turks.

"My friend," he told Joel, "I have long admired your constancy & courage. I now find you are true to me as well as to your country. I have treated you with great severity, but you must allow that I have had uncommon patience; for I have always felt something at the bottom of my heart which told me, that man cannot lie. God has rewarded you for all your suffering. We shall be friends forever."

Joel was so relieved he couldn't keep back his tears.

Negotiating the treaty with Tripoli took up two months. The business with Tunis dragged on and on. The Bey of Tunis was slippery as an eel. The Dey of Algiers blustered and threatened and even declared war on him, though he never got around to bringing Consul Barlow his enemy's head as he'd promised. In the end after an endless haggle about the price the Tunisian Bey settled. Assured that the signed treaty actually was on the way, Joel got a new American agent installed in Algiers. At last he was ready to go home to Ruth. Instead of four months he'd been away sixteen.

During the latter part of his stay he'd had time to make the wine from the grapes at his gardenhouse, to attend a bear hunt, and also to do a little business. In partnership with Herculais, the French envoy, he had bought the American brig *Friendship*, sold as a prize in Tripoli, and the *Rachel*, whose captain had gotten into complications in Oran. In his next letter he told Ruth triumphantly that she was the halfowner of a fine vessel.

Soon he was writing her in the highest spirits from the lazaret at Marseille rhapsodizing about the beauty of the very letters of the name of Marseille. The weather was delicious. In front of him, when he stepped out of his door, was the steely blue bay that stretched sparkling between the ashwhite hills and steep islands with their white forts that hemmed in the crowded town and the land-locked harbor bristling with masts and tackle and sails drying. The quarters were comfortable. The food was excellent. There was clear water for swimming. It was such a relief to be out of Algiers that he actually enjoyed the quarantine station.

Joel wrote daily letters to Ruth, mostly in lively and affectionate French. One day he enquired whether he should cut off the mustaches he'd grown in Barbary ". . . I wear long mustaches—long beautiful and black—(a little gray, however). Do you wish to cut them here, or do you wish to see them & cut them yourself? It is necessary to say why I let them grow. There is a proverb which is only too true, although very humiliating for humanity. *Who makes himself mutton, the wolf eats;* nowhere is this so useful as in Barbary. I discovered that on arriving there, and as I am a lamb at heart, it was necessary for me to conceal this character beneath the exterior of some other animal, & my mustaches give me very nearly the air of a tiger, a beast which the wolf does not eat. They have been very useful in my business: I attach to them no value, except as a souvenir of the services they have rendered me. I place them on your altar: pronounce their fate . . ."

Never a girl who cared much for adventure, Ruth wrote him to cut them off.

More years went by before Joel could disentangle himself from his shipping partnerships, his speculations in wine and brandies and the various import and export ventures he had become involved in as a result of his trip to Algiers. The Barlows lived comfortably in Paris through the Directory and the XYZ business and the rise of Bonaparte. Each revolution in France made them a little richer. It wasn't until the fall of 1804, when their friend Jefferson had almost completed his first term in the White House, that Joel and Ruth sailed home to America.

They settled, as a result of Jefferson's fervid urging, on an estate which Jefferson picked out for them on a hill overlooking Georgetown and Rock Creek, which they named Kalorama.

The United States the Barlows came home to was very different from the land they had left twenty years before. Everywhere the new nation was outgrowing the old colonial limits. With the admission of Ohio the striped flag sported seventeen stars. Foreigners were pouring in. New Englanders and Virginians were moving toward the new lands in the Ohio valley. Progressive minded men were moving west. Among his old associates who had stayed home Barlow found an immense change of outlook.

The bitter party battles of Washington's last term and of John Adams's administration had left men and women whom he had known as openminded youngsters, casehardened into political fanatics. Black was black and white was white. The defeated Federalists had sullenly retreated into conservative shells. It was only the Republicans who still cherished the gay dreams of 1776, the prospects of a golden age.

A religious cleavage added to the virulence of party hatreds. In Washington's day deism had been a respectable belief. Now, especially on account of his recent translation with Jefferson's help of Volney's *Ruines*, the Bible of republicans and Bonapartists in Europe, Joel found himself regarded as an arch fiend by his old friends in Connecticut. Jefferson's Washington City, the only place in America where he could fit in, was considered as a city of destruction by his old cronies among the Hartford wits.

Another Connecticut Yankee, the Reverend Manasseh Cutler, colonizer and botanist, left a record of this state of mind. When he attended the Seventh Congress as a representative from his new state of Ohio, he arrived expecting to find the smell of brimstone everywhere. But in spite of his New England prejudices he had to admit that Jefferson did not wear horns and a barbed tail. His surprise shows through the phrasing of his journal and his letters home. Like most westernminded men who were accustomed to the rawness of new settlements, he couldn't help enjoying Washington City. He wrote home describing the beauty of the Potomac scenery, the magnificence of the Great Falls, the impressiveness of the view from Jenkins' Hill.

He described with relish the meals he ate at the President's house when, in due rotation, his turn came to be one of a dozen congressmen invited to dine at the President's oval table. He wrote with enthusiasm of the rice soup, the round of beef, the turkey, mutton, and ham, the loin of veal, the cutlets of mutton or veal, the fried eggs, the fried beef with which the table was piled. The cookery had a European flavor. He regarded with some suspicion a newfangled "pie called macaroni, which appeared to be a rich crust formed with strilions of onions . . . very strong and not agreeable," he added. He found the ice cream marvelous: "crust wholly dried, crumbled into thin flakes." Then there was "a dish like a pudding, inside white as milk or curd, very porous and light, covered with cream sauce," which he found very fine.

After dinner Mr. Jefferson took his company into what he called "the mammoth room" to see the five hundred pound cheese the Republican citizens of Cheshire, Massachusetts, had sent the President with the advice that not a crumb of Federalist curd had gone into the making of it. Those who were interested were allowed to examine odds and ends of bones of an actual mammoth and the Indian sculptures and paintings which were already beginning to accumulate there.

The Reverend Cutler, perhaps mollified by the excellence of the desserts, reported that he found the President's conversation less "licentous" than he had expected and his dress "quite decent." He was astonished too, so he wrote his family, to see him at the church services held in the new temporary House of Representatives which had been erected during the preceding summer in the foundations of the south wing of the Capitol.

These services, conducted each Sunday by a preacher of a different denomination—once a woman officiated in the pulpit—became as much as the horseraces and the picnics at the Great Falls one of the diversions of the new capital. They were the main gathering place of Georgetown and Washington society. Everyone came dressed in his best. The services were enlivened by the brassy strains of Captain Burrough's marine band. Mr. Jefferson, who arrived with his loose-limbed mountaineer walk, tall and erect in his buffcolored clothes and wooly waistcoat, with his rusty graying hair still caught in a queue behind his long head, was usually accompanied by his secretary, slight darkhaired Captain

Meriwether Lewis. Two seats toward the front were invariably reserved for them.

Jefferson had chosen as his secretary an army officer of twentyeight whose life was linked with his in many various ways. Meriwether Lewis came of that great family of Lewises that was scattered through the valley and piedmont sections of Virginia. One great uncle had married Washington's sister. Another was the diarist of the pioneering survey of the confines of the Fairfax grant carried on by Jefferson's father Peter and Joshua Fry in 1746. Through his mother he was descended from the Quaker Meriwethers, who were the first settlers in Albemarle County. When Meriwether Lewis's father died his mother married one of the Franks family Jefferson was allied with by his sister's marriage. He went to school in Albemarle with Matthew Maury, who was continuing the elder Maury's school on the Mountain where Jefferson got his early education.

Jefferson first became interested in Meriwether as a youngster in Albemarle. Besides being a famous coon and possum hunter, he showed more than a mere woodsman's interest in the birds and beasts and insects and the vegetation of the forests. A captain at eighteen, he was detached for recruiting service at Charlottesville. Immediately he started pestering Jefferson to let him go along on the French naturalist Michaud's botanizing and exploring expedition into the Western Waters. The dream of his life was to explore the headwaters of the Missouri.

As soon as Jefferson was elected President he had Meriwether Lewis detached from Wilkinson's command on the Mississippi for service in Washington. Immediately the two of them started plotting a reconnaissance of the continent. It was illfated John Ledyard's old plan in reverse. Now as President, Jefferson was at last in a position to turn this long dreamed of project into reality. In Captain Lewis he found a deputy whose life was what his life might have been if he had been a man of the outdoors instead of a man of letters.

The planning of the expedition to explore the westernmost of the Western Waters went along with the conduct of a strange game of hazard with the unpredictable Bonaparte. In this game Robert R. Livingston, the new American minister to France, and Talleyrand in Paris; and Madison as Secretary of State and the French minister Pichon in Washington all played their parts; the grand strategy was Jefferson's.

Ever since Talleyrand had spied out the land during his exile among the Americans, the ci-devant bishop had nourished an ambition to restore to France preponderance in America. For that purpose he egged Bonaparte on to force the Bourbon court of Spain to return to him, by a secret treaty signed at San Ildefonso, the great Louisiana tract west of the Mississippi, which included New Orleans on the eastern bank, and which France had transferred to Spain in the weak-kneed days of the dying monarchy. There had been many rumors as the intrigue proceeded, but the people of Ohio and Kentucky and Tennessee got their first concrete intimation of the new status of Louisiana when the Spanish Intendant suddenly suspended the right of deposit at New Orleans.

Before Joel Barlow left for home, Livingston had arrived in Paris to negotiate the points at issue between France and the United States. He had been instructed to try to trade American claims, for the spoliation of their commerce during the Directory's undeclared war, for New Orleans or at least for a port in West Florida.

Now Jefferson sent off Monroe, whose term had expired as governor of Virginia, as minister extraordinary to both France and Spain with instructions to offer anything within reason, to whichever government he should discover to have the territory near the mouth of the Mississippi in its control, for its cession to the United States. His bargaining point was his threat to ally himself with England in the new war which already loomed large on the horizon.

Jefferson admired Livingston's keenness and wit; but in Monroe he had absolute confidence; besides it gave him pleasure to right the wrong done his fellow Virginian when he had been abruptly recalled from Paris by the Federalist administration.

Bonaparte meanwhile, having been forced by his failure in Egypt to forgo his dreams of eastern empire, had begun to interest himself in Talleyrand's plans for expansion to the west. First the revolting Negroes of Santo Domingo must be crushed, slavery restored there, and that island fitted out as a base for a landing in Louisiana. Bonaparte sent off one of his best generals, the Leclerc who had married his handsome sister Pauline. With him went a brilliantly equipped expedition.

Faced with the restoration of slavery, the Haitian Negroes resolved to fight until they died. It was a war of massacre and countermassacre. The Negroes hid out in the hills. Another enemy appeared that Leclerc could not drive off into the hills. Bonaparte's brotherinlaw saw three fourths of his army die before the yellow fever took him. Reinforcements under the son of old Rochambeau of Yorktown died as fast as they landed from the ships.

As Bonaparte, lolling in the tubful of warm water clouded with eau de Cologne in which he did his private thinking at St. Cloud, scrutinized the butcher's bill of his Louisiana venture he decided suddenly that to fight the Haitian Negroes, the yellow fever, and the British fleet was too great odds. To keep Louisiana out of the hands of England he would cede it to the United States.

Livingston proved a good horsetrader. Though in his first surprise at Bonaparte's change of mind he fumbled a little and tried to insist that New Orleans and West Florida were all he was authorized to buy, by the time Monroe arrived

in Paris the two parties had virtually agreed on the cession of Louisiana in return
for a sum which, including the damages for spoliation which the United States
agreed to pay to its own citizens, amounted to approximately twenty million
dollars. Monroe's arrival with full powers clinched the deal.

When Jefferson and Lewis first planned the expedition to the sources of the
Missouri it had been thought necessary to procure passports from the French
minister. Now, unless they should stumble into the region the sea otters came
from, in the mistily imagined sounds north of Columbia River, which still formed
a dim no man's land where British and Spanish and American and even Russian
claims conflicted, the entire journey could be made on American soil.

Lewis had induced one of the redheaded Clarks of Virginia and Kentucky
whom Jefferson had known all his life, George Rogers' younger brother William,
to go along as joint leader, and was already recruiting his explorers out of the
western settlements. Jefferson took such pleasure in writing their instructions
that they scanned like poetry:

> "The object of your mission is to explore the Missouri River & such
> principle stream of it, as, by it's course & communication with the
> waters of the Pacific Ocean, may afford the most direct and practi-
> cable water communication across this continent, for the purposes of
> commerce . . .
> "Your observations are to be taken with great pains & accuracy, to be
> entered distinctly, & intelligently for others as well as yourself, to
> comprehend all the elements necessary, with the aid of the usual
> tables, to fix the latitude and longitude of the places at which they
> were taken."

Jefferson himself had experience as a surveyor as a young man.

> "Several copies of these, as well as your other notes, should be made at
> leisure times and put into the care of the most trustworthy of your
> attendants, to guard by multiplying them, against the accidental losses
> to which they will be exposed. a further guard would be that one of
> these copies be written on the paper of the birch, less liable to injury
> by damp than common paper."

Jefferson had written his daughters on birchbark from Lake George. One
of his hobbies was finding uses for the natural products of the American forest.

> "You will therefore endeavor to make yourself acquainted," he went on,
> "With the names of the nations and their numbers;

Lafayette, one of the most painted men of his day, in the military uniform he so loved to wear

*A sketch by Benjamin West for a painting of the shrewd Americans who out-
witted the British and the Bourbons in negotiating the peace treaty that established
American independence. John Jay, John Adams, Benjamin Franklin and his grand-
son William Temple Franklin, secretary to the commissioners, and Henry Lauren[s]
standing behind. Never completed because the British commissioners refused to pos[e]*

Volatile harddrinking Thomas Mifflin cut more of a figure in Pennsylvania than in Continental politics. Copley's painting of Governor Mifflin and his wife showed Copley at the peak of his early realist style before he underwent the influence of the school of Rome

A worried unglamorous Hamilton painted by Charles Willson Peale about 1791 when Hamilton as Secretary of the Treasury was beginning his political battle with the Jeffersonians

"Toot" Fulton, new rich and successful, painted by C. W. Peale's son Rembrandt

Like Fulton, S. F. B. Morse who invented the telegraph started life as a portrait painter. Late in Eli Whitney's life Morse painted his fellow inventor

Jefferson as President by Rembrandt Peale

the extent & limits of their possessions;

their relations with other tribes or nations;

their language, traditions, monuments;

their ordinary occupations in agriculture, fishing, hunting, war, arts,
 & the implements of these;

their food, clothing, & domestic accommodations;

the diseases prevalent among them, & the remedies they use;

moral & physical circumstances which distinguish them from the
 tribes we know;

peculiarities in their laws, customs & dispositions;

and articles of commerce they may need or furnish & to what extent.

"And considering the interest which every nation has in extending &
strengthening the authority of reason & justice among the people around
them, it will be useful to acquire what knoledge you can of the state of
morality, religion and information among them, as it may better enable those
who endeavor to civilize & instruct them, to adapt their measures to the existing notions & practises of those on whom they are to operate.

"Other object worthy of notice will be

the soil & face of the country, it's growth & vegetable productions;
 especially those not of the U.S.

the animals of the country generally, & especially those not known in
 the U.S.

the remains and accounts of any which may be deemed rare or ex-
 tinct;

the mineral productions of every kind; but more particularly metals,
 limestone, pit coal & salpetre; salines & mineral waters, noting the
 temperature of the last, & such circumstances as may indicate their
 character.

Volcanic appearances.

climate as characterized by the thermometer, by the proportion of
 rainy, cloudy & clear days, by lightning, hail, snow, ice, by the
 access & recess of frost, by the winds prevailing at different
 seasons, the dates at which particular plants put forth or lose their
 flowers, or leaf, times of appearance of particular birds, reptiles
 or insects."

Jefferson further instructed Lewis to treat the Indians he would come into
contact with "in the most friendly and conciliatory manner which their own
conduct will admit . . . if a superior force . . . should be arrayed against
your further passage, & inflexibly determined to arrest it, you must decline it's
further pursuit, and return. in the loss of yourselves, we should lose also the
information you will have acquired. by returning safely with that, you may

enable us to renew the essay with better calculated means . . . we wish you to err on the side of your safety, & bring back your party safe, even if it be with less information."

He didn't want Lewis and Clark to leave their bones like poor Ledyard in some heathen grave.

It was on December 20, 1803, that General Wilkinson, in command of the United States Army, and Governor Claiborne of Mississippi Territory had the pleasure of seeing the tricolor hauled down and the stars and stripes hauled up on the flagstaff in front of the Cabildo in New Orleans.

In the following May on a rainy day, Captains Lewis and Clark and their small party started up the Missouri River. They travelled in a covered keelboat accompanied by two sixoared open pirogues. By the last week in August they were far up the stream. They had killed their first buffalo and established relations with the Sioux Indians at Council Bluffs.

They spent that winter in a fort built of cottonwood logs opposite the mouth of the Knife River near the walled villages of the Mandans. There they came upon one of the treasures of the expedition, the squaw Sacajawea who was the wife of a French voyageur whom they hired as an interpreter. She was a Snake Indian and proved irreplaceable by her knowledge of Indian lore and of the languages of the tribes they were to meet in crossing the mountains.

On April 5, 1805 having sent the keelboat back to St. Louis with dispatches and ethnographic collections for President Jefferson, they set off up the river.

"Our vessels consisted of six small canoes, and two large perogues. This little fleet altho' not quite so respectable as those of Columbus or Capt. Cook, were still viewed by us with as must pleasure as those deservedly famed adventurers ever beheld theirs; and I dare say with quite as much anxiety for their safety and preservation. we were now about to penetrate a country at least two thousand miles in width, on which the foot of civilized man had never trodden; the good or evil it had in store for us was for experiment yet to determine, and these little vessels contained every article by which we were to expect to subsist or defend ourselves. however, as the state of mind in which we are, generally gives the colouring to events, when the imagination is suffered to wander into futurity, the picture which now presented itself to me was a most pleasing one. entertaining as I do, the most confident hope of succeeding in a voyage which had formed a darling project of mine for the last ten years, I could but esteem this moment of my departure as among the most happy of my life."

Living off the buffalo, deer, elk and antelope they shot as they went along, they worked their way upstream past the mouth of the Yellowstone. On their way through the Bad Lands to the Musselshell they shot their first grizzlies and were suitably impressed by the power of these enormous brutes.

June 13 they arrived at the great falls of the Missouri.

Portaging their boats and equipment around the immense stretch of falls and rapids took them three weeks.

July 15 they started up the canyon of the upper Missouri through the mountains westward. Bighorn sheep looked down on them from the cliffs. At a point where three forks joined to make the main river they named one stream the Jefferson, another the Madison and the third one the Gallatin. It was up the Jefferson River that they proceeded. The water was low. It was only with endless labor that they dragged up the canoes over the slippery rocks. They were tortured by boils and intermittent dysentery. Where the Jefferson River forked "we called the bold rapid and clear stream *Wisdom* and the more mild and placid one which flows in from the SE *Philanthropy* in commemoration of two of those cardinal virtues which have so marked that deservedly selibrated character (Thomas Jefferson) through life."

At last Sacajawea recognized a landmark: the Beaver's Head.

Meriwether Lewis made an entry in his journal:

"the Indian woman recognized the point of a high plain to our right which she informed us was not very distant from the summer retreat of her nation on a river beyond the mountains which runs to the west. this hill she says her nation calls the beaver's head from a conceived resemblance of it's figure to the head of that animal. she assures us that we shall either find her people on this river or on the river immediately west of it's source; which from it's present size cannot be distant. as it is now all important with us to meet with those people as soon as possible I determined to proceed tomorrow with a small party to the source of the principal stream of this river and pass the mountains to the Columbia; and down that river until I found the Indians; in short it is my resolution to find them or some others, who have horses if it should cause me a trip of one month. for without horses we shall be obliged to leave a great part of our stores, of which, it appears to me that we have a stock already sufficiently small for the length of the voyage before us."

They sank their boats in a pond and Lewis started overland in search of the continental divide. August 10 he ran into a party of Shoshones. They had dogs and an abundance of horses. He communicated with them through the interpreter Drewyer who knew the sign language. He smoked the pipe of peace with them and managed to buy horses from them.

Now the expedition could ride. With Sacajawea's help they found Indian trails that led them across the bare enormous mountains to settlements of the

Nez Percés. They found a navigable stream flowing towards the Pacific. They lived on dried salmon and a starchy root called camass that was nearly the end of them. Hardly a man could walk from pain in the bowels. They made a long camp where they built their own dugouts Indian fashion. They left their horses with the Nez Percés, buried their saddles in a cache and set out in their new canoes.

They owed their success to their sympathetic understanding of Indian ways and to their willingness to eat dog when they had to.

By the middle of October they were coasting down the swift Snake River. They met on its banks fishing Indians everywhere; Sacajawea's presence reassured them. To get away from the tiresome diet of dried fish they started to eat dog. Horsemeat had been a staple for some time. On the whole expedition it was the fact that they were willing to eat dog that saved them. By the end of October they were navigating the Columbia past peaceable villages where people lived in great board lodges covered with mats.

They entered a region of fogs and caught glimpses of a snowy mountain they surmised to be Mt. Hood. Rain became continual. The green stream of the Columbia was tidal; the water too salty to drink. November 7 Clark reported "Great joy in camp we are in view of the Ocian, this great Pacific Octean which we have been so long anxious to see."

It turned out to be merely a broad reach of river. The seas were too great for further progress by canoe. November 14 Lewis got his first sight of the Pacific. At last on November 18 Clark led his men to a point which Lewis had visited a few days before.

"after dinner to a Small rock island in a deep nitch passed a nitch in which there is a dreen from Some ponds back; the land low opposite this nitch. a bluff of yellow clay and Soft Stone from the river to the commencement of this nitch. below the countrey rises to high hills of about 80 or 90 feet above the water. at 3 miles passed a nitch. this rock Island is Small and at the South of a deep bend in which the nativs inform us the Ships anchor, and from whence they receive their goods in return for their peltries and Elk skins &c. this appears to be a very good harbor for large Ships. here I found Capt. Lewis name on a tree. I also engraved my name, & by land the day of the month and year, as also Several of the men. . . . this cape as also the Shore both on the Bay & Sea coast is a dark brown rock. I crossed the neck of Land low and ½ of a mile wide to the main Ocian, at the foot of a high open hill projecting into the ocian, and about one miles in Si(r)cumfrance. I assended this hill which is covered with high corse grass. decended to the N. of it and camped . . . men appear much Satisfied with their trip beholding with estonishment the high waves dashing against the rocks & this emence Ocian."

They wintered on the Columbia River in a stockade they named Fort Clatsop for a small nearby tribe of the Chinooks. In the middle of March of 1806 they started upriver for home. Again the horses of the Snake Indians were a lifesaver. At twelve noon on September 23 of the same year they were back in St. Louis with the loss of only one man, Sergeant Floyd who died of appendicitis on the first leg of the journey. Lewis and Clark brought back an enormous mass of information about the country the illfated John Ledyard had dreamed of exploring. They carried out Jefferson's instructions to the letter. They satisfied his lifetime aspiration to see a trail blazed across the mountains to the Western Ocean.

A People of Craftsmen
and Mechanics

CHAPTER 3 ☼

R ICH AND POOR MOST AMERICANS WERE BROUGHT UP TO WORK WITH their hands. Isaac, the slave who had been blacksmith at Monticello used to tell in his old age of how happily Mr. Jefferson whistled and sang while he was at work making brass castings at the portable forge he had in his study. A professional silversmith like Paul Revere could turn his hands to almost any craft from engraving plates to the making of false teeth and delicate mathematical instruments.

The words artist and artisan were interchangeable. Many an artisan turned to painting signs and ornamenting coaches in slack periods or to limning portraits or painting overmantels. It was natural that Charles Willson Peale who had started life as a saddler and learned to paint should also become the inventor of mechanical contraptions. From copying and mending old tools to inventing new ones was one short step.

Many of Benjamin Franklin's discoveries in the realm of electricity were made with apparatus he put together himself. As the course of the war tended to concentrate the brains and enthusiasms of the colonies in Philadelphia the country around teemed with craftsmen.

Most important to the survival of Washington's Continentals and of the pioneers who started surging west across the Appalachians even before the war was over were the accurate rifles turned out in Lancaster on the Conestoga road. William Henry, the Lancaster gunsmith who had encouraged young Benjamin West to take up the painting of "History" was one of the first Americans to put his mind to the problem of how to apply the steam pump the English used in their mines to the propulsion of boats. Mechanical invention was in the air Lancaster boys breathed.

Another Lancaster man, of the generation that followed Benjamin West's, became the most eminent example of a painter turned engineer. Robert Fulton was born in the outskirts of that industrious little city during the Stamp Act agitation. His father, a tailor who had taken to farming and failed at it, died while Fulton was still in his smock. From an early age he had to help support his mother. The family managed to get him apprenticed to a jeweller in Philadelphia. This was a step up for a tailor's son.

The slender bright eyed youth proved extremely skillful with his fingers. He became expert in weaving and pleating the designs made out of locks of their loved ones' hair which people liked to wear in lockets and rings. Mourning rings were a profitable item with the jewellers. Sometimes a lock of the hair of the dear departed would be made part of the design of a funerary picture arranged to hang on the wall.

From painting disconsolate figures in Grecian tunics posed beside urns and under weeping willow trees, Fulton took to painting the miniatures that were another part of the jeweller's stock in trade. By the time he was twenty he was listing himself as a miniature painter in the Philadelphia city directory.

By the following year he must have been free of his apprenticeship because in June of 1786 he was advertising a shop of his own:

"Robert Fulton, mineature painter and hair worker, is removed from the northeast corner of Walnut and Second Streets to the west side of Front Street, one door above Pine Street, Philadelphia."

These were Philadelphia's great years as a center of the arts and sciences. Tom Paine had turned his hand from political propaganda to the designing of an iron bridge of girder construction to replace the bridge of boats over the Schuylkill. Franklin was back home. Racked by gout and the pain of the stone that was eventually to carry him off, he had taken up his abode with his daughter and her family at the house he had built for himself years before on Market Street. Regarded with wonder and adoration by his fellow citizens, he had helped his old opponent John Dickinson dispel the frenzied political feuding that had tormented Philadelphia during the war. He served a term as President of Pennsylvania and resumed his presidency of the American Philosophical Society.

David Rittenhouse.

Visitors to the city counted themselves lucky if they caught a glimpse of the old philosopher on some fine afternoon seated among his friends under the mulberry tree in his yard. Foreigners were taken to stare at him. Like Niagara Falls he was one of the wonders of the new nation. Those were fortunate indeed who were invited to his table. Among the chief ornaments of the Wednesday afternoon dinners where he entertained his philosophical friends were amusing Francis Hopkinson, who was writing Jefferson whimsical accounts of the hot air balloons that were getting to be a fad in Philadelphia, and sober Rittenhouse.

The Americans considered Rittenhouse, right after Franklin, as their leading mechanical genius. The same age as Washington, David Rittenhouse was the son of a Mennonite farmer whose elder brother had inherited the first paper mill to be established in the colonies. At an early age he had turned from plowing his father's farm to the more congenial work of carpenter and joiner. The story was told that he had inherited from one of his uncles a chest of tools and a volume of the English version of Newton's *Principia*. Carpentry was too easy. At eighteen he was already building clocks. Meanwhile he read Newton and pondered on the laws of the universe.

His fame in the colonies dated from his construction, all on his own, of what was then known as an orrery, a model of the solar system which showed the motion of the planets and of their moons when you turned a crank. In the course of his mathematical researches Rittenhouse had become friends with Dr. Smith of the College of Philadelphia. When the energetic Dr. Witherspoon, getting wind of the orrery, rode over from Princeton and bought it for three hundred pounds for Nassau Hall, Rittenhouse had to set right to work to produce another for Dr. Smith.

He took up the making of mathematical instruments and joined Dr. Smith in the observations of the transit of Venus across the face of the sun which absorbed the interest of the philosophic world at home and abroad in June of 1769. He became eminent as a surveyor and during the war occupied the arduous post of Treasurer of Pennsylvania. Now in his fifties he was turning his mind to some research in optics which Hopkinson had suggested to him. Though he found lecturing impossible he conducted laboratory experiments for the students in natural philosophy at the college. Recently he had become interested in the plans of a hard-drinking mechanic named John Fitch to move a boat upstream against the current of the Delaware by the use of a steam engine.

This John Fitch was a Connecticut man. He had lived an erratic and wandering life. His mother died when he was tiny. His father had taken him out of school when he was eight to work him on the farm, leaving him—as he put it in his bitter autobiography, "crazy for learning."

Like many an American inventor to come he was spurred on to inventing laborsaving devices by his hatred of the tiresome repetition of chores on the farm. He ran away to sea. He studied a little surveying. Like Rittenhouse he took to building clocks. He married and settled down and for a while operated a brass factory with some success, but a quarrel with his wife set him to wandering again.

He was a successful silversmith for a while in Trenton, New Jersey. During the war he repaired rifles and guns for the New Jersey Committee of Public Safety. When the redcoats destroyed his workshop he followed the army to Valley Forge. As a sutler, selling beer and tobacco to the troops during that terrible winter he collected $40,000 in continental paper which he converted into patents on Western land. When he went out to the Ohio to look over his holdings his keelboat was captured by a band of Indians who were fighting for the British and he found himself interned on an island in the Great Lakes. There with improvised tools he set up a good business making brass buttons for the soldiery.

The coming of peace found him penniless. Like many another American he dreamed of the great fortune that would come to him from his western lands, but he had no way of selling them. He had his living to make. Somehow he hit upon the idea of building a steamboat. He whittled out a model and carried it to Philadelphia to try to interest the philosophers at the college.

Immediately a ruckus broke out between the supporters of Fitch's project, which was to use flat broad paddles attached to an endless chain on either side to drag the boat through the water and the design of a man named James Rumsey who was planning a steamboat to be propelled by a jet of water squirted out of the stern.

James Rumsey was a Marylander who started life as a blacksmith and worked as a millwright and contractor and builder. Sometime towards the end of the war, when the springs in western Virginia began to attract planters from the soggy southern lowlands as health resorts during the "sickly season" of summer, he opened an inn at Berkeley Springs, not far from Cumberland on the Virginia side of the Potomac.

A little boom town grew up at these springs which its promoters were calling Bath in the hope of rivaling the fashion and frenzy of the great English resort. When Washington rode west in 1784 to look over his land holdings and inspect the progress of the Potomac canal he was so much interested in, he stopped at Rumsey's inn. Under injunctions of secrecy Rumsey showed him a model of a twohulled boat which, using the force of the current on a central paddlewheel, poled itself upstream.

Washington was so much impressed by Rumsey's talents that he immediately hired him to put up houses on some lots he had invested in at the springs, and eventually got him appointed chief engineer for his canal. About the same time that Fitch began to appeal to Congress for a patent on his paddlewheel boat, Rumsey, who had scrapped his poles as unwieldy, came out with a plan for jet propulsion activated by a steam pumping engine.

Immediately the Philadelphia philosophers divided into two bands. Franklin and some of his friends favored jet propulsion while Dr. Smith and the professors at the College of Philadelphia favored Fitch's scheme. Long before either craft had proved its worth Fitch and Rumsey and their backers were quarreling about which of them had been the first to invent a steamboat.

During the period of the controversy young Fulton was industriously painting miniatures and portraits in oil at his shop just back of the waterfront where all the longshoremen were agog with Fitch's fireboat. Through his sitters some echoes of the conversations at Franklin's dinner table must have come to his ears. If he stepped into a neighborhood tavern for a mug of ale he may have heard Fitch himself drunkenly declaiming over his grog on the wealth and glory that would come to him as the inventor of the first steamboat.

During the winter before Fulton set up on his own as a painter he had suffered from a hacking cough. His friends told him he was threatened with consumption and packed him off to take the waters at Bath. There if he didn't actually meet Rumsey himself he must have heard talk of Rumsey's mysterious plans for a boat that crawled upstream like a bug.

Robert Fulton was a young man on the make. He was skillful with his hands. He wanted to rise above the artisan level into the world of elegance and wealth where the young ladies whose features he limned and whose locks of hair he pleated into such dainty patterns moved to the rustling of silk and the pad of satin. Somewhere the seeds must have been sowed in his mind that were to germinate years later. The man who invented a steamboat would be famous and rich.

Meanwhile he was doing quite well as a painter. He accumulated friends and patrons. It was taken for granted in Philadelphia society that to establish oneself as an American painter one must go to London to study with Benjamin West. Fulton set to work to save up money for his passage. Friends helped out. In the summer of 1787 he set sail for London with forty guineas in his pocket and a letter of introduction to the most prominent American in England.

1787 was a great year in Philadelphia. The constitutional convention sat all summer behind closed doors at the State House. Fitch's steamboat was launched and ponderously moved, belching smoke, not only downstream but up. He named it the *Perseverance*. One day Fitch took a party of awestruck convention members for a steam around League Island. Later in the fall he invited some of the Supreme Executive Council and a group of professors from the new university which had taken the place of the college to steam up to Bordentown with him.

Andrew Ellicott, the surveyor who laid out l'Enfant's plan for Washington City, was one of the party and so was David Rittenhouse. It was largely due to Rittenhouse's approval that Fitch was able to raise funds to build the new and larger vessel, for which William Thornton, the amateur architect who was soon to win the competition for the national capitol, designed the cabin. By 1790 Fitch's steamboat was making regular trips between Philadelphia and Trenton, carrying passengers at five shillings a head and averaging a speed of seven miles an hour. The coaches made it a little faster. The public failed to patronize the steamboat, the enterprise failed and Fitch died a disappointed drunkard in a frontier tavern in Bardstown, Kentucky.

At West's painting rooms Fulton was received with the unfailing consideration with which the great man met young painters coming to him from America. West found him lodgings, introduced him to the great masters, gave his paintings the same kindly criticism he gave all the others.

During those years so many young men were bringing paintings every morning to seek Benjamin West's nod or frown that rows of benches had to be installed to accommodate them while they waited. For Fulton it was a starving time, but he found friends to lend him money until after four years he managed to get a few pictures hung at the Society of Artists and two at the National Academy.

He found a patron, a peer with a country seat in Devonshire. Orders followed but barely enough to pay his bills. Painting was not to be Robert Fulton's path to fame and fortune.

Canals were building all over England. Engineers were scarce. What engineers there were were interested in steam propulsion as a way of hauling barges through canals. Fulton gave up designing historical paintings with such pathetic subjects as *Mary Queen of Scots in Prison* or *Lady Jane Grey Awaiting Execution* and took to designing canals. All the energy of his mind turned to engineering. Perhaps due to a chance encounter with James Rumsey, who was in London looking for backers for his jet propelled boat, Fulton's mind turned to steamboats.

Fulton was a most likable fellow. Almost overnight he became the fashionable inventor. Benjamin West's painting rooms, as well as a school of painting, were a school of the social graces. They were frequented by the best minds in England as well as by the fashionables who frequented Buckingham House. Fulton found himself friends with Robert Owen and with Dr. Dalton and the poet Coleridge. He moved to Manchester. He corresponded with Pitt's brotherinlaw the mechanical minded Earl of Stanhope. This whole circle of ardent spirits then looked on revolutionary France as the promised land. In 1797 Fulton crossed to France to try to interest the Directory in his projects.

French engineers had been thinking about steamboats longer than the Americans. In the early seventeen seventies a Count d'Auxiron and a Marquis de Follenai had experimented with a steamboat which was sunk by the indignant watermen of the Seine. In 1783, the year before Jefferson arrived in France as American minister, another French noble, a man named Jouffroy, using an Englishtype pumping engine, actually made a steamboat move against the slow current of the Saône.

During the period when Jefferson was first making his acquaintance with the French scientists and philosophers the Parisian Academy of Sciences was torn by the virulent debates the idea of steam navigation aroused wherever it was suggested. He had heard of Rumsey's experiments before leaving the States and wherever he travelled he had his ear cocked for rumors of steam navigation. On his tour of the Midi in the spring of 1787 he visited a steam grist mill at Nîmes under construction by an Abbé d'Arnal, who was also planning a steamboat.

The year before, during his travels around England with John Adams, he had seen a far more successful mill near Blackfriars Bridge in London. Matthew Boulton was just putting the finishing touches on the machinery when Jefferson visited him there.

"I could write you volumes on the improvements that are making here in the arts," Jefferson wrote Charles Thomson a couple of days later. "One deserves particular notice because it is simple, great, and likely to have extensive consequences. it is the application of steam as an agent for working grist mills . . . I hear you are applying this same agent in America to navigate boats . . ."

In spite of the fact that Boulton was enthusiastically a King's man Jefferson must have had much in common with him. It was their mutual friend, Jefferson's beloved teacher William Small, who had brought Boulton the manufacturer into partnership with a fellow Scotsman named James Watt who had ideas about condensing steam. It was out of their collaboration that the first really practical steamengine had come.

When Small, tired of the chills and fevers of Williamsburg and of the hostility which met his efforts to turn William and Mary into a real university on the Scottish pattern, made up his mind to go home to Britain, admiring American friends put him in touch with Benjamin Franklin. Franklin had conducted electrical experiments in Boulton's laboratory. Now pleased as always at the opportunity of bringing two fellow philosophers together, he gave Small a letter to Matthew Boulton.

Matthew Boulton was the son of a silverstamper. He had made money by initiating in Birmingham the manufacture of silver plate, which before his time had been the monopoly of Sheffield. He and Small took an immediate liking to each other. Since Birmingham had recently lost the medical services of a Dr. Roebuck, who had moved to Scotland to set up a plant for manufacturing sulphuric acid, Boulton, who was always trying to get interesting people to settle around him, induced Small to take up the practice of medicine there.

Boulton had just finished building a new plant on his grounds at Soho which was reputed to be the handsomest factory architecturally and the best organized for production in the whole Midlands. He was a pioneer in the use of various types of presses and in assemblyline methods. Already he was stamping out mother of pearl buttons in quantity. Later he was to experiment with the mass production of a onewheeled clock Small had been tinkering with in Williamsburg. His great success in the use of assemblyline methods was to come along after Small was dead, in his invention and installation of new machinery for the London mint.

Jefferson himself had just had his first experience with an experiment of this sort. That winter he had been helping Thomas Barclay, the consul general, make a purchase of muskets for the state of Virginia, and had written Governor Patrick Henry enthusiastically of a new method of fabricating guns with standardized parts: "An improvement is made here in the construction of the musket, which may be worthy of attention. it consists in making every part of them so exactly alike that every part of one may be used for the same part in any other musket made by the same hand. the government here has examined & approved the method, & is establishing a large manufactury for the purpose. as yet the inventor has only completed the lock of the musket on this plan. he will proceed immediately to have the barrel, stock and their parts executed in the same way. I visited the workman. he presented me the parts of 50 locks taken to pieces & arranged in compartments. I put several together myself, taking the pieces at hazard as they came to hand & found them to fit interchangeably in the most perfect manner. the tools by which he effects this have, at the same time, so abridged the labour that he thinks he shall be able to furnish the musket two livres cheaper than the King's price."

Standardization of parts, assemblyline production and mechanical power were indeed the three prerequisites for the industrial epoch about to begin which was to turn topsyturvy so many of the philosophers' preconceptions about the nature of man.

If Jefferson heard anything from Boulton about Dr. Small's last years when he and Boulton met in Paris during the following autumn, there is no trace of it in his surviving letters. As soon as the firm's royalties from the steam engine gave him a little leisure Small's protegé, Watt, now settled in the congenial atmosphere of Birmingham, had turned to exploring the composition of water. It was as one of the discoverers of the fact that water, hitherto considered an "element," was made up of oxygen and hydrogen, that he was received by Lavoisier and his friends at the Academy of Science in Paris. He and Boulton had been invited to France by the royal government on the pretext of modernizing the elaborate system of pumps that provided Versailles with water, known as *la Machine de Marly*. The French seem to have hoped they could be induced to set up a plant there to build steam engines. Although their conversations with French scientists, at one of which at least Jefferson was present, were cordial and frank, no manufactory was established.

Boulton and Watt went home without accomplishing anything. When Watt did look over the pumps and waterwheels at Marly, the complication and extravagance of the mechanism filled the frugal Scot with horror. He wrote a friend that the Machine ought to be considered a national disgrace rather than a wonder of the world and that he'd left about four hundred recommendations for improvements, but that he doubted very much whether anything would come of them.

Watt and Boulton, however much their imagination was stimulated by the progress of theoretical chemistry in France, went home to Birmingham more convinced than ever that Great Britain would lead the world in the practical application to industry of machine production.

Jefferson of course believed the same thing. He never tired of exclaiming over the perfection of the mechanical arts as he had seen them in England. It was the consequent stratification of society that filled him with foreboding. He early understood the price the people of Britain would have to pay for their primacy in manufacturing during the century to come.

Jefferson all his life was of two minds in relation to the inventions that were ushering in the era of mass production. An inventor himself—his mouldboard for a plow was the first designed according to mathematical principles—he felt the greatest enthusiasm for labor-saving devices. As a statesman he dreaded the effect on republican institutions of the mass society he saw developing in consequence of their application to manufacturing.

During his strifetorn years as Secretary of State to the new Federal administration in New York and Philadelphia the part of his multifarious duties he most enjoyed was the granting of patents. It was during these years that an enterprising Providence merchant named Moses Brown set up his textile mill at Pawtucket. In spite of all the efforts of King George's government to prohibit the export of the plans for new inventions a young mechanic who had worked in Arkwright's famous mill in England managed to smuggle himself aboard a ship bound for New York. He had no need to smuggle out any plans because he carried the whole elaborate machinery, by which Arkwright wove cloth in one continuous process, in his head. Moses Brown pounced on him and before long the two of them had duplicated Arkwright's looms in Rhode Island. All that was needed now for the setting up of a great textile industry was a convenient way of cleaning the cotton. One of Jefferson's last acts before resigning as Secretary of State was to write Eli Whitney, congratulating him on his plans for a cotton gin. He added that as a private citizen he wanted to order one of Whitney's gins to work on his own plantation.

A few years later Whitney invested his earnings from the cotton gin in a plant at Mill Rock, Connecticut, for the assembly line production of muskets for the Federal government, according to a plan very similar to that which Jefferson had described to Thomson years before.

Though Jefferson abhorred the idea of setting up manufactures in America he was entranced by canals. It was canals that would link the Potomac, which he and Washington hoped to see become the main artery of American commerce, with the Ohio and the "Western waters." Sail was notoriously inefficient on canals. Mules and oxen were slow. If a steam engine could provide the motive power the opening up of the Western country would be assured. When James Rumsey arrived in France looking for a French patent on his steamboat, Jefferson did everything he could to help him.

When Jefferson packed up to take his daughters home to Virginia he left Rumsey's negotiations with the French Academy and his steamboat in the hands of his good friend Joel Barlow whom Rumsey described as "a steady clever man." That is how it happened that when Fulton and Barlow met after Rumsey returned to England Barlow's head was already full of steamboats.

White's Hotel was still the center for Americans in Paris. It was at White's that Joel and Ruth Barlow and Robert Fulton met for the first time. The Barlows were entering their prosperous years. They had moved out of their apartment on the rue du Bac and were staying for a time at White's while they looked around for a comfortable house that had a garden. When they met the lanky curlyheaded young Pennsylvanian they both immediately fell in love with him.

He fascinated Joel with talk of his devices for putting barges through locks. He had worked out a system for moving canalboats up and down on inclined planes. Besides his canals he had plans for a weaving machine and a marble cutting machine and for a boat to be propelled by steam and for a submarine for the defense of blockaded harbors.

Every afternoon he was getting himself drenched trying out on the placid green Seine an underwater torpedo that would blow up enemy warships. He was a lively plausible sanguine fellow, remarkably goodlooking. He and the Barlows hit it off immediately.

When Joel and Ruth went to live in their roomy new house with its acre of garden on rue Vaugirard, out near the Invalides, Fulton went to live with them and for the next seven years that followed he was a member of the family. For some reason they called him "Toot."

Toot was full of ideas on every subject under the sun. With Barlow's help he took to studying languages and higher mathematics and physics to remedy his

Meriwether Lewis by St. Memin.

William Clark, the highspirited Billy of the expedition's records.

Rittenhouse's orrery.

Model of Fitch's steamboat.

Matthew Boulton.

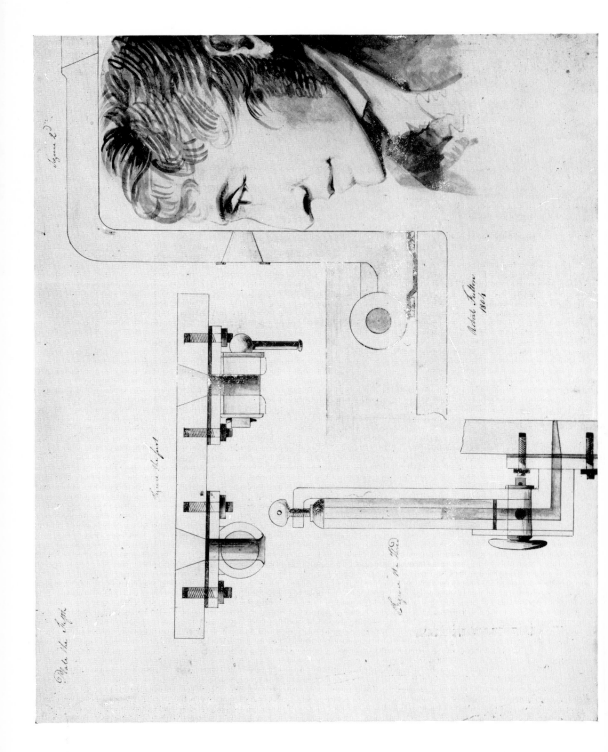

Fulton's "plunging boat" the Nautilus.

Oliver Evans.

Fulton's first steamboat.

The Port of Charleston in the early steamboat era.

Horatio Gates whose career in the Revolutionary War had been a series of rankling frustrations, at last had his brief hour.

Benjamin Franklin carved in wood by William Rush.

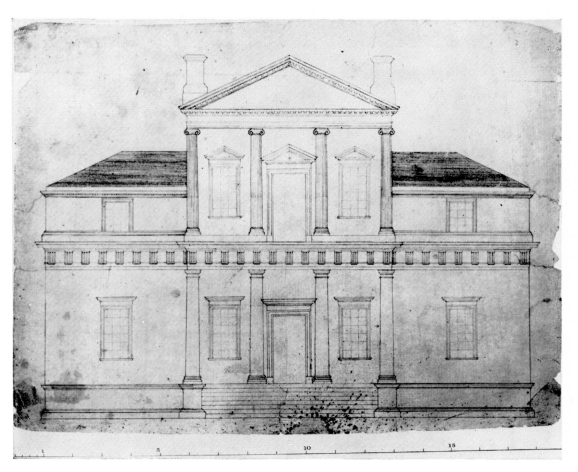

Jefferson's first plan for Monticello—front elevation.

Jefferson's Virginia State Capitol, a water color by Benjamin Latrobe.

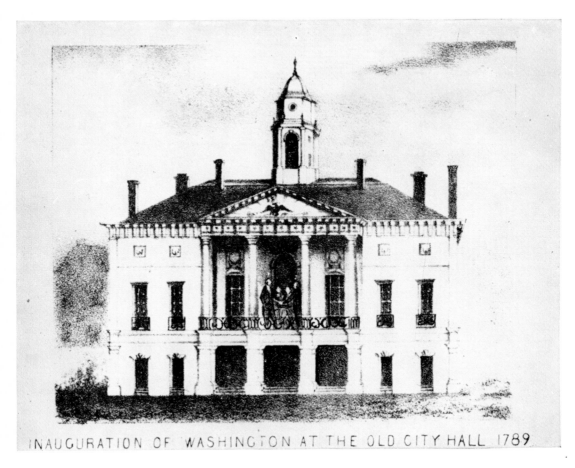

INAUGURATION OF WASHINGTON AT THE OLD CITY HALL 1789

L'Enfant's Remodelled Federal Hall.

Annapolis.

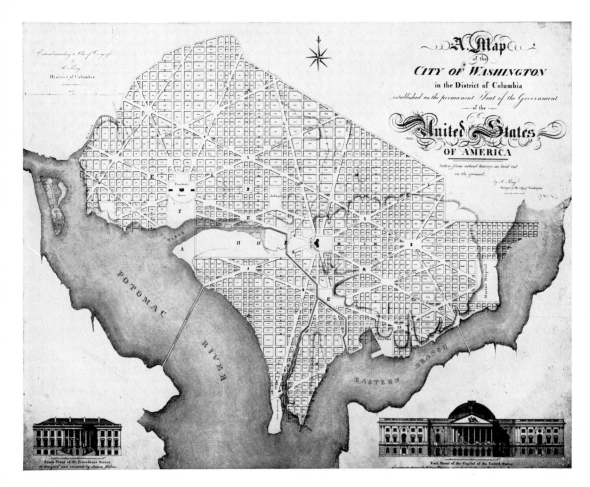

L'Enfant's plan of Washington, D.C.

Dr. William Thornton by St. Memin.

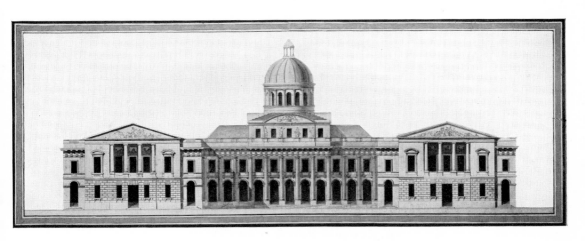

Hallet's elevation for the Capitol facade.

*Benjamin Latrobe who became Jefferson's most con-
genial collaborator in the building of Washington City.*

Latrobe's realization of his dream.

The White House and St. John's Church as Latrobe and Jefferson left them.

almost total lack of education. When war between England and France started up again, Toot's canals were laid on the shelf and he began putting all his time in on his submarine. Since Bushnell's attempt on a British battleship in the Hudson River in '76 with a turtleshaped contraption that he propelled with a scull underwater it had been a Yankee notion that something could be done for harbor defense with a submarine boat.

With Barlow's help, and his advice, and his money, and his introductions to officials, Toot worked out a submarine that really dived. What eventually stopped him was that there was no really efficient method existing at the time for propelling it. It was built of wood, and driven through the water by a screw on the stern which was turned by a crank inside. On the surface it sailed like a catboat. He called it a plunging boat and named it the *Nautilus*.

He tried the first seventyfoot model out on the Seine between the bridges in Paris, and the next year at Havre managed with his fullsized model to go some hundred yards underwater, to turn around and to return to his starting point. The French navy became interested and let him blow up a sloop in the harbor of Brest the following summer with a submarine bomb planted by his plunging boat.

The Barlows were as worried as a hen that's hatched out ducklings when Toot blithely entered into a contract with the French to blow up a British manofwar for them. Toot actually went out hunting for a Britisher along the coast of Brittany, but the *Nautilus* was too slow to catch up with one, probably very fortunately for Toot. When he found he couldn't go further with his submarine he started to work in earnest on drawings and specifications for a boat to be propelled by steam along the surface.

Meanwhile he helped out Barlow with a suggestion of how to use some lots he had acquired an interest in near the boulevard Montmartre. In England, Toot had visited a circular painting of a view of London that people were paying admission to see. Some Scotchman had rigged it up and called it a panorama. So Toot set to work to put up a circular building on Barlow's lot and to paint a *Burning of Moscow* on it. It was only moderately successful as a moneymaker, but later, with some other enterprising Americans, they added a second panorama, this time of the Battle of Tilsit. The battlepiece was a hit and thereafter panoramas of notable events were one of the typical shows of the Paris boulevards. In his spare time Fulton made sketches for illustrating the edition Barlow had in project of a new version of *The Vision of Columbus* that he was going to call *The Columbiad*.

The Barlows and Toot Fulton lived comfortably together in the big house on the rue Vaugirard. Joel had his library and Toot his studio and workshop. They grew their own vegetables and their strawberries and raspberries and peaches in the garden. They had breakfast parties out under the trees in good weather and big cheerful dinners in the stately diningroom the Barlows never could quite manage to finish furnishing.

Without taking part in it, they watched the transformation of France. As Bonaparte's military victories bowled over the ancient regime in one country after another, the Republic One and Indivisible became the broodhen of a nest of subordinate republics. As the republics multiplied, order and property beeame the watchword.

The rights of man were forgotten. After Hoche's death, Bonaparte became the pillar of order. By this time Joel Barlow, watching the astonishing Abbé Sieyès, like a magician at a children's party, bringing each time he was asked a new and odder constitution out of his hat, had decided that the republic had never been a republic at all.

In a series of transformation scenes, as lurid as Toot Fulton's panoramas, the Convention had given way to the Directory, the Directory to the Consulate, the Consulate to the Empire; and suddenly France was back in the vigorous authoritarian mood of Louis Quatorze and Richelieu. It was a far cry from the Revolution of the World.

Though his heart revolted at the new order, Barlow couldn't help enjoying its benefits. After Bonaparte's whiff of grapeshot, Barlow's investments in French funds rose in value more than enough to make up for the money he lost in his shipping speculations by putting too much good-natured confidence in other men. With Napoleon's every new infringement of the Rights of Man, Barlow's *rentes* rose in cash value.

He had his own traveling carriage now, with a pair of neat white horses. Ruth, whose illhealth was the only shadow on their happiness in these prosperous years, kept touring the wateringplaces. When Joel couldn't go on account of business in Paris, Toot, who lived with them in perfect confidence like a younger brother, was her cavalier. It was when he went with Ruth to Plombières in the summer of 1802 that in a little stream he dammed up for the purpose he finished his experiments with a clockwork model of the paddlewheeldriven steamboat which later became the *Clermont*.

When Joel Barlow finally arrived in Washington City to take up his residence it was with his portmanteau full of the great projects that he and Toot Fulton had been working out in their spare time. The new capital must have a national university that should be the center of a national educational system. It should include a school of mines, a school of roads and bridges, a conservatory of art, a national library and museum of painting and sculpture, a military school,

a mint, a veterinary college, an observatory. Washington must be the center of a
network of national highways and canals linking all the rivers.

Steamboats were on everybody's mind. Without steamboats the American
states could never take advantage of their enormous network of inland waterways.
On the Hudson they were experimenting with steam ferries. A couple of years
before the Barlows settled at Kalorama, a Delaware millwright named Oliver Evans,
who had long been operating an automatic flour mill, had set up a plant in Philadelphia to build steamengines. He had been besieging Congress for patents for
all sorts of devices: a boiler for distilling water, a plant for making ice, a machine
that spun steel wire, an early bulldozer to level roads. For the townfathers of

Oruktor Amphibolos.

Philadelphia in 1804 he produced a steam dredge to clean silt out of the city docks.
This dredge was propelled by a paddlewheel. To get it down from his foundry
to the river he mounted the thirtyfoot barge on wheels which he turned by a
flywheel from his steam engine. He entertained the inhabitants of Philadelphia for
several days by driving the world's first amphibian around the circle which surrounded their fine new waterworks before heading it for the river. There it was
floated off the wheels and their carriage to operate successfully as a dredge. Being
somewhat of a publicist as well as an inventor he gave his contraption the re-
sounding name of Oructor Amphibobos.

All the elements that would produce a successful steamboat were ready at
hand for American mechanics and boatbuilders. A man was needed with the
necessary combination of skills to weld them into a successful commercial en-

terprise. This man turned out to be Joel and Ruth's dear Toot.

Fulton had stayed on in England to sell his torpedo to the British and to super-intend the building of an engine for his steamboat by Boulton and Watt. In September 1806, he wrote Joel from London: "My situation now is, my hands are free to burn, sink, and destroy whom I please, and I shall now seriously set about giving liberty to the seas by publishing my system of attack. I have, or will have when Parker sends me my two thousand pounds, 500 sterling a year, with a steam-engine and pictures worth two thousand pounds. Therefore I am not in a state to be pitied. I am now busy winding up everything, and will leave London about the 3rd inst. for Falmouth, from whence I shall sail in the packet the first week in October, and be with you, I hope, in November, perhaps about the 14th, my birthday, so you must have a roast goose ready . . . I have made out a complete set of drawings and descriptions of my whole system of sub-marine attack, and another set of drawings with description of the steamboat. These, with my will, I shall put in a tin cylinder, sealed, and leave them in the care of General Lyman, not to be opened unless I am lost. Should such an event happen I have left you the means to publish these works, with engravings, in a handsome manner, and to which you will add your own ideas—showing how the liberty of the seas may be gained by such means, and with such liberty, the immense advantages to America and civilization: you will also show the necessity of perfecting and establishing the steamboat and canals on the inclined plane prin-ciple. I have sent you three hundred complete sets of prints (of Fulton's drawings for *The Columbiad*) by the *Orb* directed to Mr. Tolman, New York, value £30 . . . How shall we manage this winter, as you must be in Philadelphia for the printing, and I want to be at New York to build my boat? I am in excellent health, never better, and in good spirits. You know I cannot exist without a project or projects, and I have two or three of the first order of sublimity . . . Mr. West has been retouching my pictures, they are charming."

Fulton had managed to induce Boulton and Watt to build him a steam-engine that fitted his specifications, and after all sorts of difficulties had ob-tained permission from the British government to ship it to America. It was Joel Barlow who doped out the shape of the boiler. He took a patent out for it in Paris. Robert R. Livingston, the American minister, had put in the capital, and whatever he had learned from his experience with Nicholas Roosevelt's not too successful venture on the Hudson. Toot was certain he would succeed where poor old Fitch in Philadelphia and Rumsey on the Potomac and all the others had failed. He had worked everything out with scale models and could even predict the speed of his steamboat. As soon as he arrived in New York he set to work getting the hull constructed. The boat was eventually named the *Clermont* after Robert R. Livingston's place up the Hudson.

On August 17, 1807, the paddlewheels started churning the water of the North River at a dock near the state's prison, and, after only one false start, the steamboat clanking and puffing, with a somewhat worried group of friends on board feeling under their feet the strange vibration of the afterdeck, moved smoothly out into the stream.

Toot wrote Barlow, who had settled down, he thought forever at Kalorama: ". . . My steamboat voyage to Albany and back has turned out rather more favorably than I had calculated. The distance from New York to Albany is one hundred and fifty miles. I ran it up in thirty-two hours and down in thirty. I had a light breeze against me the whole way, both going and coming, and the voyage has been performed wholly by the power of the steam-engine. I overtook many sloops and schooners beating to windward and parted with them as if they had been at anchor . . ."

Going through the narrow reaches under Storm King through the mountains the passengers joined in singing *Ye Banks an' Braes o' Bonny Doon*. At another point of the journey Livingston, in the highest spirits, announced Robert Fulton's engagement to his young cousin Harriet. Toot Fulton had made good. He was marrying into one of the great families of New York.

Later that fall the *Clermont* was somewhat rebuilt and put into regular service as a packet up the river, and renamed the *North River*. The *Paragon* a new and bigger steamboat with more passenger accommodations went on the ways immediately. *Neptune's Car* followed and several bluntend steamferries and later, when the war with England began, Fulton designed and built a huge twinhulled floating battery or steam frigate named the *Demologos* or, more popularly, *Fulton the First*. The Fultons settled down to raise a family on a fine estate up the Hudson. Their first boy they named Barlow.

Toot Fulton was in the chips. One of the first things he did with his money was to publish, using engravings he had made in France from the paintings the great Benjamin West had condescended to retouch, a handsome edition of his friend Barlow's *Columbiad*. With all his soul he agreed with the poet's explanation of his aims in the introduction:

"My object is altogether of a moral and political nature. I wish to encourage and strengthen in the rising generation, the sense of the importance of republican institutions."

Both of them had turned their backs on Europe. Fulton had come to believe that his steamboats and his submarines in American hands would establish forever the freedom of the seas which would eventually make possible such a Republic of the World as the philosophers dreamed would usher in those "prospects of a golden age" inaugurated by the great principles of the Declaration of Independence. Like most of the inventors and engineers of his day he believed that

the age of steam would make possible some eventual Parliament of Man fore-
shadowed by Barlow's lines:

> Where system'd realms their mutual glories lend
> And well taught sires the cares of state attend;
> Through every maze of man they learn to wind,
> Note each device that prompts the Proteus mind:
> What soft restraints the temper'd breast requires
> To taste new joys and cherish new desires,
> Expand the selfish to the social flame,
> And rear the soul to deeds of nobler fame.
>
> But now no more the patriotic mind
> To narrow views and local laws confin'd
> 'Gainst neighboring lands directs the public rage,
> Plods for a clan, or counsels for an age;
> But soars to loftier thought and reaches far
> Beyond the power, beyond the wish of war;
> For realms and ages forms the general aim,
> Makes patriot views and moral views the same,
> Works with enlightened zeal to see combin'd
> The strength and happiness of humankind.

The Prison Ship, *one of the illustrations for the Columbiad on which Fulton lavished so much care and which Benjamin West generously retouched.*

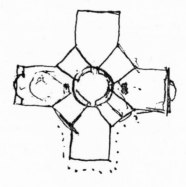 

Jefferson's rough sketch for the projected Capitol.

A People of Builders

CHAPTER 4

THOMAS JEFFERSON USED TO SAY THAT HE CONSIDERED ARCHITEC-
ture the most important of the arts "because it showed so
much." Jefferson was responsible, more than any other single man, for the introduction into America of the Greek Revival style. As the statebuilders searched the
histories of the Greek and Roman republics for models for their institutions, the
architects studied the classical forms rediscovered by Winckelmann and his school
of Roman archaeologists. They wanted to put up dwelling houses and public
buildings that would express the ambitions for human dignity and social order
which Barlow was expressing in his couplets. For them the style of the Greek
Revival stood for those "prospects of a golden age" on which they had set their
hopes for mankind.

Jefferson became one of the leading architects of his day. His influence did
a great deal to form the architectural ideas of men like Thornton and Latrobe and
Mills. In all his designs, from his forgotten work at Williamsburg to the final

establishment of a distinctive style in the University of Virginia he sought always proportions that would enhance the human figure.

His mind was already full of plans for building when, in the summer of the repeal of the Stamp Act he took time off from his law studies to drive to Philadelphia in a two wheel chair. The pretext was to get himself inoculated against smallpox. An eager curious young man, he wanted to see the world. In his pocket he carried a letter from his friend Dr. Gilmer to Dr. John Morgan, a Philadelphia physician freshly arrived from Europe.

A Palladian Villa.

Dr. Morgan was just the man Jefferson needed to put him in touch with everything and everybody. The young physician, already among Philadelphia's best known, had travelled to England armed with that indispensable letter from Dr. Franklin. After some study under Dr. Fothergill in London, he had moved on to Edinburgh. There he had followed the lectures of James Watt's scientific patron, Joseph Black, on physics, and won his degree with a thesis on the nature and formation of pus which remains one of the few medical works of the time not to be later discredited.

"Laureated" by the town fathers of Edinburgh he crossed to the continent for the grand tour. In Rome he visited the museums and antiquities and made careful notes which survive with a fragment of his journal to this day. He met Angelica Kauffmann, and all the cognoscenti of Winckelmann's group. Dr. Morgan treated "Miss Angel" for some ailment and in return she not only presented him with her portrait but painted his.

As full of enthusiasm for painting and architecture as for medicine, he collected paintings as he travelled, bought copies of Titians and Veroneses and drawings attributed to the great masters and jotted down what he was told about the architectural proportions of the colonnades and the rules of fenestration. On his way north from Padua he went to Vicenza, visited Palladio's palaces, marveled at his triumphal arch and at his magnificent reproduction in wood of a Roman theatre. He procured, so he noted, "a pretty exact plate" of Palladio's theatre.

Dr. Morgan arrived home bursting with the beauty of classical ruins. "As to the grandeur of the ancients," he had written Dr. Cullen from Italy, "from what we can see of their remains, it is most extraordinary. Arts with them seem to have been in a perfection which I could not have imagined. Their palaces, temples, aqueducts, baths, theatres, amphitheatres, monuments, statues, sculptures were most amazing. The soul is struck at the review, and the ideas expand."

He settled in a fine house and unpacked his collection of paintings and,—what must have been particularly interesting to Jefferson—, his architectural drawings which included a temple façade by Mansart, and a plan of a country house; and his curiosities of interest to natural philosophers: geological specimens, a piece of Bologna phosphorus, marbles and petrifications of various types, a stone in the form of an ear, a specimen glass eye and a hair ball from the stomach of a cow. A story persisted in his family that he brought home the first umbrella ever seen in Philadelphia.

As he visited Dr. Morgan's collections undoubtedly Jefferson's "soul was struck and his ideas expanded" by this fresh glimpse into the European world of fashion and science and elegance and evolving thought he had first seen through the eyes of the great Dr. Small in Williamsburg. Morgan's talk of the marvels of the antique background must have stirred up all Jefferson's longings to travel abroad. With the family at Shadwell dependent on his management of the estates, and his way to make as a lawyer, that was now out of the question. The notion may have started sprouting in his mind that here in America, on the shaggy hills of his own Virginia, a civilization could be built, new, separate and superior. This was the aim to which, more explicitly than any other man of his generation, he was to dedicate his life.

A civilization meant a setting. Man's setting was architecture. Through Richard Taliaferro, his friend George Wythe's fatherinlaw, he was already familiar with some of the builders' manuals so much in use at the time. As early as the summer of 1763 his thoughts had turned to building himself a house of his own in Williamsburg. "No castle, though, I assure you," he wrote his college friend John Page, "only a small house which shall contain a room for myself and another for you."

As soon as Jefferson returned home from his trip up the coast he started to build himself a house. He was already steeped in Palladio when he designed the first version of Monticello. It was typical of his radical and personal approach to everything he handled that he immediately worked his way through the superficially fashionable elements of English palladianism and came to grips with the basic problem.

He wanted a manor house which would afford airy rooms and plenty of windows through which to look out on the big Virginia hills and the blue plain that moved him as much as music. He wanted a manor house which would combine under one roof the barns, storehouses, harnessrooms, butteries, pantries, kitchens, toolsheds, stables and carriagehouses that were essential to the functioning of a plantation.

Palladio's villas were a combination of dwelling house and barn. "There must be proper covers made for everything belonging to the *Villa* in proportion to the product of the Ground and the number of Cattle and contiguous to the main house," wrote the sixteenth century Italian (this is Leoni's translation), "that the Master may easily go everywhere sheltered, without being hindered from minding his business by either Snow or Rain or the scorching heat of the Sun. This will serve also to shelter the Wood and other numberless country provisions, which too much moisture of the Air, or the heat will spoil: besides that such Piazzas will make the Building look much greater."

When the style was adapted for the British noblemen (of whom Jefferson's schoolmaster Maury had written that their vast annual revenue ranked them with, "nay set them above many, who, in other countries, claim the royal Style and Title") the practical features that attracted the frugal Italians were forgotten.

Jefferson's design for Monticello went back to Palladio's practical villa; which was essentially a farmhouse flanked by sheds, and by skillful use of his hilltop managed to go Palladio one better by establishing the working part of the building in the wings built into the hill and lighted by loggias which could be used to shelter his equipment. Their roof he used as a terrace from which to enjoy his unobstructed view.

Thus Monticello embodied in its structure the basic plan of his life, and of the lives he wanted for his friends and neighbors: a combination of practical American management of plantations large or small with the freedom enjoyed by the British noble which warranted (to quote again from schoolmaster Maury's letter) "his indulging himself in the Enjoyment of that calm Retreat from the Bustle of the World, of that studious Leisure & philosophical Repose which furnish him with the happiest of Opportunities, not barely of making transient visits to, but even of fixing his Residence, within those sacred Recesses, sequestered Seats & classic Grounds which are the Muses' favorite Haunts."

Jefferson threw into the building of Monticello all his capacity for original planning and for meticulously detailed work. Whether or not he had already designed the porches at Shirley and the Randolph-Semple house at Williamsburg as Waterman suggests in his *Mansions of Virginia*, by the time he tackled the plan for the first version of Monticello he was enough of an architect to make innovations in his own right.

The war, public service, his beloved wife's death, the difficulties of a widower trying to raise a brood of small girls—everything took Jefferson's mind off architecture during the stormy decade that followed. It wasn't until he was established in Paris as American minister that he found the leisure to study the art "that showed so much."

Outside of the diplomatic grind, he had been entrusted with two commissions which gave him real pleasure to execute. One was to find a sculptor worthy of carving a statue of Washington and the other was to furnish the state of Virginia with plans for a new capitol.

For the sculptor he immediately picked Houdon whose seated figure of Voltaire was already famous. Houdon at fortyfour was undoubtedly the best sculptor in Europe. He had won the grand prize at the Beaux Arts at eighteen and hurried off to Rome and Winckelmann. After ten years of studying fragments of Roman copies of Greek fragments, through which artists were beginning to reimagine the cool purity of the Attic style, Houdon carved a Diana so thinly draped that she caused great scandal when she was exhibited at a salon in the Louvre. Catherine of Russia, who was the patron of the avant garde arts of the time, carried the naked lady off to St. Petersburg. As a result Houdon found himself with orders from all the "enlightened" European courts.

When Jefferson went to see him he consented to leave the statues of kings unfinished and to make the hazardous voyage to America to do a head of the greatest man of the age. They agreed it was absurd to try to work from a portrait when the original was at hand at Mt. Vernon.

A certain amount of republicanism already went along with a taste for the Hellenic. Attracted by George Washington's glory Houdon agreed to do a bust for considerably less than he charged royalty, but insisted that his life must be insured at ten thousand livres for the benefit of his family in case he perished on the Atlantic. For Houdon the professional attraction of the trip was that beyond the bust he hoped to win the commission for an equestrian statue of Washington which Congress had voted. He was taken ill when the time came for him to sail, but Jefferson finally managed to pack him and a couple of his workmen off on the same ship with Dr. Franklin, who, finally released from his embassy, was being conveyed to Havre, amid the blessings and bon voyages of all France, in a royal litter.

In the execution of his second commission for the state of Virginia, Jefferson found himself embarked on the full current of the same classical revival which had helped clear Houdon's style of baroque angularities during the years he studied in Rome. Ever since Jefferson had drawn up the first bill for the removal of the Virginia capital from Williamsburg to Richmond he had been exercised about what sort of buildings would be constructed there. He had slipped into his bill the clause which he hoped he could turn into something new and fine: "said houses shall be built in a handsome manner with walls of Brick and Porticos, where the same may be convenient or ornamental."

At some early date he had already been experimenting with a tentative sketch of a plan to transform the governor's palace in Williamsburg into a temple-form building with columns in front and back. From the moment he first opened a copy of Leoni's *Palladio* he must have been taken with Palladio's drawings and measurements of the Maison Quarrée (he always followed Palladio's spelling of the French "*carrée*") at Nîmes.

As Jefferson pondered an architecture which would express the essence of the young republic his mind settled more and more on the Maison Carrée. Now in Paris he discovered a man who had recently published a set of drawings of the Augustan temple even more carefully measured than Palladio's had been.

Charles Louis Clérisseau was dean of the academy of painting and sculpture which had its seat in a set of apartments in the Louvre. He had returned from Rome after years of study. Under Winckelmann's influence he had measured the ruins at Nîmes, and crossed the Adriatic to Spalato on the Dalmatian coast to sketch Diocletian's gigantic palace there.

On this expedition Clérisseau took with him a young Scot named Robert Adam, the son of the William Adam, also an architect, whose *Vitruvius Scoticus* had simplified the palladian villas for the benefit of the short purses of the Scottish lairds. Robert Adam and his brother, who had followed him to Italy, went back to Britain with their heads full of the delicate tracery of Pompeiian decoration, and became the fashionable designers and decorators of the period. They put their stamp so effectively on the English taste of the time that it is hard to think of the later Georgian except as the Adam style: the style of the Adelphi, the brothers liked to call it.

The capitol at Richmond planted this classical revival in the New World. Both in England and America, and in Russia too, the style in its various forms stemmed directly from Clérisseau's album of archaeological drawings.

When Jefferson went around to Clérisseau's studio, soon after arriving in Paris, the elegance and balanced strength of the Greek temple form burst on him anew. Immediately he bought Clérisseau's book on Nîmes, and engravings of Baalbec and Palmyra, and of the mighty temples at Paestum which architects were barely beginning to look upon with favor.

At Clérisseau's for the first time, Jefferson found himself with the resources of a proper architect's drafting room. Modelers and draftsmen were ready to put his amateur's improvised sketches into a form usable by a contractor. He learned to work with a hard pencil. Henceforth his architectural drawings had a professional air. He bought enough coordinated paper in Paris to last him most of his life. In Clérisseau's portfolios he could thumb through pictures of about everything that had been so far unearthed of the Greek and Roman heritage. He kept coming back to the Maison Carrée.

He was choosing Roman architecture at the moment when it was nearest to Greek. "We took for our model," he wrote Madison of Montpelier, "what is called the Maison Quarrée of Nîmes, one of the most beautiful if not the most beautiful & precious morsel of architecture left to us by antiquity. it was built by Caius & Lucius Caesar, & repaired by Louis XIV & has the suffrage of all the judges of architecture who have seen it, as yielding to no one of the beautiful monuments of Greece, Rome, Palmyra, & Balbec, which late travellers have communicated to us. it is very simple, but it is noble beyond expression, & would have done honor to our country, as presenting to travellers a specimen of taste in our infancy, promising much for our maturer age."

"Would have," he wrote, in the past tense, because he had received the news that the undertakers appointed by the Assembly were already laying the foundations for a capitol and was afraid that they would go ahead with the building without waiting for his plans which Clérisseau's draftsmen were at that moment drawing up.

Clérisseau seems to have been surprised and delighted to find in this tall angular envoy from the Virginia mountains "un vrai amateur de l'antiquité." He furnished the archaeological information, but the plan was essentially Jefferson's. For simplicity, or perhaps because he despaired of getting Corinthian capitals properly executed in America, he changed the order of the porch to Ionic and thereby helped give the whole school of architecture which was to follow in the United States its distinctively Ionic flavor. He designed the interior chambers for the House and Senate and the conference room between, which the constitution called for. The arrangement of the windows was Jefferson's, and it was he who insisted, against the Frenchman's advice, on following exactly the proportions indicated by Clérisseau's own measurements of the actual temple at Nîmes.

It is likely that Clérisseau sketched a good deal of the decorative detail. His draftsmen polished up Jefferson's drawings, and to make sure the undertakers in Virginia wouldn't go wrong they made a scale model in plaster, which is still preserved in the now very much transformed state capitol in Richmond.

The drawings and the model were finally shipped off to Monroe in Virginia, who was urged to make sure they were executed even if it meant tearing down some of the work already done. "Do my dear friend exert yourself to get the plan begun on set aside," Jefferson wrote Madison, "& that adopted which was drawn here. it was taken from a model which has been the admiration of sixteen centuries; which has been the object of as many pilgrimages as the tomb of Mahomet; which will give unrivalled honor to our State, & furnish a model whereon to form the taste of our young men."

Jefferson never quite admitted that he was the author of this first adaptation of the classical temple form to modern uses. He tried to give the impression that he had merely made suggestions to an established European architect who had drawn up the plan. Patrick Henry was governor of Virginia, and although their correspondence was polite, rightly or wrongly Jefferson suspected that the "great whale" and his friends would oppose any project of his just because it was his. Then too he feared the Assembly would be suspicious of so novel a building if it came from a fellow Virginian.

He had reason to be uneasy because he was far in advance of the taste of his time. His design anticipated Napoleon's rebuilding of the Madeleine by twenty-two years. Although there had been small models of temples on the great English estates, as in the gardens at Stowe, the temple form was not put to practical use in England until well along in the nineteenth century. In America the capitol at Richmond became the prototype from which developed the style of the early republic.

In spite of the efforts of Madison and Monroe Jefferson's original plan was changed by the commissioners in charge of construction. The pitch of the roof was altered, a bastard type of Ionic capital was used on the porch, the fluting was left off the columns and three ugly windows were put in the pediment to give light to the attic. Even so, in its essence the transformed temple remains to this day as Jefferson planned it. From Latrobe's watercolor of Richmond in 1796 you can get an inkling of how elegantly the capitol with its high white porch stood guard on its hill over the clapboard houses and the log huts and the shanties and rattletrap fences of the raw little town at the falls of the James. Monsieur Clérisseau could never have guessed how admirably, translated into wood in the years to come, the Ionic style would express the civic dignity of the republican frontier.

When Jefferson returned from Europe in 1789 his plan was, after settling his daughters with their cousins and aunts, to sail back to France to see what he was looking forward to as the glorious accomplishment of a moderate revolution. Before that he hoped to steal a little time for rebuilding Monticello somewhat on the plan of the hôtel de Salm he had so admired in Paris.

From his brotherinlaw's home at Eppington he wrote his friend Short whom he had left in charge in Paris, to describe the new buildings at Richmond. Way's new bridge across the James, carried on pontoons and boats, was twenty-two hundred feet long; the locks on the Westham canal were completed. "Our new capitol, when the corrections are made, of which it is susceptible, will be an edifice of first rate dignity, whenever it shall be finished with the proper ornaments belonging to it (which will not be in this age) will be worthy of being exhibited along side the most celebrated remains of antiquity. it's extreme convenience has acquired it universal approbation," he added with understandable pride. It was stirring to see that the building he had worked so hard on had already taken form in stone and mortar. "There is one street in Richmond," he added, "(from the bridge straight on towards Currie's) which would be considered as handsomely built in any city of Europe."

When instead of returning to Paris Jefferson accepted the post of Secretary of State he found Congress sitting in New York in l'Enfant's remodelling of the old State House. The adventurous Frenchman's adaptation of the Louis Seize styles of his native Versailles to the American scene for Federal Hall, as it was called, was to be the forerunner of one trend in American building, as Jefferson's Richmond capitol was the forerunner of another. In Washington City both styles were to fuse.

Though Jefferson's political differences with George Washington multiplied as the years went on the two men found it easy to agree on one subject. That was in the establishment of a capital city below the falls of the Potomac.

As early as his term in the Continental Congress just before he went to France, Jefferson had argued in favor of a federal capital on one of the waterways flowing into the Chesapeake. As soon as he joined Washington's administration he went to work with the same end in view. June 20, 1790, he was writing Monroe: "It is proposed to pass an act fixing the temporary residence of 12 or 15 years at Philadelphia, and that at the end of that time it shall stand *ipso facto* & without further declaration transferred to Georgetown. In this way there will be something to displease & something to soothe every part of the Union, but New York, which must be contented with what she has had."

Once the residence bill had passed Jefferson felt there was no time to lose. He and the President needed no bargains to make them work together for Washington City. They were both Virginians. Always happiest when they looked to the West, they both believed the Potomac valley was the natural route to the Mississippi. Washington, as a dealer in western lands, an accomplished merchant of town lots and an able promoter, was deeply involved in the Potomac and Ohio canal. Jefferson's vocation as an architect, his local patriotism, and his conviction that, if the eastern and western states were to remain united, a cheap and easy passage through the Appalachians must be opened up at once, combined to involve all the great enthusiasms of his life in the project.

When Congress adjourned in August to meet in Philadelphia in the fall, Jefferson and Madison, who was still a bachelor, travelled home together. These jaunts in Jefferson's phaeton were getting to be increasingly important to both men as their intimacy increased. They could talk as they drove. They studied the flora and fauna. They examined the buildings. They stopped at the best inns. The care with which they chose their meals did not escape the eyes of their political enemies who soon would be accusing them of scorning their "native victuals."

On this particular journey they were joined, while they were waiting on the Eastern Shore for a vessel to ferry them across the bay to Annapolis, by the young Tom Shippen for whom Jefferson had made up one of his little educational Baedekers for the European tour.

"My journey was a delightful one from Chester Town to George Town," he wrote his father, the doctor, in Philadelphia, "whether spoken of for the excellence of the society, my fare, the weather or the roads. For I overtook as I told you I expected I should my two valuable friends, Messrs. Jefferson and Madison. At Rock Hall 12 miles from Chestertown we waited all day for want of a vessel to take us over, and I never knew two men more agreeable than they were. We talked and dined and strolled and rowed ourselves in boats and feasted on delicious crabs."

Tom Shippen looked back on the trip as a great experience. Even fresh from the good inns Jefferson had been careful to recommend to him in Europe, he declared Mann's Inn at Annapolis to be "among the most excellent in the world." His words glowed when he described the meals his friends ordered: "I never saw so fine a turtle or so welldressed a dish as he gave us the second day for dinner —Everything was of a piece—Old Madeiria at £80 a pipe to season it."

They pushed on to Georgetown, where Congressman Carroll took them riding, with a cavalcade of the local landowners, over the tract of farmland and meadow that lay between Rock Creek and muddy little Goose Creek, which Jefferson already was glorifying by the name of Tiber. After dinner they rowed in a boat up to the Little Falls and admired the romantic beauty of the river. It's quite possible that, looking back from the water at the richly wooded lands of the saucershaped depression which his imagination was already filling with the white columned porches and the noble domes of the federal city to be, Jefferson was able, against the blue highlands that hemmed it about, to count seven hills.

Madison and Jefferson left their young friend on the Virginia side of the river. "My having joined these two charming men," he wrote his father again after he had torn himself away from his abounding Lee cousins, explaining that he needed more cash, "though it gave me infinite pleasure, cost me money . . . I found that I was by thirty dollars poorer than when I left you." The Virginians travelled in style.

When they drove down to Mt. Vernon the next day, they were well primed with the lay of the land. The plan of the city was the chief subject of their conversation with Washington. The three of them seem to have agreed that the best site on the Maryland shore was somewhere between the wharves of Georgetown, at the head of navigation of the tidal estuary of the Potomac, and the Eastern Branch, for which Jefferson soon dug up the old Indian name of Anacostia. Jefferson wanted the city laid out in squares (on the plan of Babylon, he said), like Philadelphia, though he wondered whether that city's ordinance placing the houses at a certain distance from the street didn't tend to produce "a disgusting monotony." It's likely that it was for this conversation with Washington that he sketched out the little plat that has come down to us of a gridiron of streets fronting on the creek.

Jefferson was in favor of a certain conformity of height and of a harmony of style. He had shipped home from France, somewhere among the immense number of crates that were now headed for Philadelphia, a collection of engravings of the best modern dwellings he'd seen in Europe, where he felt builders and architects would be able to find hints for the style of private houses. The public buildings should be modeled on the antique, either in the spherical forms that stemmed from the domed buildings of the Romans, or the cubical which originated in the colonnaded and cunningly proportioned temples of the Greeks. The waterfront along the shallow Tiber should be preserved for public walks and the houses for government officials.

Washington, as he'd shown in his rebuilding of Mt. Vernon, had a taste for architecture himself and gloried in the spacious laying out of grounds. Planning a city suited him to a T. Next month he himself rode round the edges of the marshes and up under the great trees on the hills between Rock Creek and the Eastern Branch to establish definitely where the limits of the city should be. He chose for the federal district a region ten miles square on both sides of the Potomac. The southern point of the square would include Alexandria and its wharves as far south as Hunting Creek. He hoped to find a way of taking in Bladensburg to the east. As the reporter for the *Times and Patowmack Packet* of Georgetown put it, the President "with the principal citizens of this town and neighborhood set out to view the country adjacent to the river Patowmack in order to fix on a proper selection for the Grand Columbian Federal City."

Next day he rode over the hills towards the northern right angle of the square in the direction of Elizabeth Town (now Hagerstown) where he was received by enthusiastic citizens on horseback and saluted by a company of militia presenting arms amid the ringing of church bells when he rode into town. Bonfires blazed and the windows were illuminated. At a supper served to him at the tavern the President presented the toast, "The River Potowmac. May the residence law be perpetuated and Potowmac view the Federal City."

To the Virginians it must have seemed too good to be true. Washington, never sanguine that his dearest hopes would be fulfilled, wrote of his gloomy apprehensions. Jefferson agreed with him that there was a danger that Congress might change its mind. There was no time to be lost.

As soon as he was back in his office on High Street in Philadelphia, Jefferson drew up for the President's attention a highly characteristic document which stretched Congress's vague enactment to the point where it could be put to practical use.

Speaking of his conversations with local landowners he wrote: "they were properly impressed with the idea that if the present occasion of securing the Federal seat on the Patawmack should be lost, it could be never more regained . . . & that therefore measures should be adopted to carry the residence bill into execution . . . and that the requisites were: 1st land enough to place the public buildings on; & 2ndly money enough to build them, and to erect moreover about 20. good dwelling houses to themselves, about as many good lodging houses and half a dozen taverns."

He went on to suggest various methods which could be used to pay the owners for the land turned to public use without needless expenditure of public funds. He was for playing on their hopes of rising values once the city was a going concern.

Meanwhile the President was appointing a Board of Commissioners to superintend the work and a surveyor was being found to lay out the boundaries of the district. As early as February 2 of the following year Jefferson wrote Andrew Ellicott, one of the ablest surveyors of the time, instructing him in professional language how to make his preliminary rough survey along the lines President Washington had decided on. A few days later, in spite of the wintry weather, Ellicott was writing back that he would soon submit a plan "which will I believe embrace every object of advantage which can be included within the ten miles square."

Ellicott had hardly started to carry his lines across the wooded hills overlooking the Potomac when Washington and Jefferson, in a fever to get sod turned for the foundations, sent frothy Major l'Enfant after them to draw a city plan.

Pierre Charles l'Enfant arrived in America at his own expense as a volunteer to fight the British. The son of a court painter, some of whose vast seascapes and battlepieces still hang in the gray light of the royal palaces, he was brought up at Versailles. The father drew designs for the Gobelin tapestry works. The son was trained as a painter.

In America he served with credit in the artillery, was wounded in the assault on Savannah under Laurens and discharged with the rank of major. Washington thought highly of him. He was thick with the leaders of the Cincinnati, who, after the war, sent him back to France to have manufactured for them from his own design the gold eagles which were their emblem.

He was a man of grandiloquent notions with a sense of scale that appealed to Washington. In the Federal Hall in New York he made the first essay towards a distinctive American style. In decoration he was a brilliant innovator, but he doesn't seem to have had the necessary training as an architect to execute his grand ideas.

As soon as he arrived he wrote Jefferson he'd reached Georgetown in spite of the sleet and the mud "after having travelled part of the way on foot and part on horseback leaving the broken stage behind . . . As far as I was able to judge through a thick fog I passed on many spots which appeared to me rarely beautiful and which seem to dispute with each other who (to) command." He went on in his tumultuous English: "In the most extensive prospect of the water the gradual rising of the ground from Carrollborough toward the Ferry Road, the level and extensive ground from there to the bank of the Potomack as far as Goose Creek presents a situation most advantageous to run streets and prolong them on grand and far distant point of view; the water running from spring to some distance into the creeks, appeared also to me possible to be conducted without much labor so as to form pounds for watering every part of that spot."

L'Enfant had with him Jefferson's modest sketch with its suggestion of an open mall between the President's house at one end and the house for Congress at the other. As soon as he saw Jenkins' Hill far to the east, he seized on that as a site for the capitol, and placed the President's house about on the spot Jefferson had indicated. He immediately tripled the scale of Jefferson's sketch. Jefferson had furnished him with maps of a number of European cities, but freshest in l'Enfant's mind was the plan of Versailles. It was in Versailles that he had spent his youth. So he took Jefferson's gridiron and imposed on it the arrangement of broad avenues branching out from round points, like the claws in a goose's foot, which the royal city planners of France most likely copied from the goosefoot of streets branching out from the Piazza del Popolo in Renaissance Rome.

L'Enfant was so impressed by the grandeur of the work and with his own importance as the founder of the city that he quite lost his head. He wouldn't cooperate with the commissioners. He wouldn't explain his plans. He suddenly and without warning ordered his men to tear down a house one of the Carrolls had started to build in what l'Enfant decided was the middle of one of his

favorite avenues. Before long, to the horror of Jefferson and Washington who
wanted to have the city an accomplished fact before there was too much talk
about it, he had managed to flush every local vested interest so that the Georgetown people and the speculators who'd laid out lots at Hamburgh on the Eastern
Branch and the great tribe of Carrolls were all at sixes and sevens. There appeared
a l'Enfant faction and an anti-l'Enfant faction.

*The Piazza del Popolo in Rome. An early example of the goosefoot arrangement
of streets followed in the laying out of Versailles.*

He became so embroiled that although Jefferson had him sent Clérisseau's
drawings for the Richmond capitol from which to study details, he never found
time to prepare plans for the federal buildings. He had them in his head, he
told Jefferson. "I rest satisfied the President will consider," he wrote in a breathless letter "that erecting houses for the accommodation of Government is not
the only object, nay not so important a one, as the encouragement to prepare
buildings at those principle points, on the speedy settlement of which depends
the rapid increase of the city . . . to change a wilderness into a city, to erect
beautiful buildings etc. to that degree of perfection necessary to receive the seat

of government of a vast empire in the short period of time that remains to effect these objects is an undertaking vast as it is novel."

Houses for the accommodation of government Jefferson and Washington were determined to have. The foundations must be laid before some faction reared up in Congress and squelched the whole grandiose scheme. After some further urging that l'Enfant present the plans he kept talking about but never divulged, they decided to hold a competition. In March 1792 Jefferson drew up an announcement that the commissioners would offer $500 for a suitable plan for the President's house.

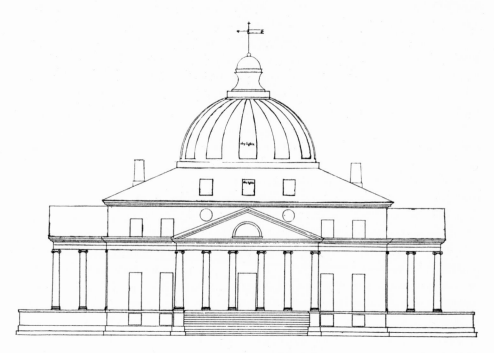

Jefferson's anonymous drawing entered in the competition for the President's House.

When few architects appeared to take part in the competition Jefferson submitted a drawing of his own, in which he set a skylighted dome, similar to the dome which had so intrigued him on the Paris grain market, on a version of his favorite Villa Rotunda. He signed it with the initials AZ and kept the secret of his authorship so close that for years the sketch, which remained among the papers of his friend Latrobe, was attributed to an Alexandria builder named Abraham Faws.

The prize was awarded to James Hoban, a young Irish immigrant who had won a fine arts medal in Dublin and been induced to come out to Charleston to design the first South Carolina statehouse. The drawing he presented was eminently practical and had a pleasing modesty which immediately attracted Washington; and Jefferson too. He was not the man to push his own project. It was part of his gentleman's code, already quaintly archaic in his lifetime, that a gentleman didn't claim authorship of designs for a building any more than he used his own name when he wrote in the newspapers or published books. But neither was Jefferson a man to neglect making his influence felt. Much of the architectural character of the White House as it stands today depends on those later additions such as the terraces and the curved south portico which Jefferson either designed or had built under his direction.

When the time came to open the competition for the capitol, Jefferson wrote the commissioners, as usual putting his own ideas in another man's mouth, that the President felt that instead of facing the buildings with stone of different colors as had been suggested, he would prefer them faced with brick, possibly above a stone watertable and using stone for ornament and trim.

"The remains of antiquity in Europe," he added, "prove brick more durable than stone." He gave the exact dimensions of the flat Roman bricks. He'd measured them himself. "The grain is as fine as our best earthenware." On that sunny long ago drive through the Midi he'd been fascinated by the beauty of Roman brickwork. The prospectus he drafted called for a brick building, gave dimensions for a Senate chamber and a House chamber to hold three hundred men and left about everything else to the ingenuity of the architect.

By this time news of the competition had spread through the states. The projects submitted for the capitol showed an unexpectedly high order of invention. A great period in American building was about to begin. In all the seaport towns merchants and shipowners and successful seacaptains were rummaging in their strongboxes for funds to pay carpenters and undertakers for mansions and public buildings of frame and brick which would express the new dignity of Americans as citizens of an independent republic.

Samuel Dobie, who'd helped in the building of Jefferson's Virginia statehouse and may have known that Jefferson had a fancy for this work of Palladio's, sent in a monumental Villa Rotunda.

Samuel McIntire, already busy ornamenting seacaptain's houses at Salem and Newburyport, with his New England version of the style of the Adelphi, worked out a highly accomplished design in the full tradition of the late eighteenth century in England, which some architects still consider his most interesting project.

A man named Diamond, probably a practical contractor with a feeling for brick construction, presented a square building set about a court that harked back even further in English taste, but struck an up to date note by indicating locations for waterclosets. There were some enlarged versions of the Annapolis statehouse. There were some intriguing experiments with oval rooms. A recently arrived Frenchman whose name was Americanized as Hallet drafted a dome over a pediment supported by Ionic columns which presented a compromise between the ornate dome of the Invalides and the beautifully simple dome of the École Mazarine in Paris. He had been talking to Jefferson, who wanted a domed building and who had made a vigorous little sketch of his recollections of the great domed church on the hill above the students' quarter on the left bank of the Seine.

When the drawings were shown to Washington the President found only one which satisfied his sense of pomp and his desire for great scale. This was a drawing submitted by a Dr. Thornton who boasted of being a rank amateur. Jefferson immediately concurred. Thornton had put the antique forms to modern use. The center of Thornton's plan was a bold Roman Pantheon set up on a sturdy set of rusticated arches. It had the New World flavor.

Born of a family of rich Lancashire Quakers on the tiny island of Jost Van Dyke off Tortola in the Virgins, William Thornton had been educated for medicine in Scotland, and being a young man of some wealth had set out on the customary grand tour. He had been captivated by the classical revival and had spent a season in Paris subject to the fascinations of the salon of Josephine de Beauharnais, whom the clinging new tunics in Hellenic style became so exquisitely. He had turned up in Philadelphia in time to dine with Dr. Franklin before he died, had married a Pennsylvania girl and had become a naturalized citizen of Delaware. Dunlap, the historian of the arts of the early republic, speaks of him as "a scholar and a gentleman—full of talent and eccentricity—a quaker by profession, a painter, a poet and a horse racer, well acquainted with the mechanic arts."

Thornton claimed that he'd never thought of architecture till he saw an advertisement in a Philadelphia newspaper of a competition for a library. He bought himself some books, fudged a set of plans and carried off the prize. Now President Washington could think of nothing but his elevation of the façade for the national capitol.

Jefferson and the commissioners had already virtually engaged Hallet and approved his project. It was a case which demanded more than a normal amount of healing oil to keep everybody happy. February 1, 1793, Jefferson wrote Daniel Carroll, now retired from Congress and appointed a commissioner: "Doctor Thornton's plan of a capitol has been produced and has so captivated the eyes and judgement of all as to leave no doubt you will prefer it . . . It is simple, noble, beautiful, excellently distributed, and moderate in size . . . The Doctor will go with it to your meeting in the beginning of March. In the meantime, the interval of apparent doubt may be improved for settling the mind of poor Hallet, whose merit and distresses interest everyone for his tranquility and pecuniary relief."

The prize had no sooner been awarded to Dr. Thornton than it became apparent that it would be impossible to erect the building as planned. The columns of the portico were too far apart, there was no way indicated to support the floor of the central peristyle, there was no headroom on the stairways and important parts of the interior totally lacked light and air. It was up to Jefferson to get the plan into practical shape.

Hallet had been awarded second prize. Jefferson, who recognized the Frenchman as a competent technician, promptly engaged him to work on Thornton's drawings. He called in Dr. Thornton, Stephen Hallet, Hoban and a practical contractor named Carstairs to a conference on ways and means. Dr. Thornton brought along a certain Colonel Williams who claimed all difficulties could be handled by the use of "secret arches of brick" for support.

Jefferson abhorred the notion, but he kept his feelings to himself. He managed to keep all these gentlemen pulling together to the extent that by hook or by crook, by August 15 of the same year, he had a set of workable drawings ready to send on to Washington City. Somehow, in spite of all the burnings and reconstructions and the thousandfold modifications of the original plan, the capitol, as it at present stands, has, in the relationship of the dome to the general mass and balance of the wings, more affinity to Jefferson's tiny sketch than it has to Thornton's original plan.

Meanwhile a miasma of contention arose from the muddy flats of the Potomac. Though many loved him and all admired his talent, nobody could work with l'Enfant. His disregard for money was epic. He was too grand to study ways and means. For him it always had to be rule or ruin. Jefferson wrote tactful letters. Washington sent one of his personal secretaries with soothing explanations to try to induce the major to cooperate with the commissioners. The secretary was rebuffed. Washington took the rebuff as a personal slight, closed his thin lips over his uncomfortable dentures and set his great jaw and retired into his implacable dignity.

For years l'Enfant, with his mighty imaginings unrealized, haunted the unfinished city, the first of a long train of injured men waiting for redress. When Ellicott resigned in a huff as surveyor, Jefferson wrote begging him to keep his complaints out of the newspapers. In the end Thornton, too, in spite of the sudden establishment of his reputation as America's leading architect, joined the ranks of the disappointed. The federal city seemed to devour men of talent.

As Jefferson's collaboration with Washington's administration became more and more uneasy, his personal influence diminished at the federal city. The project was beset by every difficulty conceivable. Flocks of speculators rode in, bought lots on borrowed money, took fright in the panic that followed the inflation of the stock in Hamilton's Bank of the United States, sold at a loss and were ruined. The streets were a morass. At high tide the creeks backed up into the lowlying lots. Clumps of unfinished buildings moldered in the scrubby undergrowth. There was never enough money to pay the workmen. There were never enough workmen to do the work. When workmen arrived they found no houses to live in.

Washington and Jefferson were both stubborn men. Each in his own way, they pushed the work on the government buildings on through inconceivable disappointments. It was not till the triumph at the polls in 1800 of the western settlers and the farmers and planters and the mechanics and tradesmen who made up the Republican Party that the survival of Washington City was assured.

Jefferson as President in the fresh air of the new century was able to take full charge of the work in progress. He appointed Benjamin Latrobe as surveyor of the public buildings. Latrobe was a really great architect, a man of true originality who was able to reconcile Jefferson's meticulous taste with the grandiose plans inherited from l'Enfant and Thornton. His artistic education had been steeped in the classical revival. In Cockerell's office in London he'd learned to prefer an Attic plainness to the spindling elegances of the Adam taste. He was a competent engineer versed in the mechanical inventions which were transforming European society. Jefferson found Latrobe's inventive mind stimulating and congenial; together they were able, pulling down the bad workmanship and shoring up the good, to complete the White House and Capitol's two wings and to set the print of their fresh republican style on the government buildings so that Washington City became the radiating center of this first great period in American architecture.

After his own retirement Jefferson was to write Latrobe, when at last he too resigned, like the others, disappointed, underpaid and resentful after having devoted years of his life to the Capitol: "I shall live in the hope that the day will come when an opportunity will be given you of finishing the middle building in a style worthy of the two wings, and worthy of the first temple dedicated to the sovereignty of the people, embellishing with Athenian taste the course of a nation looking far beyond the range of Athenian destinies."

THE END

Index